Sanatana-dharmamrta-sindhu

"The Nectarean Ocean of the Eternal Natural Way"

Sanatana Dharma:
The Eternal Natural Way

Sri Dharma Pravartaka Acharya

Sanatana Dharma:
The Eternal Natural Way

Sri Dharma Pravartaka Acharya

ISDS

Omaha, NE, USA

2015

International Sanatana Dharma Society
13917 P Street
Omaha, NE 68137

www.dharmacentral.com

Other Works by Sri Dharma Pravartaka Acharya

The Vedic Way of Knowing God

Living Dharma: The Teachings of Sri Dharma Pravartaka Acharya

Radical Universalism: Are All Religions the Same?

Taking Refuge in Dharma: The Initiation Guidebook

The Shakti Principle: Encountering the Feminine Power of God

The Art of Wisdom

The Dharma Manifesto

Sanatana Dharma: The Eternal Natural Way

The Sanatana Dharma Study Guide

The Vedic Encyclopedia

Vedanta: The Culmination of Wisdom

The Dharma Dialogues

The Dharma of Wellbeing

All these works can be purchased at:

www.dharmacentral.com

Table of Contents

**Chapter 3 Epistemology in Literary Form: The Scriptures of
Sanatana Dharma**   87

xiv

Dedication

The present work is dedicated to Sri Ramanuja Acharya
(1017–1137 AD), the greatest philosopher and reviver
of the authentic Sanatana Dharma tradition in history.

Introduction

Who among us has never, at some contemplative point in our lives or another, asked the truly big questions, questions about the ultimate meaning of the world we find around us, and of our lives within it? Questioning the reason for our human existence is a very natural pursuit on the part of any intelligent human being (*manushya*). Indeed, unlike any other species of life, God has gifted human beings alone with the unique cognitive ability to engage in self-reflection upon our very own existence as human beings. To be human means to question what it means to be human.

It is especially when such existential questions arise in our minds that we find ourselves understandably turning to those precise fields of knowledge that deal most directly with such questions: the inseparable sister fields of religion and philosophy. Many philosophers, both Western and Asian, from the beginning of time, have attempted to discern the nature of existence. Whether we are speaking of Thomas Aquinas and his metaphysical distinction of existence and essence, Søren Kierkegaard and his attempts to come to grips with the problem of existence from a Protestant perspective, the hopeless ennui preached by the Existentialists of the 20th Century, or the Samkhya, Yoga and Vedanta schools of Sanatana Dharma with the inward seeking imperative for which they are so well known, the nature of our existence has been forefront in the minds of some of history's greatest thinkers.

The most basic of all philosophical questions that can be asked is: Why do human beings exist? In order to sufficiently analyze this question, the question itself really needs to be divided into three closely related questions: a) Why do we exist at all? b) Why do we exist as human beings? c) How are we meant to live such that we can achieve our life's ultimate purpose? In the following book, I will be answering this universal query of life's ultimate meaning from the perspective of the most ancient religio-philosophical system on earth, Sanatana Dharma: the Eternal Natural Way.

According to the ancient wisdom of Dharma, we exist because it is our very innate nature to exist. The sacred scriptures of both Yoga and Sanatana Dharma, known as the Vedic literature, teach us that our true, innermost nature is that we are what is called *atman* in the ancient Sanskrit language, or eternal units of pure consciousness. We have the transcendent Absolute (Brahman, or God) as both our causative and substantial source, and as the ontological sustainer of our existential being.

Having God as our underlying source, it necessarily follows that we naturally share in many of God's essential attributive qualities. Because we participate in God's innate attributes - and if not to a quantitatively equivalent degree, then certainly to a qualitative one - we too share in many of God's innately positive, spiritual qualities. One of those attributes that both God and we have in common is necessary existence. In other words, both God and we ourselves (*atmans*, or souls) are eternal by our inherent nature. Consciousness is eternal. God and individual *atmans* cannot but exist. To truly go out of existence is simply not within the realm of our capability, either conceptually or in reality.

Never was there a time when we came into being, and never will there be a time when we cease to exist. So, in a way, we exist because we cannot but exist, being purely spiritual beings in essence. Such is our nature, for it is also the very nature of God, the ultimate source of our being. Such are the teachings of Sanatana Dharma, the Eternal Natural Way.

A deeper question than the principle of necessary existence, however, is: why is it the case that we were even gifted with necessary existence to begin with? Sanatana Dharma answers this in the following manner. Brahman (God) is One (*ekam*). But as a natural result of the free-will overflowing abundance of the Infinite, God decides to become more than One. God thus becomes One-with-attributes (*vishishta-advaita*). Consequently, in addition to Brahman (the Absolute), we also have *atman* (individual selves) and *jagat* (materiality, or the Creation). As *atman*, we have our own individual existence in attributive relationship with Brahman (God) in order to know, and love, and serve Brahman.

The second part of our question on human existence – "why do we exist as human beings?" – can then be understood from understanding the first part. As beings who partake in God's necessary existence and attributive nature, we are currently in a state of self-imposed separation from God due to our self-destructive fascination with illusory ego and the objects of ego. It is our individual, free-will choice to revel in ego, and the subsequent selfishness and self-centeredness that result from ego, that produce the various layers of illusory self that we mistakenly identify with our true, spiritual identity.

The "human person" is in actuality a complex symbiosis comprised of several distinct aggregates, including physical body (*deha*), emotions (*abhitapa*), mind substance, (*manas*), intellect (*buddhi*), illusory ego (*ahamkara*), the vital force (*prana*), and ultimately *atman* as the source of consciousness and animating source. While the "human person" is an artificial and temporal construct comprised of these many elements, it is the *atman* alone that is the true self, and that is eternal, actual, beautiful, indestructible, wise, and blissful by its own inherent nature, having God (Brahman) as its source of being.

We thus find ourselves in human form (and sometimes other forms!) in an endlessly unsuccessful attempt to selfishly enjoy ourselves in the illusion that we can have a meaningful existence without the benefit of God's love. We are identifying with the temporal instead of the eternal, with the shallow instead of the profound, with the material instead of the spiritual, with the illusory instead of the real.

This thus leads, finally, to our third primary philosophical query: "how are we meant to live such that we can achieve life's ultimate purpose?" The meaning of life in human form is to reverse this negative and self-defeating tendency to serve our illusory ego, and to instead once again serve God. We are here, as human beings, to transcend our merely human nature, to re-embrace our true identity as eternal spiritual beings, and to partake of the divine nature that is our birthright, that is our natural state of being, and that is our true home. We are here to know, and to love, and to serve the Divine.

In Sanatana Dharma, God is presented as the source of all goodness, acceptance, compassion, and non-judgmental love. God is embraced and loved without restrictions, without fear, without force, without jealously, and without loss. This is a very different conception of the Absolute when compared to the notion that we find in the much more historically recent Abrahamic religious constructs of Judaism, Christianity and Islam.

Unlike in the Abrahamic religions, in Sanatana Dharma we find a concept of God as not only consisting of a thoroughly transcendent source of reality, but also as a lovingly imminent and intimate friend who provides us all with a means for achieving immediate knowledge, and a direct and ecstatic experience of Him.

The path of Sanatana Dharma offers us such profoundly philosophical works as the *Bhagavad Gita, Upanishads*, and *Vedas* for the unfailing guidance and knowledge necessary to comprehend life's meaning. It also offers us a systematic path of spiritual practice that leads directly to a profoundly personal experience of the Divine. This path includes the ancient and highly effective processes of Yoga, meditation, *puja* (meditational worship ritual), and selfless devotion to God, or *bhakti*.

To truly know the answer to the meaning of human life, however, it is not enough ultimately to merely engage in an intellectual understanding of Truth. Rather, we need to personally experience the sweet taste of Truth as the immediate and uninterrupted presence of God in our hearts and in our lives. To experience the profound bliss of God's presence in your life, and to truly know why we have the joy of existence, we must explore the profound depths of spiritual realization that Sanatana Dharma has to offer.

Sanatana Dharma (commonly referred to erroneously as "Hinduism") is a spiritual path that has existed since before the beginning of time. It is a path that is both ancient in origin, and profound in its understanding of the nature of reality. Sanatana Dharma is completely unlike any other religious tradition in existence. Rather than reflecting the dogmatically inclined expressions of denominationalism, sectarianism, and divisive religious doctrines that are of more recent origin, Sanatana Dharma is a spiritual expression of the divine intelligence that naturally underlies the more empirical aspects of our cosmos. Sanatana Dharma is the Eternal Natural Way. As such, this path represents the pre-religious, primordial essence of all true spirituality, philosophy, and yearning to know the higher Reality, as well as the very foundation of any and all attempts to establish any civilizational constructs based upon such eternal ideals.

Despite the fact that Sanatana Dharma is one of the most ancient and profound philosophical cultures known to humanity, I have had the sad experience over the last four decades of my personal study of the world's many diverse religions of witnessing the perpetuation of more misconceptions, stereotypes and outrageous caricatures about Sanatana Dharma than exists about every other religion on earth combined! Even more troubling than the perpetuation of so many misconceptions about this noble religious tradition has been the fact that so few leaders, scholars, or even so-called "*gurus*" of Sanatana Dharma have ventured to correct these gross misconceptions. It is one of the goals of *Sanatana Dharma: The Eternal Natural Way* to correct the record about what Sanatana Dharma actually is, and what it actually teaches.

During my public discourses and spiritual presentations on Sanatana Dharma, I am invariably asked by my students if I can recommend a good book that serves as a well written, systematic, accurate and conclusive introduction to the philosophical world-view, historical and social factors, and practice of Sanatana Dharma. Sadly, I have always had to answer no to this question. There had been no such book available for sincere seekers who wished to understand Sanatana Dharma in its pristine and authentic form.

Remarkably, every book that currently exists that purports to be an introduction to Sanatana Dharma falls far short in a number of respects. The two primary poles in which these books fail at their task are that they are either written by a) well-meaning, but ultimately woefully unknowledgeable and unqualified, adherents of the tradition, who thus miss the very philosophical essence of Sanatana Dharma; or are b) well-written academic treatises penned by biased professors and scholarly researchers who inevitably gut the spiritual tradition of anything of spiritual, experiential, practical and aesthetic value, and who thus miss the very spiritual essence of Sanatana Dharma.

The first group consists primarily of unknowledgeable and unqualified "*gurus*" for whom Sanatana Dharma is relegated to being merely an expression of personal cultural heritage, if not merely a moneymaking venture. For the latter group of academicians, Sanatana Dharma is nothing more than a dead relic of the past whose sole value consists in providing material and literary data for the uninterrupted churning out of speculative academic theses. For both groups of authors, Sanatana Dharma is merely a means of fostering a career and making a profit. For both groups of authors, Sanatana Dharma is not a living tradition meant to be practiced and experienced, but a tool to achieve material success for themselves as authors. Both groups have failed in their attempts to explain the path of Sanatana Dharma in a manner that fully reflects the path as it truly is.

The "Sanatana Dharma" that is the subject of this specific book is necessarily an ever-living and eternal Sanatana Dharma. It is a Sanatana

Dharma that is life-transformative. This book, thus, presents Sanatana Dharma on Sanatana Dharma's own terms alone.

Sanatana Dharma: The Eternal Natural Way is a work that has been over forty years in the making, but that has in actuality been crucially missing from the annals of world literature and religious discourse for the last several thousand years. This book is a work of scholarship, it is a philosophical-spiritual treatise, it is an untold story about the survival of an ideal, but more importantly, it is a revolutionary manifesto signaling the beginning of a wholly new era in humanity's eternal yearning for a grasp of reality that makes immediate and vibrant sense. It is a call to arms for all those whose lives are dedicated to manifesting Truth. It is a rebirth of unbridled idealism, and a signal that hopefulness is again alive in our age. The focus of this book is living and dynamic Dharma, and not merely a static concept.

Sanatana Dharma: The Eternal Natural Way is designed to be the first English language *summa theologica*, a theological summary, and a systematic theological and philosophical exposition of the entirety of the Sanatana Dharma world-view. The overall organizational outline of the book is a multipart structure. The Sanskrit name of this work is ***Sanatana-dharmamrta-sindhu*** - "The Nectarean Ocean of the Eternal Natural Way". Accordingly, the work is divided into several sections in the form of "Waves". These four sections are: A) the Foundations, B) Philosophical Grounding, C) Socio-Historical Grounding, and D) Grounding in Practice. It is my hope that this work will serve as a comprehensive general guide in your personal exploration of the ancient tradition of Sanatana Dharma.

Aum Tat Sat

Sri Dharma Pravartaka Acharya
International Sanatana Dharma Society
Omaha, Nebraska, USA
August 22, 2011
www.dharmacentral.com

Introduction to the Second Printing

It has been four years since *Sanatana Dharma: The Eternal Natural Way* was first published. In that time, the book has successfully filled a tremendous need on the part of those sincere spiritual seekers who long desired a systematic introduction to the world-view of Vedic philosophy. The numbers of people who have read, appreciated and benefited from this work have innumerable. As the author of the book, people's praise of my work has left me tremendously humbled and grateful.

With this new printing, we have expanded the work to include several other important topics that were not covered in the first printing, as well as to expand on several topics that I felt needed a more in-depth treatment. This last version of the book is now the definitive and final edition of *Sanatana Dharma: The Eternal Natural Way*. It will be available both as a paperback book, as well as in a hardcover edition.

In addition, the International Sanatana Dharma Society has grown tremendously as a global movement dedicated to Vedic restoration since the first edition was released in 2011. These positive organizational developments necessitated the reworking and updating of several sections of the book in direct reflection of that positive growth.

I have also now authored a companion book, *The Sanatana Dharma Study Guide*, which was written with the purpose of helping serious readers, students, teachers and Sanatana Dharma study groups in better understanding this book. *The Sanatana Dharma Study Guide* includes many hundreds of Vedic scriptural citations that correspond with, and scripturally support, each of the sections of this book, which were too numerous to include in the book itself. I strongly recommend that you read *The Sanatana Dharma Study Guide* in conjunction with this book. May this second printing of *Sanatana Dharma: The Eternal Natural Way* fulfill the same mission that the first printing accomplished of introducing the Vedic world-view to sincere spiritual seekers everywhere.

Aum Tat Sat

Sri Dharma Pravartaka Acharya
International Sanatana Dharma Society
Omaha, Nebraska, USA
February 22, 2015
Dharmacentral.com

Acknowledgements

There are so many people who have supported and encouraged my work over the decades to whom I owe an enormous and sincere debt of gratitude. While the following list is far from exhaustive, it is at least an attempt – however small - to offer acknowledgement to some of the people to whom I owe the most. It is my hope that this small offering pleases them all.

My spiritual teachers: Sri Narada Muni, Sri Ramanuja Acharya, Sri B. R. Sridhara Swami, Sri Bhaktivedanta Swami Prabhupada, Sri Swami Jyotirmayananda, Sri Tirumalai Krishnamacharya, Pujya Sri Swami Dayananda Sarasvati, Dr. David Frawley (Sri Acharya Vamadeva Shastri), Sri Pandurang Shastri Athavale.

My early Yoga *asana* teachers: Sri Dharma Mittra and Sri Swami Bua.

My colleagues, friends and supporters: Paramacharya Palaniswami of *Hinduism Today Magazine,* Dr. Keith Yandell, Dr. David M. Knipe, Dr. Klaus Klostermeier, Dr. Robert Thurman, Dr. Georg Fueurstein, Dr. Subhash Kak, Dr. Deepak Chopra, Sri Swami Nirbhayananda, Sri Swami Sivadasa Bharati, Sri Vishal Agarwal, Dr. Subhash Kak, Sri Vrindavan Parker, Stephen Knapp, Yogi Baba Prem, B.A. Paramadwaiti Swami.

To all of my disciples, without whose tremendous encouragement, support, trust and love I could have accomplished little.

I thank Arjuna, Dharmaraja, Ms. Kalpana Mathema and Ayyangar M

14

Komanduri for their wonderful transcription assistance. Thank you to Subhadra for your wonderful editing help.

My special thanks are offered to Srimati Tulasi Devi Mandaleshvari, my chosen successor, for her brilliant layout and design, as well as the beautiful cover art of this book. Her amazing creativity and aesthetic expertise made the creation of this book possible.

First Wave

- The Foundations

Chapter 1   The Eternal Natural Way

1.1.1 The Two Approaches to Our Cosmos

We live in a world that we know is infinitely complex, overpoweringly beautiful, and often times deeply mysterious. From time immemorial, human beings have peered into the heavens and contemplated the meaning of the world around them, and the meaning of their own lives within this world. When we human beings do begin to contemplate the meaning of our reality, there are really only two mutually exclusive conclusions that we can possible come to. And we must choose between one of these two possible explanations.

The first way of viewing reality tries to convince us that the world we see around us is ultimately devoid of any real and lasting meaning. That everything happens in a thoroughly random manner. That the world is an inherently chaotic place, without an ultimate purpose, or any higher principle governing what happens in our cosmos or what happens to us. We are alone. This uninspired response to the mysteries of the world around us is the typical secular materialist response. It is the depressing conclusion that the atheist comes to. This atheistic way of viewing reality is now the dominant world-view, purposefully and systematically foisted upon us for over two centuries by those who control public discourse and culture.

The second way in which we can choose to see our world tells us just the very opposite of the above pessimistic and ultimately hopeless scenario. This second way envisions the universe around us as being full of deep

18

meaning and alive with exciting possibility. Our cosmos is understood to be a reality in which, while oftentimes seemingly chaotic or confusing at a cursory glance, is in actuality governed by a higher and benevolent intelligence. It is a reality in which a nuanced order, balance, harmony and purpose lay hidden behind every important occurrence. Ours is a cosmos that is ruled by Natural Law. Though each and every one of these eternal principles of this Natural Law are not necessarily all known to us at all times, they are nonetheless discernible by those among us who are wise, patient and sensitive enough to listen to the quiet whispers of nature and to humbly open ourselves to the many lessons to be learned from Her. When we fully realize the nature and power of this Natural Law, and live according to its wise guidance, then we are living in harmony with the cosmos, and we open ourselves to experiencing the peace, health, joy, sense of oneness with all of creation and with every being in creation, and deep sense of meaning that each of us, in our own way, yearns for. This second response to the mystery of our cosmos represents the optimistic and hopeful world-view of Sanatana Dharma, the Eternal Natural Way.

1.1.2 Normative Religion Versus Sanatana Dharma

The spiritual path of Sanatana Dharma, or "The Eternal Natural Way", is the most ancient spiritual culture and tradition on the earth. Indeed, it is "*sanatana*", or eternal. It is the original spiritual path of the Cosmos, and of the Earth, itself. To one degree or another, it forms the archetypal antecedent of every other later religion, denomination, and spiritually minded culture known to humanity. Such South Asian religions as Jainism, Buddhism and Sikhism; all pre-Abrahamic indigenous religious expressions; and to a more indirect degree, the Abrahamic religions of

Judaism, Christianity and Islam, all owe the spiritual and mystical content
of their various formal religions to the pre-sectarian reality of the Eternal
Natural Way, or Sanatana Dharma. Before there were any of the major
world religions that we are familiar with today, there was Sanatana
Dharma.

Religion represents the outer form of spirituality, but Sanatana Dharma
represents the more important inner heart of all spirituality. While Sanatana Dharma represents the world's most ancient continuously practiced
spiritual tradition, it is nonetheless not to be understood as a tradition in
the normative sense of the modern term "religion". For, being the most
ancient of humanity's spiritual expressions, Sanatana Dharma predates
"religion" in the current denominational, sectarian, or dogmatic notion.
Rather, Sanatana Dharma is pre-religious in both the historical and organizational sense.

Before there were any rigidly organized denominations, sects, faiths, or
theocratic dogmas in the contemporary normative sense of these terms,
there was the Eternal Natural Way. Previous to the concept of wars
waged in the name of a jealous god, or the persecution of people who
had a differing religious belief, or religion used by evil men to conquer,
divide, and subjugate large portions of the human race, there was the
Eternal Natural Way. Sanatana Dharma harkens back to a time in human
history when spirituality arose naturally as an organic and vital expression
of living beings' innate core essence as eternal consciousness expressing
itself in the temporal and material world, when sanity and humility ruled
the domain of spiritual expression, and when life was lived joyfully in
accordance with transcendent Reality.

Sanatana Dharma is today commonly misnamed "Hinduism". While the term "Hinduism" is perhaps a more familiar term for this ancient spiritual path, and is often still used by practitioners of Sanatana Dharma as a matter of practical convenience, the term "Hinduism" is in actuality not more than 350 years old. The word "Hinduism" arose under the British colonial rule of India as a legal and demographic term to designate those living in British India who were not Muslim. Thus, even Buddhists, Jains and Sikhs were mistakenly lumped under the artificial term "Hinduism" by the colonial bureaucrats despite the fact that these were completely different (and much later) traditions from Sanatana Dharma.

More, "Hinduism" is not a term that is historically rooted within the tradition itself. The word "Hinduism" is not found anywhere in either Vedic or classical Sanskrit, nor in any of the recognized sacred scriptures (*shastra*) of this spiritual path. Rather, the proper name of this spiritual tradition, the name that is found throughout the scriptures of the tradition, is "Sanatana Dharma", or the Eternal Natural Way. Additionally, followers of Sanatana Dharma are not properly referred to as "Hindus", but as "Dharmis", or followers of Dharma. Consequently, throughout the entirety of this book, we will use only the proper terms Sanatana Dharma and Dharmi(s) to refer to the path we are revealing, and to the followers of that path, respectively.

I have been on a mission since around 1988 to encourage practitioners of the Vedic path to abandon the incorrect terms "Hinduism" and "Hindu", and to instead use the respective terms "Sanatana Dharma" and "Dharmi". In the first several years of my campaign, this was a very lonely mission for me. In the first fifteen or so years of my campaign, even most Vedic leaders were very slow to adopt the proper name of our spiritual path, if at all. Today, however, we have seen many millions of followers of the Vedic tradition who have now proudly embraced the beautiful and philosophically meaningful terms "Sanatana Dharma" and "Dharmi" as their own. Indeed, these terms are now quickly becoming household words globally.

1.1.3 Uniqueness of Sanatana Dharma

As an extension of its pre-religious nature, there are several astounding factors about Sanatana Dharma that make this tradition radically different from every other major world religion being practiced today. Among these unique features is the fact that no scholar or historian has been able to trace its origins to any particular date or era in human history. Unlike Sanatana Dharma, every other world religion has a historical point of origin, a time in which we know that the particular religion in question was founded. Judaism, for example, is approximately 3800 years old. Christianity is roughly 2000 years old. Islam was founded about 1400 years ago. Buddhism, Taoism, and Confucianism can all be traced back what scholars of religion have referred to as the Axial Age and are thus all roughly 2500 years old. No scholar, historian or religious authority, however, has ever been able to conclusively state when Sanatana Dharma was founded. In fact, no one can venture to pinpoint the founding of Sanatana Dharma to within even a millennium of its origin.

This is not a surprising occurrence to followers of Sanatana Dharma because it is understood that Sanatana Dharma was never "founded" within the context of history, or even of time itself. Rather, Sanatana Dharma is, as its name implies, the "Eternal Natural Way." Being a transcendent metaphysical principle and set of eternal natural laws, thus necessitating

22

that Sanatana Dharma transcends both time and space, it preexisted the creation of the material cosmos itself, and it will continue to exist even after the universe itself ceases to be. Sanatana Dharma always was. Sanatana Dharma is. Sanatana Dharma always shall be.

In the same manner that the origins of Sanatana Dharma cannot be located anywhere within the scope of human history, another unique factor about this tradition is the fact that there is also no one individual person, or any collection of such persons, who can be said to be the founder, originator, or creator of the tradition. This, again, makes Sanatana Dharma radically different from every other world religion. Every other world religion has a founding prophet, sage, or mystic who inspired the creation of the particular tradition. Abraham (and to a lesser degree Moses), for example, is usually seen as the founder of what later came to be called Judaism. Jesus is the mystic-sage indirectly responsible for the later birth of Christianity. For Islam, the founder was indisputably Mohammed. For Buddhism, the Buddha is said to have inspired the later organizational form of that religion. Taoism was started by Lao Tzu, and Confucianism by (as the name implies) Confucius. Unlike these other religions, however, no one can say that there was any one individual who suddenly came up with the bright idea to start a new religion called "Sanatana Dharma".

Rather, multiple aspects of the religion of Sanatana Dharma were revealed, and re-revealed, over an infinite stretch of time by many enlightened sages known as *rishis*, whose existence have spanned the whole of history, from the earliest dawn of creation several billions of years ago, down to our present day, and stretching into the future beyond. The *rishis* did not invent, create, develop, or evolve the spiritual reality of Sanatana Dharma. More, the truths of Sanatana Dharma were not existentially dependent upon the revelatory activities of the *rishis*. Rather, the truths of Dharma eternally preexisted their earthly manifestation.

In the same way that Sir Isaac Newton cannot be said to be the "creator" of the principle of gravity, but was merely responsible for the restatement of this unalterable fact of physics in a manner that his contemporaries could understand, the *rishis*, too, only revealed certain unalterable and eternal facts of metaphysics in such a way that the common human being could then have access to this knowledge. Indeed, it is primarily the transcendent and eternal truths revealed by these many *rishi* sages over time that form the bulk of the revealed scriptures of Sanatana Dharma.

1.1.4 The Vedic Revelation

All too often, Western and Abrahamic inspired scholars of religion will make the artificial and highly biased distinction between those religions that they call the "Religions of the Book", namely the Abrahamic religions of Judaism, Christianity and Islam, and falsely juxtapose these "Religions of the Book" with every other religion that lay outside of the Abrahamic revelatory-matrix, and who supposedly are not based upon a recognized set of scriptures. This is in actuality an artificial, chauvinistic and highly inappropriate distinction that is based more upon an ugly sense of religious bigotry than anything remotely purporting to be objective scholarship. Like the Abrahamic religions, Sanatana Dharma is also based upon a revealed scriptural canon that is held as both sacred and authoritative by its followers, and can thus also be appropriately termed a "Religion of the Book" to at least the same degree as the Abrahamic religions can. In the case of Sanatana Dharma, our vast collection of sacred scriptures is known by the general Sanskrit term *Veda*.

The word *Veda* is an interesting and unique term in that the literal translation of the word *Veda* means simply "knowledge", deriving from the Sanskrit verb root "*vid*", meaning "to know". Thus, rather than merely being a parochial record of a particular sect, people or culture, the literature known as the *Veda* represents knowledge in its most pristine and transcendental of forms.

The Vedic scriptures do not consist of only one brief work, but rather constitute a vast and diverse library of sacred literatures. There are many hundreds of volumes in the Vedic scriptural canon. There are so many sacred books within the Vedic cannon, in fact, that these works are traditionally organized into entire subgenres of literature. For example, the genre known as the *Upanishads* consist of 108 profoundly philosophical texts. Likewise, there are 36 major and minor *Puranas*, which are large books that record the ancient histories of all humanity (*manushya*), the very smallest of which is the size of the entire Bible! There is the *Mahabharata*, which is the largest epic poem ever written in world literature, and which, with over one-hundred-thousand verses, is roughly eight times the size of the Iliad and the Odyssey combined. Then there are such other genres of sacred literature as the *Samhitas*, the *Brahmanas*, *Aranyakas*, *Tantras*, *Sutras*, *Pancharatras*, *Agamas*, and others, all of which contain multiple volumes of sacred texts under each heading. So vast is the total canon of Vedic sacred literature that it would take a good part of a person's lifetime to read them all! To merely read is, of course, not the same as to understand. To actually understand the full profundity and depths of their spiritual meaning could take lifetimes of concerted spiritual growth.

That being said, the question sometimes arises as to why it is necessary to have such a large, and seemingly unwieldy, library of scriptures. After all, would it not be an advantage to have one small book like the *Qur'an* or the *Book of Mormon* as a scripture that people could have ready access to? Who in the world has the time to read such a large library of scriptures, even the most spiritual among us? The answer to these very natural questions is this: Usually, when Westerners especially think about religious or spiritual pursuit, we tend to think of such pursuits as existing outside the realm of everyday life. The philosophy of Dharma, however, teaches us that spirituality is not a part of life that is meant to be relegated merely to the realms of theology and philosophy. Rather, being an eternal culture that has the ability to reveal to us the very source and grounding of all reality, Dharma spirituality is designed to inform, and thus transform, every single aspect of the human experience in this world. This includes, certainly the spiritual, but more, it also includes the fields of science, art, medicine, politics, economics, mathematics, martial sciences, architecture, music, city planning, cosmology and cosmogony, ethics and morality, language and grammar, and every other field of human endeavor that we can possibly think about.

Dharma teaches us that all these fields, and more, can be viewed from an overtly spiritual perspective, and thus be used toward the task of self-realization and in the service of God. This being the case, Sanatana Dharma has a vast myriad of sacred scriptures that speak about each of these many fields of endeavor from a purely spiritual perspective. The Vedic scriptures, then, form not only the basis of a specific religion, but offer the very foundational knowledge necessary for the creation and maintaining of an entire spiritual civilization. As a result of this unique approach to the nature of spiritually revealed literature, the *Vedas* are understood to be the source of perfect knowledge in every realm of thought and action.

It is for this reason that all sincere Dharmis (follower of Dharma) are guided by the Vedic scriptures in all important spiritual and secular decisions in their lives. Indeed, the knowledge contained in the Vedic scriptures have been shown for the last 5100 years to be so reliable, effective and perfect that all serious Dharmis use the Vedic scriptures as the ultimate test of whether or not a statement or proposition can be trusted as reliable or not. All authentic *gurus* must be able to demonstrate that their teachings are derived directly from the Vedic scriptures, and do not merely have the teacher's own speculation or crafty mind as their source. If the Vedic scriptures uphold a proposition or practice to be truth, then it is true. If it is not upheld in the Vedic scriptures, then its truth must at the very least be questioned.

Another important factor in the issue of the practical efficacy of accessing the totality of Vedic scriptures is that in our current age (which is known in the Vedic world-view as the Kali Yuga, or Age of Conflict), there is no necessity to read the entire Vedic literature in order to have a full grasp of the philosophy of Dharma. At the very beginning of our age, over 5100 years ago, the last incarnation (*avatara*) of God, Bhagavan Sri Krishna, provided us with a scripture that forms the most perfect philosophical summation of the entire teachings of the *Vedas*. This work is known as the famous *Bhagavad Gita*, or Song of God. By fully grasping the brief 700 verses of this work, one can have a summary understanding of the full purport of the complete Vedic scriptures. The central importance of the *Bhagavad Gita* in the spectrum of the Vedic literature has traditionally been understood to be so immense that we have devoted a large section later in this book to an in-depth study of this principal scripture.

1.1.5 Who is a Dharmi?

What are the minimal prerequisites necessary for a person to be considered a follower of Sanatana Dharma? The important question of what officially makes a person a follower of any particular spiritual tradition is answered in a remarkably similar way in most of the world's larger religions, including the tradition of Sanatana Dharma. A person is an official follower of a specific religion if he a) accepts the scripture(s) of that religion as an authoritative source of truth in his life, b) accepts the essential teachings of that tradition as his own personal credo, and c) openly acknowledges that it is his religion. As an example: if a person accepts the Bible as his scripture, accepts the central teachings of Christianity, and declares himself a Christian, then he is a Christian.

In a similar manner, if a person accepts the Vedic scriptures as their spiritual guide in life, believes in the central teachings of Sanatana Dharma as they are revealed in the Vedic scriptures, and openly acknowledges that he is a follower of Sanatana Dharma, then that person is automatically welcomed into the family of Sanatana Dharma. In other words, if a person freely and consciously identifies with Sanatana Dharma, then they are a Sanatana Dharmi.

There is no official ceremony or ritual that a person needs to undertake to be accepted as a Dharmi. There is no "conversion" in the modern sense of that term that is necessary for a person to officially be a Sanatana Dharmi. Rather, if a person accepts the scriptures, the teachings and the practices of Sanatana Dharma, then they are as much of a Sanatana Dharmi as anyone who was "born" into the tradition. Being "born" into the tradition does not in any way give a person a superior status to someone who has chosen to adopt Sanatana Dharma having been "born" into a different religion.

While having a mere nominal affiliation with a religious tradition is alone not enough for salvation, of course, personally identifying with a specific spiritual tradition represents, in fact, the very beginning stage of making spiritual progress within that tradition. It is for this reason that followers of Sanatana Dharma must openly and verbally identify with Sanatana Dharma as their spiritual path. If you are a follower of Sanatana Dharma, then do not be afraid to say so!

1.1.6 Monotheistic Panentheism[1]

Another unique feature of Sanatana Dharma is its philosophy on the nature of God. As we know, there are a variety of opinions as to what constitutes the Absolute. Some religions believe in polytheism, the idea that ultimately there is a council of gods and goddesses who collectively rule over reality. Some espouse pantheism, which teaches that the totality of nature in and of itself constitutes the highest Absolute. Finally, several religions are monotheistic in their theological systems. Monotheistic religions teach that the supreme Absolute, often called God in the English language, is one, unitary, omnicomptent, transcendent being, and the

---

[1] Panentheism is not to be confused with pantheism.

source of all reality. On the question of the nature of the Absolute, Sanatana Dharma falls very clearly under the heading of a monotheistic religion. We believe that there is only one Supreme Being who is the origin and sustainer of all reality, and that the highest goal (*artha*) in life is to know, to love, to serve, and to come to an eventual state of intimate communion with the Divine Being, God.

There are many names for the Supreme Godhead in the Sanskrit language. Two of the most important, however, are Brahman and Narayana. Brahman is the more generally philosophical of these names, and designates God as the source of all abundance and growth. Narayana, on the other hand, is the more intimate and personal, and thus more important, of these two names. Narayana means "the Sustainer of All Beings".

How Sanatana Dharma expresses its view of monotheism does differ significantly from the Abrahamic monotheism found in Judaism, Christianity and Islam. The Abrahamic religions espouse what I would term an "anthropomorphic monotheism", in which their god, variously termed Yahweh or Allah (who both really represent the very same being), is seen in very materialistic, earthly and human terms by his followers.

In the Old Testament and Qur'anic depictions, for example, the Abrahamic version of this divinity is one in which their god displays many of the emotions, jealousies, hatreds and decidedly mercantile concerns of territorial acquisition and conquest that we usually associate with imperfect humanity.[2] He is often depicted rallying his acolytes to bloody

---

[2] Among many other Old Testament passages clearly illustrating the violently anthropomorphic behavior of the god of the Old Testament, please see especially: Deuteronomy 2:31-34, Deuteronomy 3:1-7, Deuteronomy 7:1-6:20:16-17,

military conquest in his name, as depicted in Joshua 6:20-21, for example:

> When the trumpets sounded, the army shouted, and at the sound of the trumpet, when the men gave a loud shout, the wall collapsed; so everyone charged straight in, and they took the city. They devoted the city to the LORD and destroyed with the sword every living thing in it—men and women, young and old, cattle, sheep and donkeys.

Likewise in Joshua 8:1-2 it states:

> Then the LORD said to Joshua, 'Do not be afraid; do not be discouraged. Take the whole army with you, and go up and attack Ai. For I have delivered into your hands the king of Ai, his people, his city and his land. You shall do to Ai and its king as you did to Jericho and its king, except that you may carry off their plunder and livestock for yourselves. Set an ambush behind the city.

It is very clear from the writings of the Old Testament and the Qur'an themselves that the god of the Abrahamic religions is viewed as a god of conquest.

Additionally, the supreme being of the Abrahamic world-view is viewed by his devotees as being remotely transcendent, distant and "other" in relation to both the creation and all created beings. God, in this impersonal view, is infinitely removed from all human beings, from all living entities, and from all the elements of nature and the natural world. Indeed, "God" in this tradition is meant to be feared and obeyed.[3] The

---

Psalms 136:17-21, Joshua 6:20-21, Joshua 8:1-2, Joshua 11:14, Numbers 31:7-12, Numbers 31:14-18, Numbers 31:25-47, I Samuel 15:1-3, Isaiah 13:13-20, Ezekiel 9:1-7, II Chronicles 36:16-17, Jeremiah 48:10.

[3] "Fear the Lord your God, serve him only and take your oaths in his name." (Deuteronomy, 6:13)

Abrahamic ontology of the divine radically juxtaposes that divine against everything else that is not specifically Yahweh/Allah, with little more to connect the creator with his creation than the shear causal fact of one having been created by the arbitrary will of the other.

The world-view of Sanatana Dharma, by stark contrast, can be termed a "panentheistic monotheism". God, for our ancient tradition, is seen not as reflecting flawed human personality traits, with all of our lesser foibles, egoically fueled emotional outbursts, and need for financial, political and territorial acquisition. The true Absolute is not anthropomorphic in nature. Rather than God being anthropomorphically inspired, human beings and all of creation are seen by Sanatana Dharma, instead, as being theomorphic, or modeled after God, having God as our ultimate source, origin and enforming principle.

God is the locus and source of an unlimited number of infinitely expansive positive attributes (*ananta-kalyana-gunaih*), and is a fully omnicompetent being; no task stands beyond God's capability to perfectly perform; no action or possibility is too great for God's power. God (Brahman) is ontologically antecedent and transcendent to both finite living beings (Atman) and material creation (Jagat) since God is the very source of existence for both of these phenomena.

Despite the transcendentally situated nature of the Absolute, however, unlike the general belief of the Abrahamic faiths, that very same Absolute is still simultaneously wholly eminent in all of creation. There is no place where God is not. Indeed, for Sanatana Dharma, it is the very presence of God within the very core of all things that gives all things their very existence ontologically, and their very *raison d'être* spiritually. God is present within all of the material creation, within all of nature, in the hearts of every living being, and ever-present within our own essential being as the very Soul of our soul, the very foundation of our being, and the sustainer of our existence. Indeed, it is understood that if you were capable of pointing to anything either perceivable or conceivable in which God were not present - you would actually be pointing to nothing at all! This is the reason why the very highest name for God in the tradition of Sanatana Dharma is the Sanskrit term "Sriman Narayana", or "the Auspicious Sustainer of All Beings."

1.1.7 Vishva Dharma: The Universal Path

Being the Eternal Natural Way, Sanatana Dharma is a world-view that is universal in nature, and that can be followed by any sincere person who is ready to know Truth. It is not relegated only to a particular people, nation, ethnicity or geographical region. Dharma is not a race, a parochial cultural expression, a nationality, or a geographically bound phenomenon. Rather, Dharma is as universally applicable a truth and a systematic methodology as are the knowledge-revealing intellectual realms of mathematics, science, logic, or philosophy. As a result of the universalism of Dharma, this path is open to any sincere seeker on Earth, regardless of the person's national or ethnic heritage. Sanatana Dharma is not a race, a nationality or an ethnicity. Sanatana Dharma is not Indian, Asian or Eastern. Sanatana Dharma is the Eternal Natural Way, and it is the spiritual inheritance of all living beings.[4]

---

[4] For a more in-depth examination of the universal nature of Sanatana Dharma, see my introduction to Dr. David Frawley's book *Universal Hinduism: Towards a New Vision of Sanatana Dharma.*

1.1.8 Ethnicity Versus Religion

A very common mistake that many make is to erroneously equate being of Indian ethnicity with being a follower of the religion of Sanatana Dharma. The two categories of ethnicity and religion are very far from synonymous. Being Indian is an ethnicity, while being a Dharmi is a religious choice. While the dual categories of ethnicity and religion are legitimate and convenient methods used to designate and understand the diversity inherent in people, the terms ethnicity and religion refer to two very distinct categories of human identity.

An ethnicity is comprised of the genetic inheritance of an individual that determines such factors as a person's race, physical appearance, IQ, biological predispositions and other physically inherent attributes. Ethnicity is an unalterable biological fact. A person is born with an ethnicity, and it is impossible to change one's ethnicity from one to another. Ethnicity is a physical phenomenon, and thus lies outside the area of personal choice.

Religion, on the other hand, is not determined by one's genes, ethnicity, race or biology. Rather, religion fall under the domain of philosophical and spiritual world-view. Religion is an intellectual, spiritual and will-oriented phenomenon, and is thus a matter of free personal choice. At some point in a person's life, whether done consciously, or by mere cultural or familial acquiescence, each person chooses to either follow a certain religion, or even to have no religion at all. More, over the course of an individual's life, that person can even change their religion multiple times. They can be a Christian as a youth, convert to Buddhism as a teenager, and then choose to follow Sanatana Dharma as an adult. We have no choice as to our ethnicity; but we all choose our religion.

1.1.9 Sanatana Dharma is not an "Indian" Religion

All too often people will make the closely similar mistake of equating Sanatana Dharma specifically with the current nation-state of India. We will often hear such inaccurate depictions of Sanatana Dharma as "the religion of India", or of the Vedic scriptures as "Indian literature". In actuality, not only are the terms "Sanatana Dharma" and "India" not synonymous, but the two actually have nothing to do with one another. Sanatana Dharma is not a concept that is bound to any one particular nation on this Earth. Rather, Sanatana Dharma pertains to all living beings regardless of their national background. It is the common spiritual heritage of all human beings, and applies to Europeans, Americans, Latin Americans, Australians, and others just as much as it does to the residents of South Asia.

The current nation of India is a very modern political-geographical construct that was founded in 1947, and that only very roughly and inaccurately corresponds to the past historical sphere of cultural influence that Dharma once enjoyed. India as a political entity is not currently a Dharmic state, nor is it even a "Hindu" state in any other sense of this term other than the fact of shear demographics. India is today as radically secular a state as is the United States or most of the nations of Europe. Modern India was founded as a nation that was designed to treat all religions as equal and that would not allow any one particular religion to dominate the cultural or political spheres. While it is true that approximately 83% of India's population are nominal followers of Sanatana Dharma, thus making India the nation currently with the highest number of Sanatana Dharma adherents, India also has a very large Muslim population, as well as tens of millions of Christians, Sikhs, Jains, Buddhists, atheists, and a smaller number of Zoroastrians and Jews. Thus, when encountering a person of Indian heritage, it would be both highly presumptuous and possibly even insulting to simply assume that he or she is a follower of Sanatana Dharma merely because the person is from India. Today's India is not a Vedic nation, and has not been one for quite some time.

There is today no nation in existence that governs in accordance with the eternal principles of Dharma. Indeed, the very last nation in history to rule in nominal accordance with Dharmic principles was the Kingdom of Nepal up until the final Communist takeover and cultural destruction of that nation in 2006. For more information on the political structure of a Dharma Nation, refer to my book *The Dharma Manifesto*.

1.1.10 The Ancient Dharmic Cultural Sphere

At one time in history, Sanatana Dharma was the predominant worldview on earth. As we look at the history of the ancient world, it becomes very quickly apparent that the further back we explore history, the more Dharmic the world correspondingly was, and the greater was the corresponding expanse of Vedic cultural and spiritual influence. If we examine at the continent of Asia at the time of the Buddha, for example, which corresponds to around 500 BC, we see that the Vedic sphere of influence covered at least two-thirds of Asia.

At that juncture in history, the Dharmic and Vedic world-view constituted the primary spiritual/cultural/civilizational organizing principle in every region of Asia ranging from much of Persia, Central Asia and Afghanistan in the West, stretching over all of South Asia, which includes today's Pakistan, Nepal, Tibet, India, Bhutan, Bangladesh and Sri Lanka, and extending as far east as all of South-East Asia, including Burma, Thailand, Cambodia, Laos, Vietnam, southern China, Malaysia, all the many islands of Indonesia, and large parts of the Philippines.

Even in the Middle East, we have seen that many of the pre-Abrahamic cultures followed forms of spirituality that were either directly and strongly influenced by the Vedic tradition, and in many cases that were completely Vedic in content. The ancient Hittite empire (currently the nation of Turkey), as well as the Philistines, Mesopotamians, Assyrians, Mitani, Arabs, and most of the peoples of the Middle East practiced religions that were clearly Dharmic. Most of Europe, as well, practiced forms of Dharmic spirituality during the Axial Age (roughly 500 BCE), including the ancient Greeks and Romans, the Germanic tribes, the ancient Slavs and the Celtic people.

On an almost weekly basis, modern archeologists and scholars uncover ancient Vedic temples, religious icons (such as sacred representations of Vishnu, Ganesha, Shiva and Shakti Devi) and other forms of Vedic artifacts in many of these diverse nations. Indeed, ancient statues of Vishnu have recently been found in Russia. This entire region, from Europe to the Philippines, once constituted the international spiritual/cultural matrix of Sanatana Dharma.

Arguably, from a more general understanding of Dharma as a natural law philosophy, the actual world-view of Dharma was itself followed under different names by almost every ancient culture and civilization on Earth, including most pre-Abrahamic Middle Eastern, European, and Native

South American and North American peoples. With the arising of the more aggressive Abrahamic religions, however, we have witnessed a 2500-year decline of the influence of Dharma in most regions of the world, and a corresponding rise in Abrahamic religious fundamentalism and secular materialism.

1.1.11 The Dharmi Population

As the number of adherents of Sanatana Dharma steadily declined over the last 2500 years, today there are only approximately one billion Dharmis still left worldwide. Demographically, this makes Sanatana Dharma the third largest religion on earth, with Christianity being the largest, and Islam occupying second place numerically. While, the vast majority of Dharmis today happen to live in South Asia and to a smaller extent in South-East Asia, we do find Dharmi populations living happily in almost every nation in the world today. There is almost no nation on earth today in which we do not find followers of Sanatana Dharma, including every nation of Europe, South America, Asia, Australasia and Africa. Recently, we have seen a natural and spontaneous revival and re-adoption of Sanatana Dharma taking place in many nations throughout the world. In several nations of Europe, such as Germany, Russia and Lithuania, Sanatana Dharma is often counted as either the first or second largest growing spiritual tradition in these nations.

In the United States alone, there are approximately 5 million Dharmis. Of these, about 2 million are of South Asian (Indian, Nepali, etc.) and Caribbean (Guyanese, Trinidadian, etc.) origin. Significantly, the other 3 million are non-Indians who have adopted and practice Sanatana Dharma to greater or lesser extents. This largely unreported latter group of non-Indian Dharmis is what I have called the "Hidden Dharmis". Many of these non-Indian, American followers of Dharma remain "hidden" simply due to the fact that they may not necessarily have consciously or vocally identified themselves as Dharmis. But this is usually despite the fact that they are nonetheless following Sanatana Dharma in actual daily practice and in their chosen world-view.

There are, for example, multiple millions of Americans who, with great enthusiasm and discipline, a) practice Yoga, b) engage in meditation, c) gain guidance from such Vedic scriptures as the *Bhagavad Gita*, d) maintain a vegetarian diet, e) believe firmly in such Dharmic concepts as *karma* and reincarnation, f) and who follow such Vedic natural health modalities as *ayurveda*. So, in effect, these millions of Americans are **practicing** Sanatana Dharma philosophy and disciplines in their daily lives - whether or not they have yet gained sufficient knowledge about their practices to clearly **acknowledge** Sanatana Dharma as their spiritual path. Despite the fact that they are enthusiastically practicing Sanatana Dharma, many of these very same American Dharmis do not necessarily consciously identify with the tradition of Sanatana Dharma as their own religion of choice. It is my hope that this book will help these millions of American Dharmis to undertand that Sanatana Dharma is, indeed, the religion that they are practicing, and that they should now openly identify with.

What we find when we look at the Sanatana Dharma community in both America and Europe is that there are actually two separate and distinct communities, one composed Indian "Hindus", and the other made up of millions of non-Indian practitioners of Yoga spirituality. More, each of these communities directly possesses what the other community lacks.

Indian Hindu Community: Members of the Indian "Hindu" community, on the one hand, have the advantage of consciously and verbally identifying themselves as Dharmis, as well as holding on to their beautiful temple, ritual and cultural traditions. The disadvantage that the Indian Dharmi community has, however, is in both fostering a deep understanding of the Vedic scriptures and in actually practicing Yoga and meditation. As a result, it is often a rare occurrence to see even one Indian "Hindu" in a typical Yoga class of fifty students. But, conversely, it is also very rare to see more than one or two non-Indians among a crowd of 500 in a Hindu temple!

The "Hidden Dharmi" Community: The "Hidden Dharmis", on the other hand, have the advantage of zealously studying the Vedic scriptures, as well as practicing Yoga and meditation, but coupled with the disadvantage of not knowing that they are part of a greater and ancient Vedic community of one-billion fellow Dharmis.

Ideally, both communities will come together in time, each providing what the other is lacking, and creating a more whole and integrated Dharma community in which all will consciously identify themselves as followers of the distinct and dignified tradition of Sanatana Dharma, while also practicing in a regular and disciplined way the actual spiritual practices that form the very core of Sanatana Dharma, which are Yoga and meditation. To merely call oneself a "Hindu", while not also practicing the lifestyle and spiritual disciplines of Dharma, is to only be a nominal "Hindu". While to practice Yoga and meditation enthusiastically, but without having the added psychological benefit of consciously identifying with the tradition and community of practitioners (*dharma-sangha*), is to be a spiritual orphan disconnected from our greater Dharma family.

Both Indian and non-Indian followers of Sanatana Dharma have very good reasons to take immense pride in their spiritual path. As we will see, Sanatana Dharma represents the most well developed philosophical world-view, and the most effective spiritual path known to human history.

Second Wave

- Philosophical Grounding

Chapter 2 The Philosophical Foundations of Sanatana Dharma

2.1.1 Dharma as a World-view

Throughout the unceasing course of human history, there have been a small number of revolutionary ideas that have served to define the nature and shape of an entire era and people. These ground-breaking ideas have been neither parochially limited, nor culturally demarcated in scope, but rather have served as meta-cultural, trans-geographical ideological principles that have assisted in guiding and molding the direction and purpose of entire civilizations and epochs in history. Such world-views are *Weltanschauung*, a German word that has no English equivalent. The closest translation is perhaps the phrase "world-perspective", or a "world-view". It is a way of perceiving reality, a way of seeing.

A *Weltanschauung* can be of either a positive and life-enhancing nature, while others can be devastatingly destructive. Some of the meta-ideas responsible for such civilizational transformation have included the world-altering ideas of theism, science, secularism, materialism, Marxism, hierarchy, equality, and democracy, among others. Of all the known ideological world-views to have arisen in human memory, the ancient principle of Dharma ("Natural Law" one can say) is by far the most important, universal, compelling, and surprisingly least known in our age, of all *Weltanschauung*. It is a world-view that has shaped entire intercontinental civilizations in the ancient past, and that is still making its presence known today. It is also the one world-view destined to shape the future of our new global civilization in the 21st Century and beyond.

As we enter the beginning stages of the 21st Century, we find that the world as we know it continues to figuratively shrink in size - and that ideas, cultures, and possibilities that in the past seemed so mysteriously remote and far from our grasp have now entered the clear purview of accessibility to us all. This is especially true of the millennia-old divide that had separated East from West, the "Oriental" from the "Occidental" world-views. *"East is East, and West is West, and never the twain shall meet"*, proclaimed Rudyard Kipling over a hundred years ago; and more wrong has a man rarely been known to have been.

Today, ideas, cultures, philosophies and world-views that were once relegated to a certain geographical area are now accessible at the click of a mouse, with many having now gained planetary influence. Today, meta-cultural ideas have the ability to affect not only traditional ethnic enclaves, or even continental civilizations, but human civilization as a whole. The concept of Democracy, for example, is no longer merely an "American idea", but has come to inspire lovers of freedom everywhere, regardless of their ethnic, social, or linguistic affiliation. Similarly, the idea of free-market economics, once a notion seen as being the sole possession of the Anglo-American world, is now an idea that has swept much of the globe – in some ways for good, and in others deleterious. In our contemporary world, "Western" ideals of freedom are celebrated by secularists in the Islamic Middle East, and conversely the Buddhist Dalai Lama has a following in the West as large as he does in Tibet. Similarly, more people practice the ancient tradition of Yoga in the United States than do in all of India, its land of original development. Significantly, many other philosophical principles at first seemingly originating from specific geo-cultural spheres in Asia, and once seen as being inaccessibly remote and mysterious notions to the West, have now become commonplace throughout the entire world. Some of these valuable principles and practices include Yoga, meditation, environmentalism, religious tolerance, vegetarianism, Vedantic metaphysics, Buddhism, and the principles of *karma* and reincarnation.

Of all of these concepts to have been reintroduced into the West in recent decades, and thus consequently reintroduced onto the world stage, the principle of Dharma is by far the most ancient, important, universal, and powerful concept in existence today. Being at one time in history an ideology whose influence spanned much of the globe, Dharma represents the most ancient and prevalent philosophical concept in the entirety of religious history. Dharma is a *Weltanschauung* like none other, because no other world-view has been as long lasting, universal in application, and culturally all encompassing. The primary teachings of Dharma were at one time as prevalent as is the idea of liberty today. The prevalence of Dharma, under a variety of different names, has been demonstrated to exist in almost every pre-Christian civilization and culture in the world. It is thus the common heritage of a large majority of the earth's inhabitants. As expressed in the specific tradition of "Hinduism" (properly known as "Sanatana Dharma"), the metaphysical concept of Dharma is both a spiritual path, as well as a comprehensive ideology and world-view that directly informs the realms of politics, social theory, economics, culture theory, architecture, medicine, religion, aesthetics, martial warfare, philosophy, ethics, mathematics, and every other aspect of human concern.

Though the concept of Dharma is the earliest concept known to humanity, it is a world-view that is hardly relegated to a hoary and obsolete past. Rather, the positive, life-affirming principles of Dharma have proven themselves to be as relevant today as they have ever been. In the following philosophical exposition and practical manifesto of Dharma, we will explore the meaning of Dharma, and how to maximally utilize the unlimited benefits that Dharma can offer us, our families, and our troubled world today.

The earliest instances of the concept of Dharma in world history are first found in the most ancient literature known to humanity, the Vedic literature of Sanatana Dharma. The *Vedas* were first composed in Sanskrit approximately 3800 BC. Previous to even this time, this literature is known to have been preserved orally, and passed down from generation to generation of priests, seers and sages before finally being committed to writing. Thus, no one can accurately date the antiquity of the *Vedas* and consequently of Dharma. Dharma is one of the most ancient concepts known to humanity.

The word "Dharma" is found repeatedly throughout the entire corpus of the Vedic scriptures, from the earliest *Rig Veda* to the *Bhagavad Gita*. There is almost no scripture in the entirety of the Vedic literature where one will not come across the word "Dharma" as the preeminent name of the religio-philosophical world-view taught in these ancient, sacred texts. Sometimes the word "Dharma" is used by itself; at other times it is used in conjunction with other qualifying words, such as "Vaidika Dharma" (Vedic Dharma), "Vishva Dharma" (Global Dharma), "Yoga Dharma" (the Dharma of Union), or more frequently as "Sanatana Dharma" (the Eternal Natural Way). The diversity of adjectival emphases will vary in accordance with the precise context in which the word is used. Of these terms, the name "Sanatana Dharma" has been the most widely used name of the path of Truth, and is used as far back as the *Rig Veda* (3800 BC), the very earliest scripture of the Indo-European peoples, and the earliest written text known to humanity. It is also the most philosophically profound and conceptually beautiful name for the path of Truth.

While some reading this work will have no doubt encountered the term "Sanatana Dharma" (The Eternal Natural Way) before, not everyone is necessarily as familiar with the full philosophical implications of the term's meaning. Thus it is necessary to explicate the term's full meaning in depth. The Sanskrit word "*sanatana*" is the easier of the two words to translate into non-Sanskritic languages. It denotes that which always is, that which has neither beginning nor end, that which is eternal in its very essence. The concept of eternality that the word "*sanatana*" is trying to convey is a radically different concept than is ordinarily understood in the Western Abrahamic religions. When the Abrahamic religions of Judaism, Christianity, and Islam employ the concept of eternality, what is usually being communicated is that *x* thing, having come into being, will never come to an end. In other words, "eternal" for the Abrahamic religions, usually refers only to the future. It is a unidirectional concept. A more accurate term for this Abrahamic concept is thus "everlasting", rather than "eternal" proper.

In Sanatana Dharma, however, the concept of eternality denotes something quite different from the standard Abrahamic notion. The Dharmic idea of eternality is nuanced with a subtlety and sophistication that is not easily copied in the West. This is the case because, eternality refers in the Dharmic context to both an infinitely non-ending past, as well as future. In this more expansive and bi-directional model of eternality, the concept of *sanatana* extends not only into the infinite recesses of the future, but into the past as well. By referring to something as "*sanatana*", the idea is that an eternal object will not only never come to an end, but that it has also always existed in the past as well. Something that is eternal has necessary existence. That is, it is not possible to even conceive of such a thing not existing. Thus, God (Brahman), the individual self (*atman*), prime materiality (*jagat*, or *prakriti*), Truth (*satya*), the *Veda* (Truth rendered into literary form), and Dharma itself all have necessary existence. They are *sanatana*. They always have been - and they always shall be.

As Sri Krishna, the last incarnation (*avatara*) of God who appeared on earth over 5100 years ago, explains in His teachings in the *Bhagavad Gita*: "Never was there a time when I was not in existence, nor you, nor all these kings. And never in the future shall any of us cease to exist." *Sanatana* means necessary existence.

2.1.2 Understanding the Concept of Dharma

Unlike the word "*sanatana*", the term "*dharma*" is a word that can be properly rendered into the English language only with the greatest of difficulty. This is the case because there is no one corresponding English term that fully renders both the denotative and the connotative meanings of the term with maximal sufficiency. When translators (and especially professors of "South Asian Studies") have attempted to translate the term "*dharma*" into English, they have often been forced to betray the real essence of the term, and have instead clumsily relied on secondary attributes of the term's real meaning. Often "*dharma*" has been inelegantly translated as "righteousness", "religion", "law", "duty", "the way", "morality", etc. While these terms are not incorrect per se, all of these attempts at translation are merely descriptions of the characteristic parts of Dharma. But the actual essence of Dharma lies behind them all.

Rather than merely communicating a nominal subject for which there can be an easy word-for-word equivalency, the Sanskrit term *"dharma"* is an attempt at communicating the elaborate nuances of a metaphysical concept. So, if we wanted to properly translate into the English language what the term *"dharma"* is actually attempting to communicate, rather than using a single word to do so, we would need to use a paragraph!

The word *"dharma"* is etymologically derived from the Sanskrit verb root *"dhṛ"*, meaning "to sustain", "to uphold", "to support", etc. And it is in these verbal derivative meanings that we can begin to clearly detect the precise idea that the term *"dharma"* is attempting to communicate.

The denotative meaning of "*dharma*" straightforwardly designates an essential attribute of x object - an attribute whose absence renders the object devoid of either rational meaning or existential significance. An existent thing's *dharma* is that which constitutes the thing's very essence, without which, the very concept of the thing would be rendered meaningless. In the pre-Abrahamic (and thus Dharmic) Greco-Roman world, the great Pagan philosopher Aristotle wrote about the inherent essentiality of all individual things, and agreed that all things have a primary essential attribute, without which it would be left devoid of meaning. Everything in existence has a *dharma* (essential attribute), because everything has an essence. Thus, essence ontologically precedes and gives both form and meaning to existence. More, any existent thing is merely the quantitative, and thus measurable, manifestation of its qualitative essence.

To illustrate the full meaning of this term, we can use the following examples: It is the *dharma*, or essence, of water to be wet. Without the essential attribute (*dharma*) of wetness, the concept and existential fact of water loses all meaning. It is literally impossible for us to even imagine what it would mean to drink water that wasn't wet. Likewise, it is the *dharma*, or essence, of fire to be hot. If we had a fire that didn't have the property of heat emanating from it, we wouldn't have fire at all. The fire's very essence would be missing. Thus, the existent fire would lose its existence due to a lack of essence. The *dharma* of space is to be expansive, and the *dharma* of time is to be ever progressing. An almost infinite number of similar such examples can be given. Thus it is the intrinsic *dharma* of any particular thing that makes it unique, and that gives its existence sustenance and meaning. Dharma sustains.

This more straightforward, denotative meaning of *dharma* is easy enough to comprehend. It is, however, when we come to the more important connotative meaning of the term "*dharma*" that we then leave the more philosophical concerns of microcosmic physics behind, and then enter the realm of the overtly metaphysical. Going from the microcosmic to the more macrocosmic significance of the term "*dharma*", we begin to understand the profound power of this concept.

For, according to the ancient Vedic tradition itself, the very empirical cosmos in which we find ourselves currently situated also has its own inherent *dharma*, its own essential attributive nature, without which the universe and reality around us becomes meaningless. Just as every individual component of the world around us has its own inherent *dharma* on a microcosmic scale, similarly, the world itself has its own inherent essential nature. In this more macro-cosmological sense, the term *dharma* is designed to communicate the view that there is an underlying structure of natural law – a natural and intelligent order - that is inherent in the very intrinsic constitution of Being itself. The universe itself has its own *dharma*.

The currently dominant secular-materialist world-view - the foundations upon which rests many of the most fundamental presuppositions, dogmas and articles of faith of modernity - postulates a world that is devoid of inherent meaning and purpose. In the opinion of post-Enlightenment era secular-materialism, our world does not have a transcendent basis upon which it depends, but rather our world is a realm that is ethically relativistic, philosophically meaningless, devoid of a Divine intelligence responsible for its otherwise obvious orderly nature, and is thus a realm that is ultimately rendered absurd.

The Vedic world-view, by stark contrast, sees the universe in a very different light. Our world, according to Dharma, is a place that is replete with inherent meaning, value, and an intelligent design underlying its physical principles and laws, as well as a transcendent purpose that, while not necessarily discernible via empirical means, nonetheless forms a very concrete spiritual basis of all empirical reality. The material, according to Dharma, finds its origin and sustaining ground in the spiritual. The measurable is grounded upon the infinite. The spiritual necessarily precedes the material. The world is here for a purpose – and that purpose is God's purpose. The word "*dharma*", in this more important philosophical sense, refers to those underlying natural principles that are inherent in the very structure of reality, ordering our world as the metaphysical backdrop to the drama of everyday phenomenal existence, and that has their origin in the causeless will and grace of God. Dharma is Natural Law. Thus, if we needed to render the entire term "Sanatana Dharma" into English, we can cautiously translate it as "The Eternal Natural Way".

52

Jean-Jacques Burlamaqui paints a picture of the symbiotic inter-
relationship between the metaphysical Natural Law (Dharma) and our
surrounding empirical physical reality in the following manner.

> Let us only cast our eyes on this universe, and we shall
> every where discover, even at the first glance, an admi
> rable beauty, regularity, and order, and this admiration
> will increase in proportion as, in searching more closely
> into nature, we enter into the particulars of the struc
> ture, proportion, and use of each part. For then we shall
> clearly see, that every thing is relative to a certain end,
> and that these particular ends, though infinitely varied
> among themselves, are so dexterously managed and
> combined as to conspire all to a general design. Not
> withstanding this amazing diversity of creatures, there is
> no confusion we behold several thousand different spe
> cies, which preserve their distinct form and qualities.
> The parts of the universe are proportional and balanced,
> in order to preserve a general harmony and each of
> those parts has exactly its proper figure, proportions,
> situation, and motion, either to produce its particular
> effect, or to form a beautiful whole. It is evident there
> fore, that there is a design, a choice, a visible reason in
> all the works of nature, and consequently there are
> marks of wisdom and understanding, obvious, as it
> were, even to our very senses.

Jean-Jacques Burlamaqui, *The Principles of Natural Law*

Thus, it is the invisible hand of Dharma that is responsible for the ordered, balanced and cyclical state of the natural world, and of reality as a
whole.

The functional characteristics of the natural laws of Dharma are somewhat akin to the principles of physics. Indeed, the principles of physics
are themselves seen as only a pale reflection of the higher and founda-

tional metaphysical laws of Dharma. Like physics, the truths of Dharma are: a) axiomatically true, b) universally applicable, c) conformable to the laws of logic, d) verifiable and replicable via the respective laws of reason and experience, e) and thus, are completely scientific in nature. Next we will explore in more depth these five aspects of Dharma.

2.1.3 Dharma as Axiomatic

"Facts do not cease to exist because they are ignored"

-- Aldous Huxley

The unalterable functionality of Dharmic principles is the metaphysical equivalent of the concrete functional reality of physics. Like the laws of physics, the laws of Dharma are axiomatically true. That is, the fact of their truth is not dependent upon one's belief system, perceptual perspective, or ideological biases. Objective reality remains ever unaltered even in the face of belief's direct challenge. If, for example, one were to attempt to deny the physical law of gravity by claiming that such a law falls outside one's area of belief, gravity remains a concrete and unalterable reality of the physical world nonetheless. If one were to make the claim that the law of gravity only works for Roman Catholics, but not for Scottish Presbyterians, such an absurd claim can be easily refuted by shear empirical reality. The simple test of this unreasonable proposition would be to ask the Scottish Presbyterian to walk off the roof of a skyscraper and to then objectively observe if the reality of physics is really applicable to him or not. Empirical reality and logical necessity invariably prevail over subjective belief. In the same way in which the laws of physics are true whether or not we wish to acknowledge their truth, the truth of Dharma too is not dependent upon our belief or faith.

As is true of the laws of physics, the natural laws of Dharma are also true irrespective of one's personal belief or disbelief in them. They exist as objective and impersonally operative laws of nature regardless of our own subjective choice of religious affiliation, philosophical outlook, ideology, or belief system. In this regard, the author C.S. Lewis has written:

> The Tao [Dharma], which others may call Natural Law or Traditional Morality or the First Principles of Practical Reason or the First Platitudes, is not one among a series of possible systems of value. It is the sole source of all value judgments. If it is rejected, all value is rejected. If any value is retained, it is retained. The effort to refute it and raise a new system of value in its place is self-contradictory. There has never been, and never will be, a radically new judgment of value in the history of the world. What purport to be new systems or...ideologies...all consist of fragments from the Tao [Dharma] itself, arbitrarily wrenched from their context in the whole and then swollen to madness in their isolation, yet still owing to the Tao [Dharma] and to it alone such validity as they posses. (*The Abolition of Man*)

These laws are axiomatic, scientific, and mathematical in nature. Thus, Dharma is not "religious" in the modern, normative application of the term. It is not sectarian, denominationally oriented, or predicated upon blind faith. While such axiomatic principles as the laws of physics are more clearly discernable via empirical means, however, the laws of Dharma do not apply primarily to the realm of physics, but to the much more important underlying reality of philosophical metaphysics.

The principle of Dharma is not sectarian, dogmatic, or faith-dependent. Rather, they are pre-religious in both essence and function. Dharma existed before there were such institutions as sects, denominations, or world religions. Indeed, Dharma serves as the basis of all later organized religion. All present-day religious denominations - and even the largest and oldest of the recognized "world religions" - have clearly defined dates of origin within the realm of time, as well as discernable founders. Judaism is no more than 4,000 years old, and was founded by Abraham. Buddhism is 2,500 years old, and was based upon the teachings of Gautama Buddha. Christianity was born some 2,000 years ago from the teachings of Jesus of Nazareth. Islam is about 1,400 years old and is the creation of Muhammad. Dharma, on the other hand, was never "founded" at any point in recognizable history, nor is there any human being who can be identified as the "founder" of this world-view. Dharma originates at a time before there was such a thing as denominationalism, before all recognizable present-day world religions came into being, and at a time when spirituality was used as a means of harmoniously uniting humanity, and not exploited as a tool to divide them into sectarian identities. Dharma has no historical point of origination. Further, Dharma has no recognized founder, or prophet, or originator, other than the direct will and causeless overflowing grace of the Absolute.

At one time Dharma was the sole expression of humanity's yearning to stretch its hearts and intellects beyond the known world, and to intimately know and experience the source of all reality. Dharma was humanity's attempt to incorporate the will of the transcendent Divine into the everyday, phenomenal concerns of this world, and to live and explore politics, economics, the arts, music, philosophy, literary expression, and life itself as an everyday, every-moment celebration of the omnipresent imminence of the Divine.

56

When the rational and divinely inspired laws of Dharma governed the world, spirituality served as a source of unity, tolerance, joy, and mutual understanding. It is only with the later rise of the denominations that religion was then used to divide people, and to aggressively conquer others in the name of a god. Being thus a pre-religious phenomenon, Dharma serves as the spiritual foundation of all later denominational expressions of spirituality, and thus, by extension, as the very source of all important civilizations on earth. Dharma is the common heritage of all humanity, whether or not individual humans today are ready to acknowledge this fact or not.

2.1.4 Dharma as Universally Applicable

The concept of Dharma is not bound by sectarian considerations. It is trans-denominational and pre-religious. It is an axiomatically based truth that is, consequently applicable for all humanity, regardless of religious affiliation, ethnicity, creed, ideology, or personal belief. Dharma is not Hindu, Buddhist, Indian, European, Persian, White, or Asian. Rather, it serves as the unifying principle underlying all the peripheral differences that seem to incessantly divide humanity. Like the unalterable truths of mathematical principles, Dharma transcends human boundaries, human prejudices, and human faults, and is thus the central ordering principle for all human civilization.

The universal applicability of Dharma is especially seen in the fact that historically, it was at one time the prevalent world-view of most of humanity. At one time, the reality of Dharma was not a matter of disputation, but was a given, and was the foundation of every civilization, nation and tribe of the ancient world. The majority of ancient, pre-

Christian cultures were philosophically Dharmic in their overall world-view, even if they were also culturally and linguistically diverse. The vast ethnic and cultural diversity of myriad human societies found its unifying center in the teachings of Dharma. The concept of Dharma, encountered in a variety of local languages and names, was accepted as the preeminent ordering principle to be understood, respected, and emulated, in a wide variety of ancient, pre-Abrahamic cultures.

Though Dharma is one, it was expressed in different ways linguistically. The Sanskrit word "*dharma*" became the word "*dhamma*" for example, in the Prakrit language of Pali, the language of the oldest corpus of Buddhist scriptures. Further east, the Chinese word "*dao*" (sometimes spelt "*tao*") has the exact same meaning as the term "*dharma*", and designates "the way" or "the way of nature". The Chinese religion known as Daoism can be rendered into English as "the Way". Confucianism, too, accepted the reality of the *dao*, or "way of nature", as the primary ordering principle of both heaven and earth. The Chinese term "*dao*" becomes "*to*" and "*do*" in both Korean and Japanese. Similarly to Sanskrit (*dharma*) and Chinese (*dao*), the terms "*to*" and "*do*" mean "the way", and is encountered to this day in such terms as Shin**to** ("the way of the spirits"), aiki**do,** ken**do,** ju**do,** and tae-kwan-**do.**

Traversing westward, the pre-Islamic Persians referred to the concept of Dharma as "*asha*", which in Gathic Avestan literally means the ordering principle of the cosmos. "*Asha*" also means "what fits" in any and every situation, in every physical, emotional, ethical, mental, material and/or spiritual relationship, as well as "truth", "righteousness", and "order". The Persian concept of *Asha*, then, is synonymous in meaning with Dharma. The pre-Islamic Persians were faithful and enthusiastic followers of the way of Dharma. While the ordering principle of Dharma has been understood and honored throughout the length and breadth of Asia, however, Dharma has been nothing less than a trans-continental, universal concept.

The concept of Dharma is also found throughout the length and breadth of pre-Christian Europe. The ancient Greeks, for example, referred to this universal ordering principle as "*physis*", from whence we derive the English word "physics". In Latin, the Natural Law is known as "*liga natura*", and played a crucial part in the formation of Roman law, which in turn serves as the primary foundation of the modern Western tradition of law. The bulk of our laws today are based upon the Natural Law (i.e., Dharmic) antecedents of the Roman world. In addition to the Greco-Roman cultures of antiquity, Dharma is found in every other corner of pre-Christian Europe. Significantly, in the ancient, pre-Christian Lithuanian religion of Romuva, the term for this universally honored principle is "*darna*", Lithuanian being the European language that is closest linguistically to ancient Sanskrit.

Similarly, the ancient Egyptians were intimately acquainted with Dharma, which they termed "*ma'at*". Among all the 300 tribes of Native-Americans found in North America, the idea of Dharma was known by too many diverse names to even adequately mention, the vast majority of which translates into "The Way" in English. We will now briefly examine more in-depth several of the shared Dharmically inspired elemental principles and practices that many of these historically Dharmic cultures had in common.

Each Dharmically-inspired ancient culture - including Persian, Tibetan, Indian, Chinese, Japanese, Thai, Indonesian, Greco-Roman, Germanic, Celtic, Mayan, and Hopi, among dozens of others, all generally shared these same elemental Dharmic values, organizational paradigms and world-view.

2.1.5 Universal Elements of Dharmic Civilizations

1. Cyclical nature of time, life and nature.

2. Historical devolution of humanity ethically, morally, spiritually, civilizationally, etc.

3. Spirit is ontologically prior and superior to matter.

4. Transmigration (reincarnation) of the soul.

5. Hierarchy of being, all categories of existent objects, and of human society.

6. Meticulous demarcation of society into the class categories of a) sage/priest, b) martial class, and c) commoners/laborers.

7. Clear cosmological division of the universe into a tripartite structure of a) the heavenly realms, b) the earthly middle realm, and c) the hellish realms.

8. Deep respect and cultivation of personal virtue, morality, honor and values.

9. Belief in ethical universals/absolutes (*dharma, te, arête*, etc.), and the rejection of moral relativism.

10. A non-anthropomorphic view of reality, in which non-humans were afforded more respect and dignity than they were during the post-Abrahamic era.

11. Personification of the natural elements in the form of myriad species of spirits, fairies, gods and goddesses.

12. Panentheism: the simultaneous transcendence and immanence of the Transcendent.

13. Profound respect for wisdom and wise-people.

14. Understanding that the Earth is a Mother Goddess and a sentient being.

15. Tolerance of other people's beliefs, forms of worship, and choice of gods.

16. Teaching through primarily oral, not written, instruction.

17. Deductive, not inductive, reasoning.

18. Employment of sacred imagery.

19. Understanding that order is a positive state to be strived after, and that disorder and chaos are negative states that must be avoided at all costs, cosmically, socially, within the family, and in one's personal life.

20. A strict host/guest etiquette.

21. Theocratic governments were universally upheld in every ancient, pre-Abrahamic culture without exception.

22. Great respect for nature and the environment.

23. Respect and worship of one's family ancestors and of the ancestors of the nation.

24. Filial piety and respect for one's elders.

25. Clearly defined gender roles in which both men and women were afforded the respect and dignity of fully manifesting their specific natures.

26. Philosophy and intellectual life were grounded in spirituality.

27. Science cooperated with natural law, and did not see itself as being artificially at war with nature, as is the case in the modern era.

28. The sacredness and crucial importance of the teacher/student relationship in the passing down of knowledge. It was understood that one could only acquire spiritual truth through the guidance of a living master, and that the student needed to be worthy of acquiring such knowledge.

29. The concept of having small, manageable cities (*polis* in Greek, *pura* in Sanskrit) and city-states. The Vedic ideal was that a city should have no more than 50,000 inhabitants. Any larger population would lead to intense urban strife.

30. The preeminence of mysticism and reverence for mystics.

31. The presence of priestesses. Dharmic and Indo-European religions all had priestesses, in addition to male priests. These included hierodules (temple servants), dedicated virgins, as well as such oracles as the Roman Vestal Virgins, the Greek Sibyls and the Germanic Völvas.

32. The importance of astronomy and astrology for detecting and interpreting large-scale occurrences and transitions in our cosmos.

33. There was no distinction between theology and philosophy.

34. Worship of the household gods by every family.

35. Offering of food to the gods before human consumption.

36. Making the main temple the central focus of the city, both in placement and social/spiritual concern.

37. The Mandate of Heaven as the basis of king's authority.

38. The concept of ever-progressing cyclical ages (known a *yugas* in Sanskrit).

39. The recognition of the four basic material elements of water, earth, air and fire.

40. The existence and preeminence in all societies of a learned and wise priest class, such as the Celtic Druids, the South Asian Brahmins, the

Latin Flamines, and the Persian Magi.

41. The existence of a specified pantheon of major divinities recognized by each people and nation.

This list of common Dharmic elements found across diverse ancient cultures can be easily greatly expanded, and is being kept purposefully brief in order to serve as a cursory illustration of the universality of Dharma and Dharmic values throughout the ancient, pre-Abrahamic world.

2.1.6 The Logic of Dharma

An unfortunate, stereotypical misconception that some harbor whenever a trans-empirical, metaphysical concept is proffered is that the discussion has now hopelessly ventured to the "mystical" and the irrational. When speaking of the logical underpinnings of Dharma, however, nothing could be further from the truth. Murray Rothbard supports this contention in the following observation:

> It is indeed puzzling that so many modern philosophers should sniff at the very term "nature" as an injection of mysticism and the supernatural. An apple, let fall, will drop to the ground; this we all observe and acknowledge to be in the nature of the apple (as well as the world in general). Two atoms of hydrogen combined with one of oxygen will yield one molecule of water — behavior that is uniquely in the nature of hydrogen, oxygen, and water. There is nothing arcane or mystical about such observations. Why then cavil at the concept of "nature"? The world, in fact, consists of a myriad number of observable things, or entities. This is surely an observable fact. Since the world does not consist of one homogenous thing or entity alone, it follows that each one of these different things possesses differing attributes, otherwise they would all be the same thing. But if A, B, C,

etc., have different attributes, it follows immediately that they have different natures. It also follows that when these various things meet and interact, a specifically de limitable and definable result will occur. In short, specif ic, delimitable causes will have specific delimitable ef fects. The observable behavior of each of these entities is the law of their natures, and this law includes what happens as a result of the interactions. The complex that we may build up of these laws may be termed the struc ture of natural law. What is "mystical" about that?

(The Ethics of Liberty)

Reason and logic are an inherent part of the Natural Way. "The natural-law doctrine usually assumes that man has a specific nature which in-volves certain natural needs..." according to the philosopher and celebrated University of Chicago professor Mortimer J. Adler "...and the power of reason to recognize what is really good for man in terms of these needs." *(The Nature of Natural Law)* The laws of human reasoning employed in the fields of philosophy and logic are seen, not only as a fair and valid means of assessing the claims of Dharma philosophy, but fur-ther, the culture of Dharma itself has led to the direct development of many of the most rigidly logical principles of reason known to the human race. Logic itself was originally developed by the pre-Christian philoso-phers of the Platonic and Aristotelian schools of Europe, as well as the Nyaya (logic) and Pramanavada (epistemology) schools of Sanatana Dharma. The invention of such principles of reasoning as the syllogism, inferential entailment, epistemology, and hundreds of other aspects of rationalism are to be directly attributed to the Dharma-inspired philoso-phers who flourished over 2000 years ago. Indeed, the fields of ethics, aesthetics, political/social philosophy, ontology, logic, phenomenology, cosmology, cosmogony, speculative physics, and theory of perception all find their origins in the work and genius of pre-Christian and pre-Abrahamic thinkers.

The principles of Dharma are not based upon superstition, religious dogma, or "mysticism" any more than are the theorems of Pythagoras, the mathematical axioms of Euclid, the Newtonian laws of physics, or Einstein's theory of relativity. Rather, the laws of Dharma are based upon empirical observation, direct non-mediated insight into the nature of Reality via the process of Yoga, and upon complete conformation with the laws of human reason and inference. Indeed, as explained by M. N. Rothbard, the universally applicable truths of Natural Law (Dharma) serve as the foundation of more conditional instances of human reason.

> In natural-law philosophy, then, reason is not bound, as it is in modern post-Humean philosophy, to be a mere slave to the passions, confined to cranking out the dis covery of the means to arbitrarily chosen ends. For the ends themselves are selected by the use of reason; and "right reason" dictates to man his proper ends as well as the means for their attainment. For the...natural-law theorist, the general law of morality for man is a special case of the system of natural law governing all entities of the world, each with its own nature and its own ends.

> (Murray N. Rothbard, *The Ethics of Liberty*)

The truths of Dharma conform to a) everyday empirical observation of the phenomenal world around us, b) with the insights and spiritual discoveries of perfected sages, and c) with our own reasoning abilities. Dharma not only conforms to logic and reason, but it forms the very historical and theoretical bases of these disciplines.

2.1.7 Dharma as Replicable

Often it is asked, how do you know if the practical claims of Dharma are factual and provable? For that matter, how do we know that any philosophical or empirical claims are true? Again, given that the propositions of Dharma are not faith-based, but are instead based upon reason and trans-empirical direct insight, it must be the case that Dharma's claims are demonstrable. The modern scientific method is predicated upon the fact that the proof that *y* **effect** is directly produced from *x* **cause** is in showing that the effect is consistently repeatable in multiple tests. In the same manner in which scientific claims need to be replicable in order to be conclusively proven to be true, the claims of Dharma too have to be clearly demonstrable through replication of effect. In other words, the claims of Dharma can be proven because any such claim that *x* **cause** leads to *y* **effect** can be proven by repetition. Practically applying the principles of Dharma in one's life and seeing if there is the promised effect will prove the claims of Dharma.

As several easily demonstrable examples: a) the Dharmic science of Yoga either does or does not produce a overall healthier state of wellness in its practitioners; b) the Dharmic practice of meditation either does or does not alleviate stress, anxiety, and depression; c) the dual metaphysical principles of *karma*/reincarnation either occur after death or they do not.

2.1.8 Dharma as Scientific

The word "science" is from the Latin "*scientia*". It derives from '*sciens*', which is the participle of '*scire*', which means 'to have knowledge of, know, understand'. Thus, the ordered acquisition of valid knowledge, both empirical and trans-empirical, forms the foundational philosophy of science. Dharmic epistemology shares in the two primary means of knowing accepted by the modern philosophy of science known as the principle of positive verification: reason and empirical observation. The replicable nature of Dharmic principles is a clear exhibition of the scientific nature of these principles.

Finally, living in accordance with Dharma assures the natural highest good and happiness for all.

> The natural law, then, elucidates what is best for man — what ends man should pursue that are most harmonious with, and best tend to fulfill, his nature. In a significant sense, then, natural law provides man with a "science of happiness," with the paths which will lead to his real happiness.

> (Murray N. Rothbard, *The Ethics of Liberty*)

Contrary to the mistake of some, the world-view of Dharma is not merely concerned with the religious and philosophical dimensions of life. While certainly rooted deeply in the realm of spirituality, and using transcendent truths as its basis, Dharma is a comprehensive and holistic world-view that comments upon all fields within its purvey. The scope of Dharma naturally extends itself to such fields as the political, social, cultural, aesthetic, scientific, ethical, religious, architectural, philosophical, medical, martial, economic, etc. Speaking specifically about the realm of economics, for example, James Schall states the following:

> The natural law, in its briefest statement, is acting reasonably, is the "normalcy of functioning" of a thing. The natural law of a market, so to speak, is its normal

> functioning, its ability to concentrate reason and good
> judgment on the production and distribution of
> goods." (James V. Schall, *Natural Law and Economics*)

The natural ordering power of Dharma is universally applicable across
the spectrum of all fields of human endeavor. Thus there is a "Dharma
of…" everything.

2.1.9 The Metaphysical Principles of Dharma

There are a large number of philosophical principles of Dharma that are
considered to be axiomatically operative in nature due to their ability to
reveal the metaphysical workings of nature that, in turn, produce our
empirical reality. The following list of these metaphysical Dharma principles is far from exhaustive, and is designed merely to shed light on a few
of these more important philosophical principles.

1. **Omnisentiency** – For the Dharmi, the world around us is seen as
being alive with sentiency and personality. Some of this life is readily seen
through the senses, while other forms of life exist on more subtle realms
and cannot be as readily detected. Consciousness – life - inhabits the four
corners of our cosmos in all its myriad forms, and is all meant to be appreciated for its own inherent value. As a result of this unique way of
perceiving reality, the Dharmi has deep respect and reverence for his surroundings, including respect for all life forms, all natural phenomena, as
well as for the Earth Herself. The trees, mountains, the oceans, rivers and
lakes, the myriad diverse biospheres, and the planets and stars are all seen
as being beneficent friends and blessings upon us all. The Dharmi never
considers himself to be at war with other species of life, but views the
diverse living entities found in nature with love and acceptance. All living

beings have an inherent right to life. Thus, the follower of Dharma lives in intimate harmony, non-violent relationship, and environmental integration with his surroundings.

By stark contrast, when modern, materialistic man looks up at the stars and ponders the grandeur of the universe, he sees primarily a cold and lifeless phenomenon. He views nature with fear and suspicion. The currently dominant Abrahamic and secular-materialist world-view sees the world of nature as consisting of dead material, periodically interspersed with what is oxymoronically termed "organic matter" (i.e., living beings). For both Abrahamists and secular-materialists, the world around us is filled with financially valuable forms of lifeless matter in the form of precious and semi-precious minerals, oil, and other resources that are here solely for human exploitation. When the Abrahamist materialist sees the Sun, to him the Sun is no more than a dead fiery rock floating in space. When he sees the Earth, he sees no more than a large ball of dirt and oceans meant for us to demarcate into nations, cities, and often violently protected private property. When he views the magnificence of a forest, he only sees acre upon acre of wood and other natural resources ready to be converted into profit. Nature, for such a world-view, is not celebrated as a precious gift from the Transcendent, teeming with multiple millions of fascinating life forms and potentially healing herbs, but is seen as merely a tool, there to be used as human beings will.

In actuality, Dharma teaches us that every corner of the cosmos is filled with consciousness and is alive with personality. The Sun, the Moon, the Earth, the lakes and trees, and Nature herself are all seen as being living persons, with their own will and inherent value, and are accordingly treated with the highest respect.

2. **Theocentricity** – The very center of concern and the ontological source of Dharma is God (Narayana), or the Absolute. God is the ultimate transcendental referent toward which all Dharmic principles are aimed. It is thus understood by all Dharmic cultures that God is the ultimate source and the ultimate goal of all reality. Dharma views God in panentheistic terms, that is, God is both the transcendent origin of all that is conceivable and perceivable, as well as the imminent sustainer of all being by the power of His life-giving omnipresence. To live a Dharma lifestyle is to live in communion with God. As Sri Krishna, the last incarnation (*avatara*) of God explains in the *Bhagavad Gita*:

"Always think of Me and become devoted to Me. Worship Me and offer your homage to Me. In this way, you will come to Me without fail. This I promise you for you are My very dear friend." (18:65)

To help us to live in such intimate communion with God is the very *raison d'être* of Dharma.

3. **Sufficient Causality** – No effect, or existent, is without a cause. Nothing exists in a vacuum, but is dependent upon an antecedent cause. Thus no event that occurs in our world is ever ultimately meaningless or wholly disconnected from other events. This principle is known is Western philosophy as the theory of "sufficient causality". In Buddhism, this Dharmic principle is referred to as *pratitya samutpada*, or "dependent origination". According to this principle, all aspects of phenomenal reality are no more than the results of antecedent causes; they do not contain the cause of their own existence within them and are thus no more than conditioned effects. Every existent is dependent upon pre-existing factors which contribute to the sense of an existent being an integrated

whole. Thus, everything has a cause. The only uncaused cause, according to Sanatana Dharma, is God, the cause of all causes (*karana-karanam*) and the starting point of the very chain of causality itself.

4. **Divine Procession** – The principle of Divine Procession postulates our relationship with God within the context of our experience in the material world as a metaphorical divine journey that consists of three successive stages: 1) the original unity of the individual soul with God, 2) the subsequent temporary separation of the soul from God due to the individual soul's ego-inspired illusion of separation, 3) the eventual reunion of the soul with God. All living beings come from God, are currently "separate" from God, and will ultimately reclaim their unity and repose in God whenever each individual soul is truly ready to do so. There is no literal eternal separation from God for any living being.

5. **Primacy of Free Volition** – Free will is one of the essential functioning attributes of consciousness. Free will is central to what it means to be a conscious, eternal living being (*atman*). It is choice, and the ability to freely make choices, that creates the volitional landscape through which consciousness can freely operate. Dharma is a philosophy of radical freedom. It teaches that each of us has the ability to create who we are, and to choose our future. Consequently, we are given the freedom to live in accordance with Dharma, or to reject Dharma outright. We have the freedom to exist in loving devotional relationship with our source, God, or to temporarily reject that relationship. Freedom, of course, can be misused. When it is misused, it is adharmic (artificial) will. When it is used to direct our awareness toward the Divine, then it is dharmic (natural).

6. **Qualitative Hierarchy** – There is a natural hierarchy of all things, beings, concepts, aesthetic capacities, and persons in accordance with their inherent quality, functionality, merit and depth of being. Quite literally everything that is perceptual or conceptual can be placed within a natural and healthy hierarchy. Depth of being is accorded to all things in direct proportional relation to their closeness to the Divine, and to their ability to reflect the Divine in their qualitative essence and desiderative outlook. All Dharmic civilizations recognized the importance of the qualitative hierarchy of all things, and used the science of qualitative attributiveness to order society in a manner that was efficient, rational, equitable and just for all.

7. **Precedence of Personhood over Individualism** – The modern materialist concept of the individual artificially atomizes persons, and subsumes their inherent personality into the amorphous mass of "the people". Thus individualism represents personality declined into a quantitative mass. Personhood, on the other hand, stresses the quality and depth of the human person, and the inherently unique differences that make us all diverse and special. Dharma emphasizes seeing the human person, not in mere quantitative terms, but in relation to the quality of the person. Trading spiritual consciousness for social consciousness leads to the dehumanization of the human person. Stressing personhood over individualism, on the other hand, reinstates the inherent dignity, uniqueness, and strengths of every human being.

8. **Cyclicality of Space/Time/Historical Trends** – All ancient cultures viewed history and time as being cyclical in progression, rather than linear. Like all other seasonal cycles of nature - the rotation of the planets, and the planets' following their natural course of orbit around the

sun - historical trends can be seen as forming a distinct cyclical pattern of growth and subsequent decline. Such a cyclical view of history led to a sense of optimism and closeness to the cycles of nature. The beginning of a radical break from this more organic view of history came about with the birth of Abrahamism 4000 years ago. For the first time in history, the ancient Hebrews viewed the progression of history as occurring in a starker linear pattern, with a clear beginning of history, and a dreaded end of history to come in an eventual eschatological Armageddon.

Time and history are not linear, but are cyclical in nature. As we examine history, we clearly see cycles of civilizational development and decline, repeated patterns from which we can learn great lessons. The great German historian Oswald Spengler was one of the first Westerners in the early 20th Century to again recognize the cyclical and organic nature of both history, and of civilizational growth and decline within the context of time. Spengler's philosophy of history is very much in accord with that of Dharma.

9. **Historical Devolution** –All ancient cultures taught the fact that there is a steady devolution of human values, an eroding of the strength of traditional civilizational forces, and an ever-increasing coarsening of human culture all occurring within the temporal backdrop of the four great ages (*yugas*) through which our universe inevitably marches. Currently, we are living in the last, and most spiritually challenging, of these four ages. Our current great age is known as the Kali Yuga, or Age of Conflict. This principle of historical devolution, when coupled with the principle of the cyclicality of time, however, leads ultimately to a positive and very hopeful assessment of human history because, as we eventually leave this more dark age behind us, we eventually re-enter the Golden Age and

begin this natural cycle of time over again. More, there are also mini-cycles within the greater ages of time that swing from bad to good and back again. Though we are currently within the dark age of Kali Yuga, for example, it is also recognized that within our particular mini-cycle we will soon be experiencing a mini-Golden Age, predicted to begin in roughly the late 2012-2013 time period. This time frame, amazingly, roughly corresponds with the ancient Mayan prediction of the end of one age on December 21, 2012 and the beginning of a new age.

10. **Transcendent Authority** - Authority, both spiritual and temporal, does not derive from the masses, but from those sources that have proven qualitative worth and wisdom. The Dharmic principle of the derivation of both authoritative knowledge, as well as spiritual, governance and social authority, is deductively derived rather than inductive. All meaningful knowledge and power, if it is to have any ultimate validity to it, derives from higher, more reliable, and transcendental authority. Such higher derived knowledge is then used to shed light on the challenges of our world.

11. **Order of Philosopher Guides** – Every Dharmic society had an elite order of wise priests and philosophers who guided society, officiated as judicial authorities, and served as the trusted preservers of Dharmic culture and civilization. Such professionally trained philosopher-priests were considered the highest order of society and were expected to lead society to higher pursuits by their own personal examples and teaching endeavors. So respected were these traditional orders that even the royalty and warriors were expected to heed their advice and rulings under the penalty of social ostracism and even impeachment of their powers for not doing so. Such orders of philosopher-priest guides were found in all Dharmic

74

cultures. These orders include: the Celtic Druids, the Hindu Brahmins, the Latin Flamines, and the Persian Magi. It is only when society is guided by the wisdom and strength of such Dharmically cultivated sages that justice, mercy, goodness, and purity abound.

12. **Philosopher-King** – The perfect ruler, according to Dharma, is a person who personifies the very highest ideals of both martial prowess and sagacious spirituality simultaneously. The ablest leader is at once both philosopher and king, sage and warrior, saint and ruler, temporal and spiritual leader. Such a perfect Dharma ruler, who combines in one person both administrative and priestly qualities, is represented in the Sanskritic tradition as the "Chakravartin" or "Rajarshi". The Buddha was recognized as a Chakravartin. The Chakravartin is also seen in Tibetan tradition in the role of the Dalai Lama, and in pre-Abrahamic Europe as Plato's "Philosopher-King". "Until philosophers are kings, or the kings and princes of this world have the spirit and power of philosophy, and political greatness and wisdom meet in one", wrote Plato, "then only will this our State have a possibility of life and behold the light of day." (Republic, Book V, 473-C) Such a ruler is seen as the human manifestation of the sovereign will of the people of the Dharma Nation.

13. **Theomorphism** – One of the important principles of Dharma can be summed up in the often repeated metaphysical adage "As above, so below." All reality is seen as a reflection of the Divine, even if imperfectly so. All things, both spiritual and material, both perceptual and conceptual, have God as their source and as the origin of the very building blocks of their essential nature. Sri Krishna explains this principle of theomorphism in the *Bhagavad Gita* when He says:

Aham sarvasya prabhavo mattah sarvam pravartate
iti matva bhajante mam budha bhava-samanvitah

"I am the source of all spiritual and material realities. Everything ema-
nates from Me. The wise who know this truth perfectly engage in
devotional service toward Me, and worship Me with all their being."
(10:8)

God is not made in man's image. Rather, we are made in God's image.

14. **Conservation of Energy -** This law of Dharma states that the total
amount of energy, known as *shakti* in Sanskrit, in any isolated system remains conserved and constant over time. As a result of this Dharmic
principle, energy can neither truly be created nor go out of being. Energy,
or *shakti*, is an eternally existent power of the Divine. Thus, energy can
only be transformed from one specific state to another specific state. The
only thing that can happen to energy in a closed system is that it can
change its outward form, but it retains forever its internal integrity as a
power of God. It is as a result of the principle of the conservation of
energy that the Abrahamic notion of an *ex nihilo* creation, or the creation
of energy and matter from nothing, is recognized as being a logical and
scientific impossibility.

2.1.10 The Divine Descent of Dharma

Dharma being both *apaurusheya* (not man-made), in addition to being a
systematic world-view with its own inherent principles, are not two mutually exclusive facts. It is both not man-made, while it simultaneously
has its own inherent and universally applicable principles that are meant
to be observed by all sincere spiritual seekers.

Understanding the precise nature of the descending flow of Dharma into our worldly perception will help us in this regard. The two manners in which the soul's divergence from the Good can be responded to are either via justice or mercy. While mercy is always understood to be the higher of the two principles, it is the duty of a judge, for example, to operate out of the principle of justice in order to both bring about a rebalanced equity of justice in the face of the divergence from the Good, as well as to hopefully reform the person who has engaged in such injustice.

In the spiritual realm, of course, there is only the love and consequent grace (*prasada*) of Brahman. In the state of pure consciousness, in the spiritual realm, there is no need for law or justice in the worldly or material sense. Injustice is not a possibility in the spiritual realm, the realm of the Good. The material world, however, is a realm of illusory divergence from this spiritual protocol. As God's grace becomes operative in our material world, there is a necessary devolving transformation of God's grace from a purely spiritual state of reciprocal love, into the necessarily more judicious form of law, principles, rules, justice, etc. Such a devolving transformation of God's grace into a lower and more concretized form is a necessity due to the now utilitarian function of that grace in direct juxtaposition to the psychologically warped sense of identity (*ahamkara*) that the illusioned *atman* is undergoing. The illusory self has placed itself in voluntary "exile" from the flow of grace, and can now only be reached by that grace indirectly via law, or Dharma. Thus, "Dharma" is the literal transformation of *prasada*, grace, in such a manner that the illusioned self can have access to that grace. A further concretization of Dharma itself occurs when Dharma, in turn, then devolves from being specifically the eternal set of metaphysical principles to then, in addition, being expressed in the form of purely physical principles (gravity, space-time, dimensionality, geometric patterning, etc.). Thus, God's grace devolves into the metaphysical reality of Dharma in order to help elevate illusioned souls back to a state of grace, and Dharma itself further devolves ontologically to form the physical laws of materiality itself.

All Dharmic principles, however, whether of a purely metaphysical nature or of a physical nature, are permeated throughout with intelligibility. Indeed, one can say that it is this very intelligibility that serves as the very glue and inherent guiding force of Dharma, of nature. Such intelligibility, too, has its natural, descending flow from the highest ontological substantial Real, down to the lower modes of materiality (as do many operative Reals [*tattvas*] that are too numerous to mention here). Thus, when we speak of the inherent intelligibility of Dharma, we are speaking of an intelligibility originating in the *buddhi*, or innate wisdom faculty of consciousness itself, which in turn has Brahman (God) as its source of origin, and not merely the idea of discursive thought. To see nature as being unintelligible or irrational is an atheistic stereotype that the Vedic view would, thus, radically disagree with. Nature is ultimately intelligent. This is because God is the very origination of nature, and God is the simultaneously source of all Truth, and the consequent possessor of all Truth.

2.1.11 The Behavioral Principles of Dharma

Dharma is understood by its adherents to be not just a philosophy and world-view, but to also be a values-based lifestyle and ethical way of life that is designed to guide our own behavior, as well as our everyday moral and ethical decisions in relation to others. The following is a short list detailing only a few of the practical Dharmic behaviors, values and principles to be lived in everyday life. By adopting a Dharma lifestyle, we can ensure a greater degree of happiness and prosperity, both for ourselves personally and for society as a whole.

1. Reverence for nature, an attraction to spending time in nature, and deep environmentalism.

2. God-centeredness. Endeavoring to experience God's presence at all times.

3. Exhibiting nobility in all of one's thoughts, words, and deeds.

4. Cultivating a life of ethical virtues and behaviors.

5. Recognition of the feminine aspect of the Divine, in addition to the masculine aspect.

6. Unity in diversity. Reconciling the diversity that we see around us to serve the greater whole, both politically and spiritually.

7. Respect for all living beings, regardless of their ethnicity or species.

8. Observing an organic lifestyle that is close to the Earth (Bhudevi).

9. Following a natural and organic approach to health.

10. Cultivating a regular and deep meditation practice.

11. Veneration and reverence for our ancestors.

12. Spiritual self-realization and psychological self-knowledge.

13. Acquiring wisdom (vidya), philosophical discernment, as well as intellectual and aesthetic discrimination.

14. Having a life of healthy wellbeing - physical, mental, and spiritual.

15. Avid cleanliness in body, mind, and surroundings.

16. Seeking excellence in all endeavors.

17. Humility.

18. Fearlessness.

19. Self-discipline.

20. Cultivating strong and healthy family units.

21. Admiration of beauty.

22. Honesty.

23. Loyalty.

24. Simplicity.

25. Truthfulness.

26. Contentment.

Dharmic principles of behavior serve to elevate and deepen us as human beings (*manushya*), and by extension elevate the entire society. Such behavioral standards constitute the Dharmic way of life, and should be cultivated in order to directly experience what it means to be a Dharmi in our practical everyday lives.

2.2.1 The Epistemological Principles of Dharma

Every religious tradition, philosophy and world-view claims to have the truth. In almost every case, in fact, even if it isn't stated overtly, the claim of every school of thought is that they alone are the sole possessor of the absolute and perfect truth and that, by implication, every other school of thought is wrong in their own claims to knowing truth.

Rather than merely being yet one more dogmatic voice in the deafening chorus of claimants to truth, the Vedic path asks all intelligent seekers to take a step back from such fanatical assertions, and to ask the following fundamental question: "By what means do you claim to even know what you claim to know?" In other words, anyone can make the statement, "I know that x is true!" But the real question is this: "How do you know that x is true? What is the means by which you have derived such knowledge, and how can you prove that this is a valid means for acquiring such knowledge?" Such questions about the validity of a particular means of knowing fall under the realm of epistemology in philosophy. We will now very briefly examine Dharmic epistemology.

2.2.2 Three Necessary Factors of Knowing

In general, there are three factors that need to be present for any successful attempt to know something. These factors are (a) the person who seeks to know (*pramatr*), (b) the object that the person seeks to know (*prameya*), and (c) the medium (*pramana*), or means, through which the seeker obtains the object of knowledge. For example: I am the seeker (a) of knowledge; the object (b) that I seek to know is the following: "Is there a glass of water on the table in front of me?"; the medium (c) that I use to answer this question is my eyes. So, again, to know something, there must be:

> A) The knower.
> B) The object of knowledge (what we want to know).
> C) The proper medium through which we know.

2.2.3 Three Ways of Knowing

Going deeper now, there are also three primary mediums (*pramana*) by which we know anything at all (what are called epistemic mechanisms). These are: A) *pratyaksha* - Empiricism, knowing through the senses, B) *anumana* - Logical Inference, reasoning, and C) *shabda* - Transcendent Word, or direct accessing of eternal truth via sound vibration. Each of these specific mediums, in turn, has a corresponding spectrum of objects of knowledge that is exclusive to it, and to it alone. *Pratyaksha* means very specifically deriving knowledge through the medium of the senses. Anything that we can know by seeing, hearing, tasting, smelling, or feeling with tactile touch falls under this means of knowing. Only material objects can be known through the material senses. The basic scientific method is a perfect example of this form of sensory knowledge. *Pratyaksha*, or Empiricism, is only able to give us knowledge that applies to the senses, and nothing more.

Anumana, on the other hand, means acquiring knowledge through purely inferential, mathematical, rational and logical means. *Anumana* means reasoning. The realms of mathematics and logic are perfect examples of the *anumana* means of arriving at knowledge. *Anumana* only applies to those facets of knowledge that are intellectual in nature. If we want to know the answer to the question, "Can Hal's brother be a married bachelor?", we don't need to know Hal's brother to know the answer to this question; we know the answer through the inherent reasoning mechanism of our intellect. Hal's brother cannot be both married and a bachelor at the same time since the two states are mutually exclusive, and to state that he is both married and a bachelor is a logical absurdity.

Through your intellect alone, you already know what the answer to this question has to be!

Neither empiricism, nor logic alone are capable of revealing truths that are transcendent and spiritual in nature, however, because they are tools that only apply to their respective objects of knowledge - the perceptual, material objects of the world; and the conceptual, intellectual objects of reasoning, respectively. The realm of spirit (God, gods and goddesses, Truth, soul, higher metaphysics, ontologically transcendent states of consciousness, etc.), being trans-empirical and trans-intellectual, cannot be known by such insufficient tools. To use the senses or the intellect alone to know transcendent truth is akin to using a sledgehammer to perform brain surgery; it's just the wrong tool. Since we cannot know the Transcendent through the non-transcendent means of *pratyaksha* or *anumana*, then what recourse are we left with?

Shabda, Transcendent Word, or *logos* (λόγος) in Greek, is the exclusive means by which transcendent truths are revealed. This is the case because *shabda*, being of the nature of the spiritual, corresponds in essence with the spiritual nature of transcendent truths. It is only via consciousness that we can know consciousness. It is only via spirit that we can know Spirit. It is only via *atman* (our individual soul) that we can know Brahman (God). It is only through *shabda* that we can know transcendent truths.

Shabda represents the essential nature of spiritual realities as they exist in the form of trans-empirical vibrational frequency (thus Word, *logos*, etc.). Truth, being an eternal and living reality, can be accessed by human beings who have purified themselves, and who have absorbed their

subjective consciousness in the Absolute supreme subjective consciousness (God), to such a degree that qualitative separation between
themselves and God has ceased to exist. At this point, the medium (*pramana*) between knower (*pramatr*) and object of knowledge (*prameya*),
which in this case is God, has evaporated. Thus, *shabda* is the only means
of knowing in which we transcend even the use of a medium.

In such a state of oneness with the Divine, the sage now has the ability
both to know the transcendent truth, as well as to reveal the transcendent
truth of the Divine for all the world to know. Thus, *Veda*, or perfect
scriptural authority comes into being as a result of such direct, non-
mediated insight into the nature of the Divine on the part of the sage.
Word, as the eternal transcendent reality revealed to sages in deep states
of meditative absorption (*samadhi*), becomes "the Word" as written scripture when these very same sages then write their realizations down.

2.2.4 Truth Verification System

For those who are still progressing toward final liberation, and have not
become enlightened just yet, the system of Shastra/Acharya/Vichara
provides the direct way in which we can verify any philosophical statement, and by which we can know if any particular truth-claim or practice
is actually in keeping with Truth and Dharma.

> Shastra = Revealed Vedic Scripture.
> Acharya = Self-realized Sages.
> Vichara = Our own reasoning capacity and experience.

If any claim-to-truth or practice that we encounter is contradicted by any of these three elements, then they are to be considered suspect. If a person claiming to be an Acharya, or *guru*, makes a statement that is contradicted by the Vedic scriptures and our own reasoning capacity and experience, then the supposed "*guru's*" statement is suspect, and consequently his very status as a *guru* is also now rendered suspect. If our own logic and subjective experience tells us one thing, but the Vedic scriptures and the Acharya contradict this, then our own intelligence and gut feeling is suspect. However, of all three elements of this system (Shastra, Acharya and Vichara), the Vedic scriptures (Shastra) is the only element that is never wrong. The Vedic scriptures always have supremacy in any contradiction with the Acharya and one's own Vichara. The problem today in the search for, and verification of, Truth isn't so much that there is not already a perfect system of knowing Truth available to humanity, but that the above system simply is no longer known or being practiced. Thus, we are revealing this system once again to the human race.

To access truth today, we must use all the above three means. We must undergo a deep study of *shastra*, the revealed Vedic scriptures, such as the *Upanishads*, the *Bhagavad Gita, Yoga Sutras, Narada Bhakti Sutras*, etc. We also need to seek out a true and authentic *guru*, or spiritual teacher, in the form of a living Acharya who is perfectly practicing and representing the Vedic tradition in an unaltered and traditional manner. Finally, we need to use our own discriminative reasoning abilities to discern whether what we are reading and hearing makes good sense to both our mind and heart.

Truth, including the very highest of spiritual and philosophical truths, can be known to us with ever-increasing depth and clarity. We can know truth, both in theory, as well as through direct experiential insight, by employing the Vedic tools of Yoga and meditation, all under the capable guidance of the Vedic scriptures, the authentic *guru*, and the power of our own sincerity and direct insight into the nature of the Absolute. This is the Vedic way of knowing.

Chapter 3 Epistemology in Literary Form:
The Scriptures of Sanatana Dharma

3.1.1 The Vedic Literature

The Vedic literature is singularly unique and unparalleled among all world literatures, both sacred and secular. The *Vedas* represents the most easily accessible window to the spiritual realm available to humanity today. Revealed directly to the ancient perfected sages (*rishis*), these works of sacred literature were first rendered into written form many thousands of years before the Common Era, and contain within their pages vividly clear glimpses into higher truths that are not available in any other known writings.

Sanatana Dharmis look to the divine writings of the Vedic literature for guidance, inspiration and higher truths in both their spiritual and material pursuits. If there are either philosophical disputes or confusions, as well as proofs or authoritative insights that are needed by a follower of Dharma, it is to the Vedic literature that he turns for objective and perfectly reliable clarification. What defines a follower of Sanatana Dharma more than any other single factor is precisely that they enthusiastically accept and abide by the teachings of the *Vedas* as the perfect source of perfect knowledge. If the Vedic scriptures do not confirm an assertion or proposition, then it is not true. If the Vedic scriptures do confirm an assertion or proposition, then it is true.

The eternal flow of Truth is a non-empirically-audible sonic reality that transcends the realm of human sensory purview or intellectual speculation, but that is nonetheless directly accessible to any sincere seeker who eventually reaches the stage of being a liberated *yogi*. Such transcendent Truth can only be known by purifying oneself through the practices of Yoga, meditation and devotional consciousness (*bhakti*) toward the Supreme Godhead, and reforming one's character to the point of dissolving illusory ego completely. It is this living, transcendent Truth that the perfected sages encounter in the yogically inspired state of non-mediated spiritual perception of the Absolute.

This transcendent realm of Truth can be compared to the overwhelming majesty and power of a mighty rushing river. That Truth is ever-dynamic, ever-fresh, unalterable, unstoppable, and alive with spiritual power. That river of Truth has the power to quench our thirst and our longing for the nectarean sweetness of Reality unlike anything else in existence. That river of Truth is the only sustenance our soul will ever need. When directly encountered by any liberated *yogi*, that mighty river of Truth is experienced in its dynamic form. When this very same *yogi* then reveals this transcendent Truth to others in the material world, however, this dynamic Truth now becomes concretized in the form of the Vedic scriptures (*Shastra*). The difference between the dynamic Truth in its original form versus that same Truth rendered into scriptural form is similar to experiencing a living river before your live vision versus taking a photo of that very same river so that you can then show the river to others. It is correct to say that the river in the photo is the same river that you saw in real life...but now rendered in such a way that you can easily transport its representation in order to show others what you have yourself seen in person. Truth is the river; scripture is an easily accessible snapshot of that very same river. Both represent the same thing. But one (the actual river) only a very small number of people can have access to, whereas the other (the snapshot) any and all can have access to.

3.1.2 Genres of the Vedic Scriptural Canon

The Vedic scriptures are a vast library of works designed to provide guidance and insight on every aspect of the human experience from an unapologetically spiritual perspective. Because there are so many individual books, as well as so many diverse topics, writing styles, communicative formats, and purposes among all these books, the Vedic scriptural canon has traditionally been organized into two main categories, and several genres within those categories.

The two main categories are *shruti* ("what is heard") and *smriti* ("what is remembered"). *Shruti* indicates those works that are traced back the closest to their original revealers. *Smriti*, on the other hand, are sacred texts that may have been passed down for many successive generations of enlightened *gurus* and their disciples before finally being placed in concrete compositional form at some point in human history. All genres of Vedic scriptures fall under the categories of either *shruti* or *smriti*. The following chart illustrates a few of the major genres of Vedic scripture.[5]

---

[5] Again, these are all broad genres of literature. Within each specific genre, there are multiple texts. For example, there are 4 *Samhitas*, 108 *Upanishads*, 36 *Puranas*, etc.

The Vedic Canon

Shruti	Smriti
Samhitas (Vedas)	*Puranas*
Brahmanas	*Sutras*
Aranyakas	*Pancharatras*
Upanishads	*Agamas*
	Tantras[6]
	Dharma Shastras[7]
	Vedangas[8]
	Upavedas[9]
	Itihasas (Two Epics)
	1. *Ramayana* 2. *Mahabharata*
	2(a) *Bhagavad Gita*

---

[6] The *Maha-Sidhi-Sarasvata-Tantra* lists the following 64 important *Tantras*: 1) *Siddhishvara*, 2) *Mahatantra*, 3) *Kalitantra*, 4) *Kularnava*, 5) *Jnanarnava*, 6) *Nila*, 7) *Vetakare*, 8) *Devi-Agama*, 9) *Uttara*, 10) *Sri-Krama*, 11) *Siddhi-Yamala*, 12) *Matsya-Sukta*, 13) *Siddha-Sara*, 14) *Siddhi-Sarasvata*, 15) *Varahi*, 16) *Yogini*, 17) *Ganesha-Vimarsini*, 18) *Nitya*, 19) *Shivagama*, 20) *Chamunda*, 21) *Mundamata*, 22) *Hamsama-hesvara*, 23) *Niruttara*, 24) *Kula-prakashaka*, 25) *Kalpa*, 26) *Gandharvaka*, 27) *Kriyasara*, 28) *Nibandha*, 29) *Svatantra*, 30) *Sammohana*, 31) *Lalita*, 32) *Radha*, 33) *Malini*, 34) *Rudra-Yamala*, 35) *Brhat-Srikrama*, 36) *Gavaksha*, 37) *Sukumudini*, 38) *Visuddheshvara*, 39) *Malinivijaya*, 40) *Samayachara*, 41) *Bhairavi*, 42) *Yogini-Hridaya*, 43) *Bhairava*, 44) *Sanat Kumara*, 45) *Yoni*, 46) *Tantrantra* 47) *Nava-Ratneshvara*, 48) *Kula-Chudamani*, 49) *Kamadhenu*, 50) *Kumari*, 51) *Bhuta-Damara*, 52) *Malini-Vijaya*, 53) *Brahma-Yamala*, 54) *Bhava-Chudamani*, 55) *Vishva-Sara*, 56) *Mahatantra*, 57) *Mahakata*, 58) *Kulamrita*, 59) *Kuloddisha*, 60) *Kunjika*, 61) *Chintamani*, 62) *Yamala*, 63) *Tantra-Devaprakasha*, 64) *Kama*.

[7] The *Yajnavalkya Smrti* (1.4-5) lists 24 *Dharma Shastras*: Manu, Atri, Vishnu, Harita, Yajnavalkya, Ushana, Angira, Yama, Apastamba, Samvarta, Katyayana, Brhaspati, Parashara, Vyasa, Sankha, Likhita, Daksha, Gautama, Shatatapa, Vashishtha.

[8] *Shiksha* (pronunciation), *Chanda* (poetic meter), *Nirukta* (etymology and lexicology), *Vyakarana* (grammar), *Kalpa* (ritual), *Jyotisha* (astronomy and astrology)
[9] *Ayur Veda* (medicine), *Gandharva Veda* (music), *Dhanur Veda* (martial science), *Sthapatya Veda* (architecture).

3.2.1 Important Scriptures

Being such a large collection of volumes, it can sometimes be confusing for the typical spiritual seeker to know where to begin in his search for spiritual answers to life's most pressing questions. Thankfully, it has been traditionally acknowledged that reading the totality of the Vedic literature is not necessary in order to access spiritual truths. In fact, many of the individual texts contain very specialized knowledge that does not pertain to everyone, but only to those individuals who wish to specialize in a very specific field of spiritual knowledge. Not all Vedic texts pertain to the general spiritual seeker. Rather, there are a smaller number of sacred works that have been recognized as both sufficient and necessary texts to help guide us spiritually and philosophically.

The most important of these is the famous *Bhagavad Gita*, which serves as a perfect and brief summation of the essential teachings of the Vedic literature. We will now briefly examine a few of the more accessible Vedic genres and individual works, followed by a much more in-depth introduction to the indispensible teachings of the *Bhagavad Gita*. These works are all available in English translation, in addition to many other languages.

3.2.2 The Four Veda Samhitas

There are four books known as the *Veda-Samhitas*. These four works are the *Rig Veda*, *Atharva Veda*, *Yajur Veda* and *Sama Veda*. They are comprised of many thousands of revealed *mantras* and hymns dedicated to God, known is this literature by the names Purusha, Narayana and Vishnu, as well as all the lesser gods and goddesses (*devas* and *devis*,

respectively). While these four books are considered some of the most
sacred books in the Vedic canon of scriptures, the *mantras* of these works
are actually designed to be recited, heard and meditated upon in the form
of transformative sound vibration, in addition to actually being studied in
the normal sense of a book. As the *Yajnavalkya Smriti* explains:

> To the twice-born (Vedic initiates), the *Vedas* are the highest
> agent of benefaction because they all teach sacrifices, austerities
> and good works. That twice-born who daily reads the hymns of
> the *Rig Veda* satisfies the *devas* (gods) with honey and milk and
> the pitris with honey and ghee. (*Yajyavalkya Smriti*, 40-41)

The recitation of the *Veda-Samhitas* is performed as a *sadhana*, or meditative practice, as well as to establish an auspicious and blessed atmosphere
upon one's environment.

3.2.3 Upanishads

The *Upanishads* are a collection of 108 books that are highly philosophical
in content. They are in the form of philosophical dialogs, discussions,
lectures and teaching sessions conducted by several ancient liberated sages that were recorded in the form of these written works. The teachings
of 1) the *Upanishads*, coupled with 2) the *Bhagavad Gita* and 3) the *Brahma
Sutras*, form the scriptural foundation of Vedanta, which constitutes the
highest philosophical teachings of Sanatana Dharma. The term "Vedanta" is composed of two Sanskrit words. "Veda" means knowledge, and
"anta" means the end, or culmination. Thus, Vedanta represents the
"Culmination of all Knowledge". Of the 108 volumes of the *Upanishads*,
several are extremely esoteric, while some are more easily understandable
by modern readers. In either case, the only way to fully understand the

teachings of both the *Upanishads* and any other sacred work of the Vedic literature is to study these works under the expert guidance of an authentic and self-realized *guru* (spiritual master). It is impossible to understand the inner spiritual essence of the Vedic scriptures without the grace of an authorized *guru*.

Of the many *Upanishads*, there are twelve that are considered the most philosophically significant. These are called the *Mukhya Upanishads*, and are especially well known due to the commentaries on them that were written by the most famous Vedanta Acharyas. The twelve major *Upanishads* are the following:

Isha Upanishad
Kena Upanishad
Katha Upanishad
Prashna Upanishad
Mundaka Upanishad
Mandukya Upanishad
Taittiriya Upanishad
Aitareya Upanishad
Chandogya Upanishad
Brihadaranyaka Upanishad
Shvetashvatara Upanishad
Narayana Upanishad

3.2.4 Puranas

The *Puranas* are 36 very large works that contain the histories of both our planet and many other planets in our universe; beautifully composed prayers; philosophical dialogs and teachings; sacred stories of humans, gods, and other amazing beings; and accounts of the creation of our universe; among many other subject matters. The typical size of any given *Purana* is the size of the entire Old Testament and New Testament of the Bible combined. A few are several times larger than the entire Bible! Of the 36 *Puranas*, 18 are considered to be major *Puranas*[10] and 18 are minor *Puranas*.[11] Of the many *Puranas*, the two most important are a) the *Bhagavata Purana* (also known as the *Srimad Bhagavatam*) and b) the *Vishnu Purana*, both of which focus to a primary degree on directly understanding the innermost nature of God.

3.2.5 Sutra Literature

There is another important genre of widely variegated texts known as the *Sutra* literature, all of which are highly philosophical in nature. The term "*sutra*" means "thread", and indicates the unique writing style of this highly esoteric group of works. Each *Sutra* work consists of a number of very short aphorisms designed to convey a maximal of philosophical depth with a minimum of words. Thus, each individual *sutra* (or "thread") aphorism is both designed to be easily memorized by students in order to

---

[10] These are the 18 major *Puranas* listed in the *Padma Purana*, (*Uttara Khanda* 236.18-21): *Vishnu, Narada, Bhagavata, Garuda, Padma, Varaha, Brahmanda, Brahma-vaivarta, Markandeya, Bhavishya, Vamana, Brahma, Matsya, Kurma, Linga, Vayu/Shiva, Skanda, Agni.*

[11] The minor *Puranas* are: *Sanat Kumara, Narasimha, Brhannaradiya, Linga, Durvasa, Kapila, Manava, Aushanasa, Varuna, Kalika, Maheshvara, Shamba, Saura, Parashara, Devi Bhagavata, Aditya, Vashishtha, Vishnudharmottara.*

ensure the preservation of the teachings over many generations, while at the same time necessitating the presence of a living master, a *guru*, to fully unravel the deepest purport of each aphorism. Every school of philosophy in Sanatana Dharma is known to have produced at least one major *Sutra* text. The most well-known of these include a) the *Yoga Sutras*, which was written by the great *rishi* sage Patanjali, and focuses on the psychology and practice of Yoga spirituality and on self-realization; and b) the *Narada Bhakti Sutras*, which was revealed by the *rishi* Narada, and is centered around the science of *bhakti* (devotional consciousness) and God-consciousness.

3.3.1 The Bhagavad Gita

Of all the individual works that are a part of the Vedic canon, it is the *Bhagavad Gita* that takes the central place of importance for human beings today. This is the case for several reasons. The *Bhagavad Gita* is a 5100-year-old work. It is the record of a conversation between Krishna, who was a direct and full incarnation (*purna-avatara*) of God, and His great devotee, the warrior Arjuna. This inspired philosophical dialog took place at the very end of the last age, Dvapara Yuga, and the beginning of our present Kali Yuga age. It is a scripture that was revealed very specifically for the people of our dark and spiritually challenging age. In its brief 700 verses, the *Gita* delivers to humanity the very essence of the teachings of the all the Vedic literature, and the ultimate conclusion of all religion and philosophy, in a manner that is more direct and easier to fully comprehend in comparison with the other Vedic texts. If one can understand the sacred teachings of Lord Sri Krishna in His *Bhagavad Gita*, one then grasps the central message of the entire tradition of Sanatana Dharma. It is for this reason that we will now spend a considerable number of pages exploring the contents of this unique work.

3.3.2 Central Importance of the Bhagavad Gita

The dramatically stirring philosophical landscape of the *Bhagavad Gita* has inspired the imaginations of thinkers, poets, philosophers, and spiritual seekers across the spans of both history and cultures. For over 5100 years, the *Bhagavad Gita* has been considered by most scholars of religion, comparative literature and philosophy to be one of the most important philosophical/religious dialogues ever written in world history.

The Sanskrit word *"gita"* can be literally translated as "song". The term *"bhagavad"* refers directly to the Absolute. The *Bhagavad Gita* is, therefore, known in English as the "Song of God." This is the case because God is known to have literally sung these beautiful and profound teachings to His disciple and friend, Arjuna. This ancient work, which is often described as the "Bible" of both Sanatana Dharma and Yoga spirituality, has directly influenced and inspired a large number of eminent Western intellectuals and artists, in addition to innumerable generations of *yogis*, poets and sages in South Asia.

Included among the important European and American thinkers who were inspired by the profound words of the *Bhagavad Gita* have been Schopenhauer (1788-1860), Ralph Waldo Emerson (1803-1882), Albert Einstein (1879-1955), Henry David Thoreau (1817-1862), Aldous Huxley (1894-1963), and Christopher Isherwood (1904-1986). When experiencing the awe-inspiringly horrific wonder of the first atomic explosion, J. Robert Oppenheimer (1904-1967), the father of the atomic bomb, is known to have quoted aloud from the *Gita* - "Death am I, the destroyer of all worlds". So profound and thought provoking are the contents of this classic of world literature considered to be, that it has been translated into nearly every language on earth, with over 600 translations in the English language alone. Multiple thousands of commentaries have been written in an ongoing attempt to uncover the true purport of this short work; and myriad cultural, literary, and philosophical allusions have been made, both directly and indirectly, to this great work in many of the world's diverse cultures. There was even a recent major motion picture called "The Legend of Bagger Vance", starring Will Smith and Matt Damon that was based directly on the themes of the *Gita*. How has this ancient work of philosophical thought, written so long ago, come to be considered of such profound importance by so many of our contemporary intellectuals, cultural icons, and spiritual seekers? We will explore the precise reasons for this phenomenon of the *Bhagavad Gita's* importance in the coming pages of this section of the book.

Despite its overwhelming influence over so many people throughout history, the *Bhagavad Gita* is itself, surprisingly, not a very large work. It is only 700 verses in length, and can probably be read in a good sitting of about three hours or so. Contained within the *Bhagavad Gita's* brief 700 verses of text, however, are several closely interrelated paths of Yoga which, if systematically and sincerely understood and practiced, have the ability to lead you to liberation (*moksha*) from the pangs of suffering (*duhka*) and ignorance (*avidya*) so seemingly common to the human experience. The goal of this short, yet powerful, work of philosophical literature is spiritual freedom!

3.3.3 The Outer and Inner Wars

The *Bhagavad Gita* is a small portion (only eighteen chapters, in fact) of a much larger literary work known as the *Mahabharata*. At over 100,000 couplets long, the *Mahabharata* is the longest epic poem recorded in the history of human literature - more than eight times the size of the Odyssey and the Iliad combined. It is one of the two great epics (*itihasas*) of the ancient Sanatana Dharma tradition. The other great epic work is the famous *Ramayana* - the story and teachings of the *avatara* (incarnation) of God known as Sri Rama.

The *Mahabharata* records the dramatic history of events that took place in the Vedic nation of Aryavarta[12] over 5100 years ago. One of the main focal points of the *Mahabharata* is the internecine rivalry that existed between two branches of the royal family of ancient Aryavarta. These two branches of the royal family are 1) the five Pandava brothers and 2) their evil cousins, the Kauravas. Having been denied their rightful claim to the throne by the duplicitous and anti-Dharmic Kauravas, and having exhausted all peaceful and legal attempts at a political compromise, the five pious and ethical Pandava princes were given no recourse but to engage in battle for control of the vast empire of ancient Aryavarta.

At the time of the Great Mahabharata War, most nations, tribes and peoples of the earth subscribed to some form of allegiance to the principle of Dharma, whether this principle was directly known by the actual

---

[12] The ancient Vedic nation of Aryavarta does not correspond to the nation-state that we today call "India". Rather, Aryavarta consisted of a very large territory that included North India, Pakistan, the Himalayan region, Afghanistan, Persia, and most of Central Asia. Aryavarta was the spiritual center of the world, and the administrative headquarters of the Indo-European peoples.

word Dharma or some other term, such as Tao, Asha, the Natural Law, the Way, or Ma'at. The war that is documented in the *Mahabharata* is said to have involved almost every kingdom and ethnic grouping known at that time. And more, it was a sacred war (*dharma-yuddha*) that was fought specifically for the preservation of Dharma, the Natural Way.

3.3.4 Earth's First World War

Any large-scale violent conflict between two rival interests that involve not only the principle parties, but which also includes a myriad of nations allied with either one or the other belligerent party, is known as a World War. In contemporary world history, two world wars were experienced in the twentieth century - both primarily centered on the European conti- nent. From 1914 to 1918 we experienced World War I, and from 1939- 1945 the world witnessed the horrors of World War II. As the twentieth century came to a close, we have witnessed what has come to be known as Africa's first World War, as roughly seven nations battled for control of the African continent's central Congo region. With the dawning of the twenty-first century, the world is experiencing another potential World War: that of Western nations versus Islamic terrorism. With hundreds of kingdoms allied against one another, the Great Mahabharata War that took place some 5100 years ago represents the first real instance in hu- man history of a World War, a war of truly global proportions.

As the first chapter of the *Bhagavad Gita* opens, the two mighty armies face each other on the sacred field of Kurukshetra, waiting for their re- spective generals to declare the official start of the war. While it is true that war of any type or dimension is certainly always a horrific affair, nonetheless, unlike the chaotic and indiscriminate killing that occurs in most contemporary wars, warfare in the ancient world was an activity that was firmly controlled by rules of conduct and etiquette. Thus, not one arrow was shot, not one blow in anger was unfurled until the appropriate moment previously agreed upon by both parties had come.

Hundreds of powerful kings, princes and rulers had previously sworn their various nations' allegiances to one side or another. Millions of soldiers, with thousands of battle elephants (the "tanks" of the ancient world), chariots, horses and weapons of every description stood in tense anticipation of the impending carnage. What was about to commence was nothing less than the very first global scale conflict in human history, truly the very first World War, with the fate of the Earth lying in the balance.

The greatest of the five Pandava princes was the righteous and courageous warrior, Arjuna. Before the start of the war, Prince Arjuna had intelligently secured the mysterious and wise Krishna to serve as his trusted charioteer. In the midst of this dramatic scene, Arjuna asks his friend and charioteer, Krishna, to drive Arjuna's chariot to a neutral and open spot in between the two large and powerful armies in order to allow Arjuna an opportunity to survey the severity of the situation. What was to unfold before Arjuna's eyes would change his life forever.

3.3.5 The Inner War

When finally there, Arjuna saw that both those individuals whom he considered his enemies, as well as those who were his allies, were all people whom he intimately knew. This was after all a fratricidal war, a war between relatives, friends and kin of the royal family. Consequently, as

Arjuna looked upon the enemy encampment, he saw as many friends, family and teachers on the side of the enemy as on his own side. Realizing the fact that he may have to kill many of these people whom he knew intimately and loved dearly, a remarkable thing happened to this otherwise courageous and mighty warrior: he loses all hope. In what appears to be the first reported case of existential breakdown recorded in written history, Arjuna shockingly breaks down into a state of full-blown depression, throws down his mighty weapons in confusion, his limbs trembling in fear, and simply refuses to fight.

Arjuna has lost hope in life's very meaning. What demonstrates Arjuna's dilemma to be a specifically existential one, and not merely a weakness of will, is the overtly philosophical guidance that he proceeds to seek from his friend and teacher (*guru*), Krishna. For Arjuna, the problem that he is currently facing is not limited to the question of whether or not he should fight. As someone who was trained in the ways of a perfect warrior since birth, Arjuna knows very well the principle of upholding the duty of fighting a just war. In addition, Arjuna is not merely seeking a quick-fix solution to the present situation that lies before him. A simple rousing talk isn't what Arjuna wants. Rather, he is seeking nothing less than the answers to life's very meaning. He is seeking overtly philosophical and religious answers to the mystery of his own existence. He is seeking to know hope and joy in his life again.

Of all the various species of living beings in existence, whether animals, plants, birds or aquatics, it is only human beings who possess the wondrous ability to consciously ponder philosophical questions. Only human beings have the tools necessary to question the meaning of our own existence – to ask the question 'why is there *something* here each time I open

102

my eyes, and not *nothing?*" The human psyche is created is such a way, in
fact, that we all have a naturally inherent tendency to think philosophically. It is a universally witnessed phenomenon that certain basic
philosophical life-questions eventually arise in all human beings - sometimes, even despite ourselves, and despite our attempts to run away from
such questions. Regardless of one's race, nationality, religion, cultural or
ethnic makeup, if one is very simply a human being, then at some time or
another in one's life, one will inevitably ask questions of an intensely
philosophical nature. Such questions include: What is the true nature of
my essential self? Is there a God? What is the nature of that God? What
is the meaning of the world that I find myself currently situated in? What
is the interrelationship of these three aspects of reality (self, God, the
world)? And, knowing all this, finally, what am I to do in order to live a
truly meaningful life, and thus achieve that ever-elusive spiritual state
known as happiness? Because of the fact that these tend to be universally
asked questions, such queries are considered to be basic philosophical
ones. As can be readily seen by anyone who chooses to pick up this
treasured spiritual classic, in the short 700 verse span of the *Bhagavad Gita*
every one of these crucial human questions - and many more - will be
addressed in deeply profound and satisfying detail.

At this time of utter confusion and hopelessness, it is to his friend, the
incarnation of the Absolute Truth, Sri Krishna, whom Arjuna turns for
guidance and relief. In his time of confusion and despair, Arjuna asks of
Krishna:

karpanya-dosopahata-svabhavah prcchami tvam dharma sammudha-cetah
yac chreyah syan niscitam bruhi tan me sisyas te'ham sadhi mam tvam prapannam

"Now I am confused about my duty and have lost all composure because of weakness. In this condition I am asking you to tell me clearly what is best for me. Now I am your disciple, and a soul surrendered unto You. Please instruct me." (*Bhagavad Gita*, 2:7)

In Arjuna's sincere and humble statement, we witness the proper attitude of submissive inquiry with which one must approach the *guru* for guidance. Having thus accepted Krishna as his teacher (Acharya) and guide in chapter 2 of the *Gita*, chapters 2-18 are comprised primarily of a philosophical dialogue between Arjuna the student and Krishna the teacher. Thus, the outer war recedes into the background as the inner war within Arjuna's very being becomes the primary focus for the greatest philosophical dialogue ever composed.

More, though the Mahabharata War was a very real historical event that took place over five millennia ago, and Arjuna was a living personality who took part in this epic war, Arjuna also serves a secondary role as a representation of "every man". Like Arjuna, we likewise often find ourselves experiencing an internal battle with our own self-doubts, fears, and questions about our place and meaning in the universe. That inner war is a spiritual reality that all living beings face, and that can only be peacefully resolved by honoring our inner demand for the spiritual and intellectual satisfaction that we seek. This has been only a very brief examination of the dramatic scenario and personal implications of the *Bhagavad Gita*. In order to take full advantage of the profound wisdom that this work has to offer, I would urge you to read the *Bhagavad Gita* yourself, with patience, humility, sincerity and openness, and experience the transformative power that the wise counsel of Sri Krishna has to offer you. We will now briefly look at the various divisions of the *Bhagavad*

Gita.

3.3.6 The Philosophical Divisions of the Bhagavad Gita

Yamuna and Ramanuja, two of the greatest philosophers and Acharyas of the tradition of Sanatana Dharma and Yoga spirituality, have taught that the *Bhagavad Gita* can be structurally divided into three separate, yet sequential and perfectly integrated, sections. Each of these three sections has six chapters.

The first division consists of chapters 1-6. This section is focused upon an exposition of the precise method and means of self-realization - or *atma-jñana* - to be used by the individual self. The stages of such self-realization are comprised of the progressive steps of a) first gaining an intellectual grasp of the nature of true self (*atman*), then b) a pursuit of *karma-yoga*,[13] followed by c) the practice of *jñana-yoga*[14] with the express aim of achieving direct non-mediated experience of the true self within. In the classical Ashtanga Yoga system, self-realization is only the first of two ultimate goals, the second of which is *brahma-vidya*, or God consciousness.

After achieving realization of self, then the *yogi* must achieve realization of God. The next group of six chapters, chapters 7-12, exposit the nature of *bhakti-yoga*,[15] which is the primary means of knowing the Absolute. The ultimate goal of *bhakti-yoga* being God-realization (*brahma-vidya*), the-

---

[13] The Yoga of engaging in meditation while simultaneously active in the world.
[14] The path of Yoga that focuses on the development of discernment, discrimination and wisdom.
[15] The Yoga of the development of devotional consciousness via meditation upon God.

se chapters describe many aspects of the nature, glory and attributes of God in some detail. Thus the first group of six chapters serves as a preparatory step toward the second set of six chapters.

Having established the dual goals of Yoga as being self-realization followed by God-realization, the last group of six chapters, chapters 13-18 of the *Gita*, now provide a philosophical and intellectual clarification of the various matters thus far propounded throughout the work. These chapters clarify the nature of the three ultimate Reals, or Tri-tattva. These three Reals are: a) the material nature (*jagat*), b) the innumerable individual selves that inhabit the world in which we live (*atman*), and the Absolute (Brahman). Everything that exists can be philosophically, categorically and experientially reduced down to one of these three elements.

All material objects, for example, whether we are referring to the objects we see around us such as a chair, a car, a building or even our own bodies, are ultimately composed of matter, and can thus be reduced to matter (*jagat*). Our innermost essence, what in Euro-American religious expression is often termed the soul, is in actuality the true self, known as *atman*. For the *Bhagavad Gita*, in addition to these two elements, there is a third. The third ultimate Real is the source and grounding of the other two. This third Real is God, or Brahman. Matter is insentient (*jada*), while *atman* and Brahman are sentient (*ajada*). Matter and *atman* are dependent, while Brahman is supremely independent, being the source, purpose and goal of all things. In the *Bhagavad Gita*, Krishna provides Arjuna with the most authoritative explanation of the nature and inter-relationship of all three of these foundational aspects of reality.

The discussion between Krishna and Arjuna proceeds in a progressive

series of successive arguments, starting from seemingly worldly appeals
to Arjuna to fight, and leading rapidly to the main purpose of Krishna's
instructions: leading Arjuna from the delusion (*moha*) he currently finds
himself in, to the liberating knowledge of his true self and God toward
which all living beings either knowingly or unknowingly aim. For readers
who take no more than a cursory glance at the first two chapters of the
Bhagavad Gita, it is in these chapters that, more often than not, one can
get somewhat easily bogged down and confused. Often such a superficial
reading will convince the reader that the goal of Krishna's discourse is
rooted in no more than His desire to get Arjuna to regain his courage
and fight. In actuality, it very quickly becomes apparent with a more patient reading that the war, while certainly a historical reality, is also a
philosophical backdrop - a dramatic tool - to lead the reader from the
comparatively superficial concerns of the war in question to a deeper
inquiry of the very nature of reality itself.

Arjuna's dilemma is not rooted in the battle about to commence around
him, but rather it is rooted in the war that he finds taking place within
himself. Arjuna's dilemma is nothing less than a historic metaphor for the
great war that each human being faces in his or her attempt to discern
truth versus untruth, reality versus illusion - the encounter with true spiritual self versus the psychologically comforting, but ultimately enslaving,
façade of false persona. Rapidly, within the space of only a few verses in
the second chapter, the Great Mahabharata War is quickly left behind,
and Krishna and Arjuna quickly find themselves inhabiting a thoroughly
transcendent realm of discourse.

After Arjuna rejects several lesser, alternate options for relieving his existential dilemma (2:26-28; 2:31-37), Krishna then explicates the Yoga

system as the surest means of achieving both philosophical certitude, as well as the practical experience of self-realization that is necessary for lasting peace and happiness. It is at the point where we leave mere intellectual speculation behind us and we then begin practicing the liberating path of Yoga that the journey to the very threshold of Truth begins for us.

Yoga is a unitary and comprehensive system designed to awaken its practitioner to the reality of his true self. There is in reality only one Yoga system, though this one system is often mistakenly seen as multiple paths in accordance with what the particular emphasis might be. As we encounter the stunningly diverse reality of the world Yoga scene today, however, there appear to be a myriad of different schools of Yoga. Some of these emphases are quite ancient and authentic in nature, such as Kriya-yoga, Hatha-yoga, Raja-yoga and Bhakti-yoga. Others, such as the modern schools of K. Pratabhi Jois, B.K.S. Iyengar and other unqualified entrepreneurial innovators with large Western audiences, are of much more recent and dubious origins. Of the many different branches of the traditional and authentic discipline of Yoga, only four are discussed at any great length by Krishna in the *Bhagavad Gita*. We will now closely examine the different approaches, philosophical outlooks and aims of these four Yoga systems of the *Bhagavad Gita*.

The speaker of the *Gita*, Sri Krishna, describes four types of Yoga, or spiritual disciplines that ensure liberation. These four dimensions of Yoga are 1) *jnana-yoga*, or the Yoga of wisdom, 2) *karma-yoga*, the Yoga of dynamic meditation 3) *bhakti-yoga*, the Yoga of devotional consciousness, and 4) the formal classical Yoga system, also known as *ashtanga-yoga* or *raja-yoga*. While these various systems of Yoga are all intimately allied as ultimately different spokes of the one wheel of Yoga, they are not presented in the *Bhagavad Gita* as being all of equal value.

After giving a detailed description of the fourth type of Yoga (*ashtanga-yoga*) in the sixth chapter, for example, the *Bhagavad Gita* seems to then imply that this form of Yoga may be too difficult and demanding if it is practiced in a vacuum, unaided by the other three dimensions of Yoga. Indeed, the vast majority of the verses in the *Gita,* both previous to, as well as proceeding this chapter, focus primarily on the practice of the other three aspects of Yoga (*jnana, karma* and *bhakti*) as being of necessary importance for a proper understanding of, and a practical technical grounding for, the classical *ashtanga-yoga* system.

While these four Yoga paths differ slightly as far as their respective technical emphases, they are all similarly oriented in their over-all approach and goal, and are thus really only one path. All of the Yoga systems taught in the *Bhagavad Gita* are in complete agreement that devotional mediation upon, and realization of, the Absolute is the central overriding activity of any real importance in human existence. The *Bhagavad Gita* presents us with a unitary system of Yoga, one clear and systematic path, wherein all four Yoga techniques of *jnana, karma, bhakti* and classical *ashtanga* are - together – all considered crucial for spiritual realization. These four supposedly different paths, in actuality, represent four aspects of one, unified, integral Yoga system. They are akin to the four sides of a square. If one of the sides of the square is missing, then the very structural integrity and being of the square is itself compromised. Indeed, it no longer is logically qualified as a "square" at all. Similarly, the complete and authentic path of Yoga spirituality must include all these four components of Yoga in order to be fully appreciated.

It is true that these four Yogas are linked by their common emphasis on devotional meditation upon, and the ultimate loving absorption of our awareness in, the Absolute. However, it is also inarguably clear that Krishna considers *bhakti-yoga*, or the discipline of focused devotional consciousness, to be not merely one component of these four branches of Yoga, but as the very essence and goal of all Yoga practice itself. Unlike the other aspects of the Yoga path, *bhakti* (devotional meditation) is distinguished by the fact that it is not only a means (*upaya*) for knowing God, but it is simultaneously also the goal (*artha*) of all human existence. As the means, *bhakti* designates devotional meditation; as the goal, *bhakti* means devotional consciousness. At no time does one abandon the practice of *bhakti*, even upon achieving liberation. Rather, devotional consciousness focused with one-pointed awareness upon the Absolute represents the very goal of the entire Yoga system. This is not true of any other system of Yoga.

3.3.7 The Unity of Yoga

The *Bhagavad Gita's* ultimate conclusion is that it is the integration of all four Yogas, with *bhakti* being both the unifying factor, as well as the goal of all paths of Yoga, that represents the highest form of Yoga. Krishna insists repeatedly that it is through this *bhakti*-based integral Yoga system presented by Him in the *Bhagavad Gita*, through the yogic path of devotional contemplation, that one can attain knowledge of, and union (*yoga*) with, the Absolute. He says:

> *bhaktya mam abhijanati yavan yas casmi tattvatah*
> *tato mam tattvato jnatva visate tad-anantaram*

"One can understand Me as I am only by devotional contemplation. And when one is in full consciousness of Me by such devotion, he can enter into My truth." (18:55)

The great importance of devotional contemplation as the primary means for attaining realization of the Absolute is stressed repeatedly throughout the entirety of the *Gita*, throughout all the Vedic scriptures, and represents the highest path in Sanatana Dharma.

Further evidence of the primacy of *bhakti* as the unifying factor underlying all four Yoga systems can be seen in regard to the *vishva-rupa* vision of Arjuna in the eleventh chapter of the *Bhagavad Gita*. After revealing to Arjuna the beatific vision of His wonderful universal form, Krishna tells him that:

bhaktya tv ananyaya sakya aham evam-vidho'rjuna
jnatum drashtum cha tattvena praveshtum cha parantapa

"...only by devotional meditation can I be understood as I am, standing before you, and can thus be seen directly. In this way you can enter into the mysteries of My being" (11:54). Significantly, the beatific epiphany of the transcendent Absolute as the source and ground of all existence was revealed to Arjuna, not because he was a great ascetic, a learned philosopher or an austere renunciate. Rather, Krishna showed Arjuna this divine vision for one reason alone: because of the advanced level of the *bhakti*, or devotional yogic absorption, that Arjuna had achieved. (11:53-55) Thus, one's inner contemplative state takes precedence over one's external ability to perform physical *asanas* (Yoga postures).

In the *Gita*, *bhakti* is seen to culminate in the final, supreme stage of total self-surrender to the Absolute. In the last chapter of the *Gita*, Krishna informs Arjuna that He is now explaining "...the most confidential part of knowledge" (*jnanam guhyataram*). (18:64) This certainly seems to indicate that Krishna is about to reveal to Arjuna His most definitive statement thus far on the subject of Yoga. He then proceeds to illustrate the kind of thoroughly theocentric consciousness necessary for one who wishes to know the Absolute:

> *manmana bhava mad-bhakto mad-yaji mam namaskuru*
> *mam evaishyasi satyam te pratijane priyo'si me*

"Always think of Me and become My devotee," declares Krishna, "worship Me and offer your homage unto Me. Thus you will come to Me without fail. I promise you this because you are My very dear friend." (18:65) According to Krishna, the *yogi's* consciousness is to be completely absorbed in devotional contemplation upon the Divine. With his mind intently meditating on God, the *yogi* will achieve final liberation, coupled with all the freedom, peace, knowledge and fulfillment that such liberation implies. Complete, loving self-surrender to the Absolute - in sincere faith and trust - is the highest path to be traversed by the *yogi*, explains Krishna:

> *sarva-dharman parityajya mam ekam sharanam vraja*
> *aham tvam sarva-papebhyo mokshayishyami ma suchah*

"Abandon all varieties of lesser *dharmas* [duties, lesser paths] and simply surrender unto Me. I shall deliver you from all demeritorious reactions. Do not fear." (18:66)

With this culminating verse, the *Bhagavad Gita* declares *bhakti*, or devotional meditation on the Absolute, to be the highest and foremost of all

Yogas.

In his commentary on this verse, Sri Ramanuja Acharya (1017–1137), the greatest philosopher in Sanatana Dharma's very long history of religious and philosophical attainments, interprets the advice in this verse as calling for "...the complete relinquishment of the sense of agency, possessiveness, fruits, etc., in the practicing of *karma, jnana* and *bhakti yogas* in the way instructed, and the realizing of ...[God]...as the agent, object of worship, the means and the end" (Ramanuja, 1991). Thus, for the *yogi* nothing less than full surrender to the Absolute, in all of his words, thoughts and actions, will suffice if self-realization is his goal.

All four of the Yogas discussed in the *Bhagavad Gita* are intimately united on a more practical basis in that they all involve different degrees of mediation on the Absolute. Indeed, meditation, and the requisite mental discipline necessary for its practice, are integral elements of any Yoga process (*Yoga Sutras*, 1.2). This similarity, however, must not allow us to overlook the important distinctions in emphasis between the integrated path of the *ashtanga/jnana/karma/bhakti yoga* system. The *ashtanga* system described in the sixth chapter focuses on the important mechanics of practice. The *jnana* system helps the *yogi* to acquire the wisdom and intellectual acumen necessary to guide the *yogi* safely along the path. The path of *karma-yoga* transcendentalizes the *yogi's* every action. Finally, *bhakti* provides the meditative content, as well as reveals the goal of the very practice of Yoga itself. It seems quite apparent that Krishna considers *bhakti*, the state of loving devotion, to be both the underlying essence and goal of *ashtanga-yoga*, *karma-yoga* and *jnana-yoga*. All four Yoga systems are thus united into one integral path, having *bhakti* as both their essence and goal.

The *Bhagavad Gita's* recommendation is that the *yogi* should develop a loving, devotional state of consciousness toward the Absolute, finally culminating in full self-surrender (*sharanam*) to that Absolute, Bhagavan Sri Krishna. It is the final conclusion of the *Bhagavad Gita* that if one truly desires real happiness, peace and fulfillment, one must know one's true self. And this is to be done in conjunction with knowing the Supreme Self, or God.

As paradoxical as it may at first appear, it is as a direct result of this surrender of self that one realizes the self. If the goal for the *yogi* is self-realization, and if this is to be achieved only by reducing the seemingly insatiable demands of the ego, then what faster and more powerful way is there to eliminate all sense of false possessiveness that to relinquish control over even his very self by surrendering that self to the mercy and loving care of God, the Supreme Self (*paramatman*)?

The *yogi* must be prepared to plunge deeply and fearlessly into the ecstatic reality of the sweet Absolute. Nothing less than this sweetness of devotion will suffice. Nothing greater than this sweetness is to be attained. This is the essential teaching of the *Bhagavad Gita*.

The *Bhagavad Gita*, and the entirety of the revealed Vedic scriptures, serves as the primary sources of transcendent wisdom, rigorous philosophical insight, and spiritual guidance that enforms the systematic philosophical world-view of Sanatana Dharma. Coupled with the living guidance of a successive lineage of realized Dharma masters (enlightened *rishis* and Acharyas) stretching back to the beginning of time, and still present in our own era, the philosophy of Sanatana Dharma originates from transcendent perfection.

Having explored the epistemological foundations of Sanatana Dharma, we will now spend the next several chapters of this book looking at the metaphysics, ontology and ethics of the Vedic world-view.

Chapter 4 Metaphysics: The Nature of Reality

4.1.1 Tri-Tattva: The Metaphysical Foundations of Reality

The philosophy of Sanatana Dharma is a systematic and comprehensive world-view designed to understand the totality of both empirical and metaphysical reality, as well as the purpose of life within that total reality. Basic to understanding the nature of reality is the metaphysical concept of the Tri-tattva, or the Three Reals, as well as the intimate inter-relationship between them. This chapter will briefly introduce the basic metaphysical concept of Tri-tattva. Chapter five will then delve deeply into the ontological issues that revolve around each of these three elements of reality.

4.1.2 The Three Reals

Dharma addresses every aspect of philosophy - from ethics, epistemology, and aesthetics, to politics, ontology, and metaphysics. This section will deal specifically with the metaphysical concept of the Tri-tattva, or Three Reals, of Sanatana Dharma, which serves as the foundation of our understanding of the reality we find around us.

The term "metaphysics" was itself first coined in the Western world by Aristotle (384 BC - 322 BC) and denotes those subject matters that lie beyond the physical world and corresponding empirical perception. Metaphysical realities may not be provable through sensory evidence, but they can be proven through logical inference and by direct experiential insight. Thus, metaphysical objects of knowledge fall under the epistemic mechanisms ranging from *anumana* (logical inference) to *shabda* (spiritual realization). Such inquiries as those concerning the existence and nature of God, soul, overall Reality, natural law, essential attributiveness, and Being ontology are some of the subjects covered by metaphysics. While innumerable volumes have been written about the intricacies of the metaphysics of Dharma, the fundamental foundations of our metaphysical principles can be stated using a more economically postulated formula.

According to Vedanta, which forms the applied philosophical basis of Dharma, all of reality – i.e., literally everything that is perceivable by the senses and conceivable by the intellect that exists in our world – can ultimately be broken down into one or another of three very basic general elements. These are called the Tri-tattvas, or the Three Reals. These Three Reals are: a) soul (Atman), b) God (Brahman), and c) matter (Jagat). Everything around us, when reduced to their simplest components, can be ultimately seen as falling into one or another of these three ontologically exclusive categories.

For an immediate example we can all relate to, we can analyze ourselves as human persons. We know that we have a physical body, which ultimately can be reduced to prime matter (Jagat). Animating our body with consciousness and subsequent vitality is our true self, our soul (Atman). Finally, the very source, ontological ground of being, and sustainer of existence (*esse*) of our very soul itself is God (Brahman). Thus, we can either empirically or inferentially observe all three instances of the *tri-tattvas* in our lives.

4.1.3 Atman – The True Self

Having the Supreme Godhead as our source, our souls participate in the positive spiritual qualities of the Absolute. Both our souls (Atman) and God (Brahman) share in the inherent spiritual qualities of necessary being and existence, eternality, wisdom, beauty and goodness. When we analyze the attributive nature of our own soul, we discover that we too possess these, and many more, positive qualities as an inherent part of our *atman*, or true spiritual self. While God possesses these positive attributes to an infinite and never-surpassed degree, we possess them to a finite and causally dependent degree. Though the positive qualities of the soul are finite, however, they are known to have God as their source. What Dharma consequently teaches is that we already possess, as the treasures of our very own soul, the various perfections that we seek endlessly and without satisfaction outside of ourselves in our daily pursuit for happiness and fulfillment in the material world. The treasures that we seek are not "out there" in endless possessions, the never-satisfied quest for power, or the illusory lies of our own selfish, egoic lower self. The treasures that we actually seek are spiritual in nature. They are a reflection of our true, spiritual self, and include beauty, wisdom, freedom, love, joy and fulfillment. These spiritual treasures we seek lay already within us as us, as the true and spiritual us. They are the natural attributes of our very self (*atman*).

More, the soul is not merely an object that we possess. Unlike the Abrahamic religions, all of which claim that the soul is something that we merely "have" in a similar manner to how we have an appendage like a spleen, a lung, or a liver, Dharma does not teach that the soul is merely an object that we happen to have. We do not *have* a soul. Rather we *are* soul. Our soul is our innermost identity and synonymous with the most intimate level of "I" that we know to be the core of our personhood.

Both God (Brahman) and soul (Atman) are of the nature of pure sentient consciousness. Thus, being spiritual, they both transcend matter itself, as well as all the limitations necessarily associated with matter.

4.1.4 Brahman – The Absolute

The Dharmic conception of God, or the Absolute (Brahman), is described in the Vedic scriptures in a way that makes our understanding of God different and more highly developed than the speculations about God that we find in the Abrahamic faiths (Judaism, Christianity and Islam). Whereas the Abrahamic faiths have what we call an Anthropomorphic Monotheistic notion of God (that is, their god is seen as being very human-like in his emotions, prejudices, demands, goals, motivations, etc.), the Dharmic conception of the Absolute is Panentheistic in nature.

Dharmic Panentheism (not to be confused in any way with Pantheism, which mistakenly says that the totality of the material universe is God, which is not an idea that Dharma in any way supports) teaches that while the Absolute is, indeed, omnipotent, omniscient, all-good, the source of all reality, and completely transcendent vis-à-vis matter, Dharma additionally teaches that the Absolute is also wholly immanent in all of creation, and in both material and spiritual realities. There is nowhere in creation where God's direct presence cannot be encountered and experienced. Thus, for the Dharmi (follower of Dharma), nature and matter can never be seen as "evil" or "sinful" or radically alienated from God, as is clearly the mistaken assumption of the Abrahamic faiths, since God lays as both the very source and inner foundation of nature! More, we can never be truly separated from our divine Source. God is always with us, and we with God. We can, however, experience the temporary *illusion* of separation due to the arising of false ego (*ahamkara*).

God (Brahman) is an infinite ocean of positive attributes (*nitya-kalyana-gunaih*). Whatever possible qualities that are recognized as good, beneficial, healthy and positive, when taken to their very highest degree, to their very furthest depths (and then exceeded!) and then their very source pointed to, all such positive qualities are seen as originating as the auspicious attributes of the Supreme Godhead (*purna-purusha*). Thus, God is the very source of all beauty, goodness, wisdom, light, healthfulness, reality, power, grandeur, bliss, eternality, knowledge, courage, being, purity, truth, vitality, auspiciousness, etc. God is consequently seen as the supremely desirable center of all concern for all living entities, all divine powers and energies, and all reality.

Both Atman and Brahman are trans-material in their essence. Both are of the nature of pure consciousness. Atman and Brahman share sentiency in common. Matter, however, as the sole non-sentient element of the Tritattva, has its own unique relationship to consciousness.

4.1.5 Jagat – The Power of Prime Materiality Enformed

Matter is only one of the many powers, energies, or "*shaktis*" of the Absolute. Matter, like all of God's many *shaktis*, is seen as being of feminine metaphysical gender.[16] For this reason all ancient traditions have always understood materiality and nature to be best understood from our perspective as a mother and a Goddess. The idea of "Mother Earth" is a universally acknowledge archetypal reality that all human cultures have recognized and honored - with the sole and very stark exception of the radically patriarchal and artificially dualist-oriented Abrahamic cultures. Having God as its source, basic prime matter is thus seen as a positive phenomenon meant to be understood, respected and utilized properly. Matter is a divine feminine energy which, especially when seen in its prime-energetic, pre-formed state, is neutral in its phenomenal ethical content, but which can be used in either a positive or negative way by living beings when our consciousness and free-will decisions interact with it. In the same way that a sharp knife is a morally neutral tool that can be used either by a surgeon to save the life of a patient or by a murderer to take the life of an innocent victim, matter too can be used in either a morally good or evil way depending upon the intent of the conscious being, or *atman*, using the matter. Matter itself, however, neither heals nor harms, being a neutral energy of God.

Originally existing in pure energetic form, matter only becomes en-formed with name and shape (*nama* and *rupa*, respectively) when it comes into intentional contact with the illusory-egoic desires of the individual *atman*. Thus begins the process of devolution that manifests the world we see around us, with all its diversity, duality, and seemingly infinite possi-

---

[16] The dual terms "masculine" and "feminine" do not have the same meaning in metaphysics, linguistics or aesthetics that they do in biology. When we refer to "masculine" and "feminine" in the former categories, we are not referring to men and women in the biological sense. Rather, in the field of metaphysics, "masculine" and "feminine" refer to functionality and the dynamics of allied inter-relationship within that context of functionality.

bility.

4.1.6 Inter-relationships Between the Tri-Tattvas

Of the Three Reals (Tri-tattva), only God (Brahman) is thoroughly independent and sovereign, with soul (Atman) and matter (Jagat) existing in
both originating and sustaining dependency upon God. Of the Three
Reals, then, it is Brahman who reigns supreme over and above the other
two *tattvas*. God, or Brahman, is the source of all. In the state of illusion,
the soul (Atman) sees itself as an exploiter of matter (Jagat), and lives in
an unnatural state of illusory separation from God. Thus, the soul psychologically finds himself in an unnatural, unnecessary and discomforting
state of self-imposed conflict (*virodha*) and adversity with God, with other
living beings, and with the material world around him. Such an unnatural
state is the source of all our suffering. However, in the most ideal of cir-
cumstances, God, soul and materiality all exist in harmonious balance,
drawn to one another through a metaphysical bond of love, and a unity
of transcendent purpose - Atman and Jagat serving Brahman, and Brahman giving Atman and Jagat their sense of purpose and operating as the
ontological source and sustaining principle of their very being.

In the specific context of the Tri-tattva that we are discussing in this section of the book, it could be stated that the ultimate spiritual goal of each
and every living being (Atman) is to come once again to a state of natural
balance in its relationship with Brahman and Jagat, understanding Brahman as our true source, and Jagat as one of Brahman's many positive
energies (*shaktis*). When we live in such a state of natural balance, we are
then living in accordance with Dharma. We are then living our lives naturally and in perfection.

4.2.1 Tri-Tattva and the Three Dharmic Paths

It has been traditionally understood throughout the very long history of
Sanatana Dharma that there are three primary spiritual paths (*margas*) that
are an integral part of general Vedic spirituality. These three paths (*tri-
marga*) are a) Vaishnava-marga, b) Shaiva-marga, and c) Shakta-marga.
Vaishnava-marga is focused on the worship of the Supreme Godhead
Narayana/Vishnu. The spiritual focal point of Shaiva-marga is the being
known as Shiva. Finally, Shakta-marga focuses on communion with
Shakti. All three of these paths are predicated upon and situated within
the Vedic scriptural/philosophical/cultural milieu. All three base their
foundational teachings upon at least one aspect or another of the Vedic
scriptures. Thus, all three of these paths have always been considered to
be *vaidika*, or legitimate Vedic spiritual paths.

What has not always been understood about the nature of these three
paths, and often even by very serious practitioners of the Vedic way, has
been the direct correlation between the three paths and the Three Reals
(Tri-tattva) that we have outlined above. It is only in properly understanding the direct relationship between these two different categories
that we then begin to understand why these three differing paths exist as
a necessary feature of Vedic spirituality.

The Vedic way presents us with a unified vision of our cosmos, and a
self-contained philosophical construct that explains that integrated cosmos. There are ultimately no inherent contradictions, confusions or
conflicting world-views anywhere within the Vedic religion. The Vedic
religion presents us with a unified vision of reality, and the Vedic scrip-

tures describe that vision with one voice. Rather than containing any contradictions, what we do, in fact, often find are a limited category of seemingly diverse courses of action authoritatively prescribed within the greater Vedic matrix that are purposefully designed to engage different individuals with differing internal temperaments in such a manner as to afford all individuals the opportunity to honor their idiosyncratic spiritual temperaments within the context of Vedic culture.

Unlike the more artificially imposed anthropology of the Abrahamic faiths, Sanatana Dharma recognized that people are all different. We all have different desires, predilections, temperaments and goals in both material life, as well as in our spiritual pursuits. More, we are all on different stages in our individual journeys toward the Divine. Some are only a step away from the final goal, others have barely begun their journey, while most are somewhere in the middle of the path. No one is the same. It is in understanding that the Vedic path attempts to offer several courses of action to reflect such psychophysical diversity that we can begin to grasp many of these supposed contradictions within the inherently integrated Vedic milieu.

It has been unfortunate that in the past both spiritually dissociated academicians, as well as many less knowledgeable Hindu teachers, have misunderstood precisely how these three spiritual paths relate to one another, and how it can be possible that three different paths can even co-exist within the unified vision of the Vedic way. Some have proffered the mistaken idea that these three paths (*tri-marga*) are all merely different approaches to the one same goal of knowing Brahman - a type of Radical Universalist "all paths are the same" phenomenon artificially inserted within the context of the Vedic tradition - when in actuality these three

124

paths clearly do not share the same goal at all. They are not merely different chosen perspectives toward the same spiritual aim. Others have taken the opposite approach and claimed that these three paths have historically been at conflictual odds with one another, warring for untold millennia for theological supremacy within the Vedic context, thus supposedly demonstrating that the Vedic world-view is not a unified philosophical system at all. Such a speculative explanation is equally untrue.

The problems with either of these two faulty propositions is that they falsely reduce Sanatana Dharma into a world-view that supposedly contains inherent contradictions within it, that is predicated upon the imperfect whims of self-motivated humans attempting to create yet another anthropomorphic conception of the Absolute, and thus reduces Vedic philosophy to the false postulation that the spiritually-inspired philosophical outlook of Sanatana Dharma is merely one more man-made attempt to construct an Absolute out of his own image. These conclusions, however, would constitute the very antithesis of the evidentiary truth, and of the divinely revealed and comprehensively unified system of the Sanatana Dharma philosophical world-view.

Though these three distinct and separate Vedic paths do have differing ultimate goals (*artha*), they are nonetheless all perfectly reconciled and non-contradictory when understood from the perspective of Tri-tattva. This is the case because the three separate goals of the three paths (*tri-marga*) of Sanatana Dharma exist by the very design of the Vedic system itself, and not merely as a result of illusory perspectival prejudices on the part of human beings. The three separate goals postulated by the three paths are meant to be understood in accordance with the inherent con-

junction of the three primary human psychological needs with their respective corresponding element of the Tri-tattvas.

In their spiritually generated insightful brilliance, the Vedic *rishis* (seer-
sages) realized that all religiously induced sentiments in various human
beings corresponded seamlessly with either one or another of three major categories of desiderative motivations. In other words, a typical
human person who commences upon his pursuit of higher spiritual attainments is motivated to achieve one of three different goals. A person
on the spiritual path is either seeking:

> A) A connection with the underflowing energies (*prakriti*) of the
> natural, yet necessarily material, cosmos; and thus communion
> with the personification of that energy in the form of Shakti De
> vi.[17]

> B) Or to achieve isolated (*kaivalyam*) realization of his internal
> self as *atman*, which is likewise personified in the being known as
> Shiva.

> C) Or the very highest goal of ultimate communion with the
> Absolute Supreme Godhead, who is Sriman Narayana.

Those attracted to (A) will follow the Shakta path. Those attracted to (B)
will follow the Shaiva path. Finally, those who wish to achieve the highest spiritual attainment of direct communion with the Absolute
(Brahman) described in (C) will follow the path of Vaishnavism. There is
a direct correspondence between *tattva*, *marga* and the *devata* (deity) wor-
shiped. The following chart shows these natural correspondences.

---

[17] Referred to alternatively as "The Great Mother", Shakti Ma, Maha Shakti, Kali,
Durga, Parvati, etc.

Tattva	Marga	Deity
Brahman	Vaishnava	Narayana
Atman	Shaiva	Shiva
Jagat	Shakta	Shakti

The Tri-tattvas directly correspond to the three most important and prevalent divinities and paths in the Dharmic tradition. Brahman is synonymous with Narayana-Vishnu, and those who wish to focus their spiritual practice upon fully knowing Brahman will follow the path of Vaishnava Dharma. The entirety of the Vedic scriptures speaks with one united and unequivocal voice in declaring Sriman Narayana to be the Supreme Godhead. All other names, positive adjectival designations, and references to lesser *devas/devis* refer to Sriman Narayana alone as His attributive components.

Atman, on the other hand, is personified in the god Shiva. For this reason, those *yogis* who are exclusively attracted to the path of self-realization will tend toward Shaiva Dharma. Lastly, the element of Jagat corresponds to the goddess Shakti. Individuals who express their spiritual yearning toward a worship of material energies, *shaktis*, and the powers of both nature, as well as the internal natural powers such as *kundalini, chakras*, psychic development, etc., have one or another form of the great Devi or Shakti as their object of meditation. These devotees of Jagat often become followers of Shakta Dharma.

In summary, then, those individual persons who focus on the accumulation of power become Shaktas. Those who focus on self-understanding alone become Shaivas. Those who yearn for surrender to God and to be empowered by Him become Vaishnavas. While all three of these paths are Vedic, they are not all equal and they do not by any means all share the same goal.

In the next chapter of this work, we will use the knowledge of the nature of the Tri-tattvas outlined above as the foundation of a more in-depth exploration of the anthropology of the human person, the ontology of God, and the cosmophysics and cosmology of Creation.

Chapter 5 Ontology: Human Person, God and Creation

In the following chapter, we will explore more in-depth the natures of a) the human person, b) God, and c) the Creation.

5.1.1 A) THE HUMAN PERSON

Throughout the history of philosophy, both Asian and Western, there have been many attempts to create a philosophical anthropology, a systematic account of the nature of the human person (*manushya*). Many post-Renaissance, Western rationalists, such as Rene DesCartes, postulated the theory of the human person consisting of only a physical form (*res extensa*) and mental substance (*res cogitans*). For such post-Enlightenment materialist thinkers as David Hume, John Stuart Mill, Karl Marx and Rudolf Carnap, on the other hand, the human person was little more than the physical element, devoid of soul, and with even the mental and consciousness elements reduced to nothing more than a neurological extension of the physical.

Sanatana Dharma, on the other hand, offers the most comprehensive and inclusive philosophical anthropology available. According to the Dharmic account of the human person, we are much more than merely an empirically physical or an intellectual being. We are multidimensional beings consisting of a hierarchically progressive spectrum of ontologically diverse elements working in close cooperation to produce the whole effect that we know as the human being. The human person consists of several elements that become increasingly more subtle and qualitatively superior to the preceding element in accordance with each respectively higher element's proximity to that which is most real: consciousness.

The following represent the primary constituents of the various elements of which the human person is composed, and which are thus responsible for the harmonious integration that constitutes a person. They are listed from the most superior, down to the most inferior elements:

Consciousness (*atman*)

Illusory Ego (*ahamkara*)

Intellect (*buddhi*)

Mind (*manas*)

Emotions (*abhitapa*)

Body (*deha*)

Of these six elements, it is only the *atman* (consciousness) that constitutes the true self and the central core of I-cognition (*aham-pratyaya*). This is due to the fact that only *atman* displays the attributes of eternality and permanence, and perfectly reflects the substantial ontological makeup of God in necessarily limited and finite (*saptika*) form. Only the *atman* truly lasts, whereas the other five elements come into being, have temporary existence, and eventually go out of being. It is the eternal *atman* who experiences the non-permanent illusory ego, intellect, mind, emotions and body as they undergo their necessary material modifications.

5.1.2 Atman

Our soul, *atman*, originates from God. Originally situated in the transcendent spiritual realm as the consciousness-energy (*tatastha-shakti*) of God, each individual *atman* originally found itself one of an unlimited number of monadic spiritual units that makes up the effulgent, overflowing rays of God's light-energy (*brahma-jyoti*). This can be understood in the same manner in which the Sun is situated in one location, but yet spreads its influence, presence and power throughout the solar system via its rays. Within the rays emanating from the Sun, we find an infinite number of atomic particles that constitute those rays. The infinite particles of light both are, and simultaneously are not, the same as the Sun. They are the Sun in the sense that they represent the same ontological substance of which the Sun is composed. Indeed, even in common language, when we see sunshine entering a window into a room, we will often claim that "the Sun is coming into the room". When in actuality, of course, if the Sun himself were, in fact, in the room, all occupants would be immediately burnt up. Thus we understand that, in a limited and qualitative sense, the Sun (the source) and the sunshine (the energy by-product) are one. But, at the same time, we also recognize that the atoms of sunshine entering our room are also not literally the Sun in that they are infinitesimal in their expanse, while the Sun is infinite in comparison. The light atoms are the effect, the dependent by-products of the Sun; whereas the Sun is the cause of the by-products.

In a very similar way to the relationship between the Sun and the light atoms of sunshine, God also is situated as an unlimited transcendental personality in Vaikuntha, the highest stratum of the spiritual realm, and spreads His influence, presence and power via His *brahma-jyoti* spiritual effulgence, which is comprised of an unlimited number of "atomic" *atmans*. These atomic (*anu*) *atmans* are you, me and every other living sentient being in existence. The individual *atmans*, or souls, are both one with God, and yet different from God. We are one with God in that our ontological substance and God's ontological substance are the same in its qualitative makeup. Both the infinite Supreme Godhead and the individ-

132

ual finite *atmans* are of the nature of pure consciousness. We are different from God, however, because each individual *atman* is infinitesimally finite in nature, whereas God is infinite. We are conditioned by-products of the Absolute, and thus we are effects. But God is the unconditioned cause of all causes, and thus the supreme source of all. It is for this reason that each individual soul is referred to in the Vedic scriptures as *atman*, or "self"; but God alone is referred to in the very same scriptures as Paramatman, or the "Supreme Self". He is also known as the Antaryamin, or "Inner Witness". Thus, all souls originally existed as monadic units of consciousness existing within the trans-temporal and trans-spacial infinite ocean of consciousness that substantially constitutes the effulgent outflowing influence of God's essential being.

5.1.3 Aham-pratyaya Versus Aham-kara:
I-Cognition Versus Illusory Ego

Within the context of the trans-temporal, spiritual reality that constitutes this light ocean (*brahma-jyoti*), consisting of an infinite number of individual souls, from where all living being originate, each soul exists only with a trace self-awareness of itself as an individual part of the greater whole that includes God and God's infinite energies. As natural individuated self-awareness eventually appears for the *atman*, the individual *atman* begins to distinguish itself in its core identity as a unique person with a sense of selfhood. Such an eventual development is a natural spiritual process for the *atman*. This natural sense of spiritual self-awareness and sense of "I" is termed *aham-pratyaya*, or I-cognition.

At this natural stage in the soul's development, the inherent power of will and the consequent free volition that is attendant upon the power of will then come into being. Choice, in other words, now becomes a newly encountered factor for the soul that needs to be explored. The two paths that the soul is faced with at this juncture of the arising of free-will and choice are: a) to now develop its new-found sense of self-awareness, free-will and personhood in a manner that is keeping with its natural constitutional position as an eternal servant of God, and to consequently explore its inherent I-cognition (*aham-pratyaya*) in eternal loving service toward the Divine; or b) to explore an artificially imposed sense of self in which the *atman* chooses to serve its own illusory ego rather than God. The illusory ego that is formed in the latter decision is known as *aham-kara* (*aham* meaning "I", and *kara* meaning "maker", or "artificial"), literally the pursuit of an artificial "I". *Aham-pratyaya* is natural to the soul. *Aham-kara* is not. When the *atman* chooses the path of *aham-kara*, or false ego, it then instigates the devolution of the illusory material energy known as *prakriti*, and proceeds to descend into the realm of illusion known as the material cosmos to follow whatever illusory pursuits his false ego leads him in, and to experience the consequent karmic implications of his unfortunate decision.

In this context, the term *"atman"* designates the true self when it is free of *aham-kara*, where as *"jiva"* is just a more technical word for self as a living being, and most especially the self as the self is experiencing the material world.

Finding ourselves having chosen to be currently situated in the realm of illusion, the ultimate, and only meaningful, spiritual pursuit of all human persons is to thus transcend our illusory egoic selves, and to reclaim our true identity as *atman*, eternal sparks of consciousness who have God as our ontological source, and God's service as our constitutional purpose.

134

It is the combination of our inherent attributive free-will, coupled with the accumulation of our individual *karmas* created by our actions within the material cosmos, that lead to the great diversity, inequalities, and varied trajectories that we see among all living beings within the material cosmos.

5.1.4 Inherent Individuality of the Atman

According to Patanjali, the fundamental essence of the individual unit of consciousness (*atman*) is that he is of the nature of *drashtur*, or experiencer.[18] As an individual experiencer who has limited perceptual expanse in the scope of his experience, each soul only has the ability to have reality expressed to its knowing faculty via its own bounded perspectival ability alone. Then, in response to that external stimulus, it subsequently has the ability to act upon that experience via its own free will volition. Anything that is external to the core experiencer (*drashtur*, which is an epistemic signifier for *atman*), i.e., anything that is experienced, is necessarily separate from, and thus not, the experiencer, or true self. The totality of this process provides a very brief synopsis of what makes me "me", and you "you", thus accounting for subjective individuality.

The individual *atmans* are always essentially distinct from one another. Thus the simplistically formulated New Age claim that "We are all one", has meaning only on the level of emotive sentiment, and not on a philosophical one. More, the infinite individual *atmans* are also distinct from Brahman (God) quantitatively, in subjectively determined indentitarian terms, and in their nature of dependence upon Brahman, even previous

---

[18] *Yoga Sutras*, 1.3.

to each individual's first encounter with false egotism. In the initial state, however, before their first encounter with egotism, the *atman's* awareness is not individuated to the point of having the internal conditions necessary to fully exercise his innate free will. It is upon such individuation, and the consequent enabling of volitional power, that the individual *atman* then has the ability to choose as a fully individuated being. It is at that point in which the element of choice fully arises that there is the possibility of the *atman's* natural sense of I-awareness (*aham-pratyaya*) becoming perverted into an artificial sense of self (*aham-kara*). It is upon the dawning of *aham-kara* in some newly individuated *atmans* that those atmans consequently fall into materiality. Whether the *atman* chooses to remain in its pure, spiritual identity as a servant of the Divine, or chooses to artificially deny its spiritual destiny and commence its sojourn in the world of materiality, the *atman*, the pure self, remains always and forever and individual being.

5.1.5 Consciousness and Personality

Personality (*vyaktitva*) consists of the integral and nuanced expression of the individual *atman's* unique qualifying attributes, engendered upon the substratum of the essential attributes of consciousness (Atman) per se. Expressed personality is the manifestation of an individual unit of consciousness especially as experienced by one or more other individual units of consciousness. Personality is, in fact, non-different from consciousness. Everything that has consciousness has personality, and everything that has personality has consciousness. Personality is an inherent aspect of both God and of all individual souls. There are no living beings that do not have personality, whether a god, a tree, a human, a mountain, an ant, or a cow.

More, each personality/consciousness is thoroughly unique and undupli-
cable as a necessary consequence of the qualitative differences inherent in
each person's *atman*, and the expression of those cumulative differences
by each individual *atman*. Indeed, if two objects – either sentient or insentient - were to share in all the exact same attributive characteristics and
essential features, with no nuanced qualitative differentiation between the
two objects, those two objects by definition would be the exact same
thing. Thus, the lack of personality among living beings would result in
comprehensive monotony,[19] discompetency[20] and ultimately would render all sentient (*ajada*) beings insentient (*jada*), since personality equates to
consciousness itself.

The modern, New Age misunderstanding of the nature of personality is
that all forms and expressions of personality are only manifestations of
false ego. They have personally experienced so many antagonistic en-
counters with the false personas of illusioned individuals that they,
consequently, now believe that any and all personality is per se inherently
flawed. As a result of this inability to distinguish the material versus
transcendent expressions of personality, many New Age followers have
an untenable aversion to the very idea of personality itself. All personality
is puerilely judged as being illusory. In an overextending attempt to reject
illusioned personality, they have disposed of personality even in the eternal and transcendental sense. Sanatana Dharma teaches that the mistaken

[19] Thus negating the necessary condition for multiplicity and diversification in
any sense or form - ontological, philosophical, empirical or even illusory (which
would then negate the possibility of the existence of diversity even in the sense
of *maya*, or illusion, thus also rendering the Advaita school incomprehensible!)
[20] A word I have created to express "an utter inability to act", which is the opposite of the established philosophical term "omnicompetency".

New Age idea of personality is far from philosophically valid.

Rather, there is clear a distinction in Vedic philosophy between the two different phenomena of a) Persona (*ahamkara*) versus b) Personality (*vyaktitva*). Persona corresponds to *aham-kara*, while personality is *aham-pratyaya*, as elaborated in section 5.1.3 above. Persona is the temporal identity constructed by the illusioned being that is the manifest result of ignorance (*avidya*) and false identification with objects and situations external to the *atman*. Persona is an artificial façade. Personality, on the other hand, is the natural manifestation (*svabhava*) of the eternal *atman*. Personality (*vyaktitva*) is the eternal nature of the individual unit of consciousness (*atman*) as that individual *atman* freely expresses itself and is perceived, both reflexively (how the *atman* perceives itself) and by others. It is non-different from consciousness itself.

We know that consciousness and personality are one and the same because both consciousness and personality share the exact same essential attributes. Any two items that share the exact same essential attributes are, in actuality, constitutionally non-different from one another. The four primary essential attributes that both personality and consciousness must have in order to exist and function are:

A) Free-will (*sankalpa*)

B) Self-awareness (*atmabodha*)

C) Awareness of things external to oneself (*samanyasthiti*)

D) A natural propensity to seek and experience joy (*ananda-aveshana*)

The elements of consciousness (*chaitanya*) and personality (*vyaktitva*) are one and the same. The factual reality of "consciousness" itself designates the individual living entity as a being who possesses awareness. Personality, on the other hand, designates that consciousness in its sui generis state as consciousness expressing itself. Personality is the expression of consciousness. Personality designates the non-geographical locus of an individual *atman* as that individual *atman* manifests the above four primary essential attributes in contradistinction to all other *atmans* and existent objects. Thus, every single *atman* is ineludibly unique and distinct. Every *atman* possesses such a locus of individual personality/consciousness, which forms the center of its being. This is the case both for the finite and dependent *atmans*, and for Paramatman (the Supreme Atman), or God.

What we are meant to transcend is our temporal, artificial persona that has come about as a direct result of ego (*ahamkara*), while fully embracing our true, spiritual personality (*vyaktitva*) that is an eternal and perfect expression of our consciousness.

5.2.1 Equality of Spirit and Hierarchy of Form

Beginning with the so-called "Age of Enlightenment" era in European history (circa 1620 - 1789), the ideological doctrine of radical human egalitarianism has become the most sacrosanct dogma in the realms of both politics and culture. Indeed, it could be said that "equality" has become the true religion of both government and the power-elite in the modern era. The movement for equality has been the foremost social-political concern globally for the past 250 years, inspiring wars, revolutions, Marxist totalitarianism, genocides, and devastating social upheaval. So central has the concept of Radical Egalitarianism been in the modern sociopolitical landscape that it has often overshadowed every other political, philosophical, and social concern we can think of.

Despite three continuous centuries of forcing "Enlightenment" era notions of equality upon humanity, however, the world's problems have only gotten infinitely worse. With more poverty, more corruption, more wars, more unethical behavior, an ever-deeper sense of meaningless in much of the world's youth, and the increasingly rapid coarsening and degeneration of traditional cultures globally, many intellectuals and spiritually oriented people are today beginning to ask the inevitable question: "Has the dogma of radical egalitarianism actually failed humanity?"

The answer to this question, from the perspective of Sanatana Dharma anthropological philosophy is neither a blatantly overt "yes", nor a "no", but rather leads us to the more philosophically sophisticated question of: "What is the nature of the human person?" For it is only in knowing the foundational ontology of man (*manushya*) that we can then understand the true nature and meaning of the otherwise abstract notion of equality. In the following section, I will explain the Dharmic view of equality juxtaposed to the materialist-oriented Radical Egalitarianism that the world has fervently pursued for the last several centuries.

The metaphysical premises of Radical Egalitarianism are based upon an outlook of empiricist materialism that views the human individual as consisting of nothing more than merely the purely physical, the body. For the materialist, human beings do not have a soul, or an intrinsic essence, that transcends the material body. The body is itself composed of nothing more than the combination of chemicals and material substances formed over several millennia via the process of evolution. The human individual, for the Radical Egalitarian, is a soulless and ultimately purposeless machine, an automaton whose only meaning lays in whatever material and economic contributions the individual can make to the greater social whole – of which the Radical Egalitarian, of course, comprises the ruling elite. Thus, one "living body" is just as good - or just as devoid of meaningful existence - as any other "living body".

Such a mechanistic view of the human individual has led not only to the notion of radical equality, but also to the consequent view that all human individuals are ultimately equally worthless. Thus we have seen the birth of the "end justifies the means" form of relativist "ethics" that has arisen amongst the atheistic Marxists, and the consequent death and genocide that has resulted from every Communist regime the world has ever known. If all human bodies are of equal worth, after all, then by logical extension no one individual is of any more importance than any other individual. Human persons are deprived by Radical Egalitarianism of all inherent worth, value and dignity. Thus all equal persons are equally expendable.

A society that sees humans as soulless is a society that sees human beings as being of no more worth than machines. And machines are simply tools, objects, to be used for the benefit of the state, or for the amorphous abstraction of "The People". For the Radical Egalitarian, the human being is no more than a means to an end, an object for their own use, rather than a subject worthy of all the dignity, appreciation, and respect that a unique human person deserves.

The Dharmic view of equality and the human person is considerably more sophisticated, compassionate, and thus ethical, than the materialist egalitarian approach. For the conscious and sincere follower of Sanatana Dharma, the human person consists of infinitely more than the mere bodily surface appearance. The old adage that one cannot judge a book by its cover comes to mind when we examine the wisdom of the Dharmic approach to understanding the philosophical anthropology of the human person.

Rather than simplistically attempting to reduce a human person to being merely the visible material body that one can immediately detect with the senses, Dharma teaches us that the typical human being is actually a multi-faceted and multi-dimensional being, with 1) a material dimension, 2) a causal (psychic/intellectual) dimension, and ultimately 3) a spiritual dimension that is not always clearly visible to the untrained eye. The human person consists of a) *deha* (physical body), b) *abhitapa* (emotions) c) *manas* (mind substance, including impressionistic data, memory, inner sense, etc.), d) *buddhi* (the rational faculties), e) *ahamkara* (false individuating ego), and most importantly f) *atman* (the true spiritual self).

According to the Dharma world-view, we certainly are beings who possess bodies – no sane person would deny this immediate and concrete empirical fact. Indeed, contrary to the unnatural and illogical conclusions that the Radical Egalitarian draws from this simple fact, from a purely physical perspective, there is actually an almost infinitely variegated degree of diversity and inequality that is clearly empirically seen. Physically speaking, no two people in the world are ever really the same. We are all different. Some people are tall, others short. One person is strong, another weak. Some need glasses, hearing aids, or other devices to "even out the playing field" (i.e., pretend that we are all physically equal!), other people are free from physical defects altogether. The tremendous diversity that we find in physical bodies alone is endless. That is common sense.

By extension, when looking at the minds and the intellectual capacities of various individuals, we clearly see that some are more intelligent than others. Some are more naturally artistic and creative, whereas some are more analytical and cerebral. Some people will have mental or emotional challenges, such as psychosis, bipolar disorder, mental retardation, or psychopathology, while others have minds so healthy as to allow them to view reality with tremendous clarity. Some have a very firm grip of objective reality, and are able to function in the world in a healthy and happy way. Others seem to live in an unhealthy inner world of purely subjective existence, convinced that their own narcissistic perception of reality should equally apply to all beings.

Egoic desires, preferences and goals, too, are as diverse in content and quantity as are the numerous people we see around us. Some desire wealth, or fame, or romantic love. Others aspire to become great world leaders. Some people, by contrast, seem to have a profound yearning to know God, and serve their fellow beings with humility, simplicity, deep compassion, and quiet determination. We are all radically different from one another. No one human being is the same as any other human being. Thus, we are all in so many ways unequal in our appearance, our abilities, our preferences, our subjective inner worlds, and our desires.

Rather than attempting to lie to ourselves and artificially fly in the face of such clearly discernable empirical facts, Sanatana Dharma encourages all human beings to acknowledge and honor our differences, respect each other, and work together in compassion, dignity and harmony, despite our undeniable recognition of all our many differences. Sanatana Dharma (the Eternal Natural Way) gives us the empowerment to live in accordance with the natural order of the universe in a manner that is beneficial to all living beings regardless of our differences. Dharmis are thus equipped to see the underlying spiritual unity within the matrix of material diversity. While the average materialist wishes to "celebrate diversity" by artificially ignoring blatant differences between people, the Dharmi wishes to honor natural diversity in a truly meaningful manner by acknowledging and harmonizing those very same differences.

For Dharma, the realm of true equality lies not on the physical, emotional, mental, intellectual, or egoic planes, but only in the realm of spirit. Having God as our sole source, sustainer, and ultimate destiny, we all share in the same parent. From a spiritual perspective, then, in the deepest essence of who we are as pure spiritual beings (*atman*), we are all the children of God.

Your true, spiritual self (*atman*) does not have color, nor dimension, nor race, nor class, nor gender, nor age designation. In spirit, you are neither a capitalist, nor a communist. You are neither Indian, nor Black, nor White, nor Arab. Rather, your true self is the eternal, perfect, blissful spiritual center of your everyday existence. Your true self is *atman*. You are *atman*.

Transcending both the bodily dimensions of life and all limited materiality, your true self finds itself currently situated in your present body due only to your own free-will desires, motivations, consciousness, and actions of the past. *Karma* is the causal antecedent of all the diverse material bodies that we see around us. While our bodies and minds are all radically different, however, the souls of every living being are all equally held in the compassionate purview of God's merciful and loving glance. To God, we are all equally His children, temporarily separated from Him due to our own misguided surrender to illusion, all occupying unequal and diverse material bodies in accordance with our own will and actions, but all destined to one day again be in His loving embrace.

Equality in the higher spiritual sense is an exceedingly important goal toward which we should all aspire. In the political realm, Dharma calls upon each of us to always be compassionate, just, and fair to all we encounter, no matter how different they may seem to us in physical appearance. The only truly pure equality that exists, however, is that equality that exists on the spiritual realm. Thus, in the transcendental eyes of the *yogi*, or pure sage, all living beings are seen with equal vision (*sama darshina*).

This concept of spiritually inspired equal vision is beautifully explained to us by Lord Sri Krishna in His famous *Bhagavad Gita* (Song of God). In the 18th verse of chapter 5, Lord Krishna instructs His devotee Arjuna in the following way:

> *Vidya-vinaya-sampanne brahmane gavi hastini*
> *Shuni chaiva shvapake cha panditah sama-darshinah*

"The humble sage, by virtue of true knowledge, sees with equal vision [*sama-darshina*] the learned and gentle priest, a cow, an elephant, a dog or an outcaste."

Indeed, it is precisely because the humble sage views the diverse beings around him, not as mere mechanistic bodies, but as each possessing a pure spirit soul (*atman*), that he does not even see the material difference between various species of life, what to speak of different kinds of human beings! To the sage, the soul of the cow, the soul of the dog, and the soul of the elephant is just as worthy of dignity, respect, and spiritual equality as is the soul contained in the human being. *Sama Darshina*, or equal spiritual vision, is the highest form of equality toward which we can all aspire – for it sees the inherent equality that exists in the spiritual essence of all living beings. It is, in fact, the only realistic form of equality that we can ever hope for. Seeing all beings as our spiritual brothers and sisters, we will then, by natural extension, offer all people our respect on the political, social, cultural, and economic realms.

The truly just society, then, is the Dharmic society, a society comprised of citizens who aspire toward the finer and nobler spiritual aspirations of life, and who thus view the world from a spiritual perspective. That nation which will most justly serve the interests of its people is the Dharma Nation, a nation in which the eternal principles of Dharma serve as the foundational governing philosophy of the state. We must make ourselves truly worthy citizens of God's eternal Dharma Nation by spiritualizing our own vision and viewing our neighbors and fellow living beings as the *atmans* they truly are. We must begin the Dharma Revolution in our own lives.

5.2.2 Varna: Understanding Your Psychophysical Nature

One of the most important pursuits for followers of Vedic spirituality is to achieve as thorough a degree of self-understanding as is possible. It is only in fully understanding ourselves, after all, that we can live effectively and happily in the world. While the ultimate goal in such self-understanding is attaining spiritual realization of our true and eternal self, because of the fact that Vedic spirituality is a holistic system that reveals the deepest nature of every aspect of ourselves, we are encouraged to understand ourselves on each and every level of our being – spiritual, psychological, emotional, genetic and physical.

As a part of this well-rounded approach to self-understanding, the ancient *rishis* (seer-sages) revealed an ingeniously insightful system of self-analysis known as *varna*. *Varna* is a scientific means of psychophysical analysis that helps us to better understands the constitutional character of our own individual temperaments. It does this by surveying our personal likes and dislikes, desires, skills, aspirations and attitudes, in accordance with four factors: our karmic history, genetic makeup, environmental formation and personal ability to transform ourselves through our own will power. Examining all of these inherent factors in-depth, we are then understood, as an integrated whole, to fall into one of four general categories of psychophysical type. These four types, or *varnas*, are a) Brahmana, b) Kshatriya, c) Vaishya, and d) Shudra. Below is a very brief description of each of these four *varnas*.

Brahmana: Generally speaking, if a person has the natural and innate tendencies of intellectualism, spirituality, cleanliness, scholarliness, cultural and aesthetic sophistication, and is devoted to the philosophical study of the Vedic scriptures and the practice of Yoga *sadhana*, then he falls into the Brahmana type. Brahmanas are calm, even-tempered and kind in temperament. Fulfilling occupations for Brahmanas include teaching, writing, the priestly profession, counseling and advising, etc.

Kshatriya: If, on the other hand, an individual has the natural and innate tendencies of leadership, politics, martial sciences, as well as managerial and administrative capacities, then he is a Kshatriya. Kshatriyas tend to exhibit the behavior of gravitas coupled with energetic exuberance. For Kshatriyas, such professions as the military, politics and administration are the most fulfilling.

Vaishya: That person who has the natural and innate tendencies of production, entrepreneurship, agriculture, bartering, and innovative creativity is considered to have the qualities of a Vaishya. Vaishyas are very passionate and high-energy people. Vaishyas enjoy such professions as business, agriculture, trading and selling.

Shudra: Finally, that individual who takes natural and innate pleasure in working creatively with his hands in such professions as woodworking, construction, masonry, lifting and carrying, and medical surgery, and who has such qualities as loyalty, earnestness, faith and service, is a Shudra. Shudras differ from the other three *varnas* in that the other three *varnas* all involve the use of discursive cognition in their respective professions, but the Shudra *varna* does not. Rather, Shudras primarily employ subdiscursive thought, that is, thought that is dictated by emotional and sensory input, rather than by intellectual analysis. Shudras are happiest in those professions in which physical labor and skill is emphasized.

When we understand which of these four *varnas* is most reflective of our own internal nature, we then have the guided ability to access our fullest inner potential in very practical ways, including choosing a course of education, a profession, and even a husband or wife that will make us most happy as a unique and dignified individual person. It also has to be noted that, while most people tend to fall into one *varna* type or another, there are some individuals who will sometimes fall into two *varnas* simultaneously. Also, it is possible to have one's *varna* change from one to another in the course of one's lifetime. Thus, a person may start off as a Kshatriya, for example, and eventually become more of a Brahmana. Or a person who was a Brahmana originally may eventually become a Shudra later in life. More, while *varna* types might sometimes be intergenerational, the *varna(s)* of one's parents do not play the decisive role in a child's *varna*. The parents might both be Shudras, for example, while one or more of their children might end up being Brahmanas. *Varna* designation is a fluid as is the power of human will. For this reason, we can only understand a person's *varna* on a case-by-case basis. *Varna*, then, is more of a scientifically accurate indicator of one's natural tendencies than a series of rigid boxes that individuals are expected to inhabit. *Varna* is a tool of self-discovery which, if properly understood and applied, can help each of us to better understand ourselves, and which can help the social body of any given nation function in a more scientific and just way.

Please refer to the companion book, *The Sanatana Dharma Study Guide*, for practical exercises that will help you determine your *varna*.

5.2.3 The Three Personality Types

As has now been established, human beings are all different from one another in a vast myriad of ways, too numerous to count. In addition, these many ways in which humans are different in any given category can be calculated as being either superlative or lacking, either better or worse in qualitative and/or quantitative value. No two human beings are the same. More, no two human beings are equal in the inherent sense of individual personhood. While spiritually all sentient beings, including human beings, are qualitatively equal in substantial form (i.e., in their pure ontological makeup), in the realm of name and form that consists of the material world, the modern dogma of equality simply does not pertain. Thus, all human beings – as is true for all beings in existence, both human and non-human, both sentient and insentient – can be placed in specific categorical levels within the hierarchical chain of being.

All instances of human nature fall into one of three distinct categories that form a vertical, hierarchical spectrum. These three human natures are a) divine (*daivika*), b) innocent, commonplace humans (*laukika*, or *samanya*), and c) demonic (*asurika*). This vertical hierarchy looks like this:

Divine

Innocent / Commonplace

Demonic

On one far side of this hierarchical spectrum, we have those individuals who are of divine nature. These consist of approximately 4% of any given human population. Those persons who are of divine nature are inherently good, compassionate, spiritual, wise, pure, cultured, etc. On the opposite far side of the hierarchical spectrum, we have those human persons who are of inherently demonic nature. These demonic persons are also roughly 4% of the human population. Demonic individuals are what the modern field of psychiatry has termed psychopaths, or sociopaths. Demonic people revel in the pain of others. They have zero empathy, compassion or healthy love for others. They take pride in their ability to conceal their true motivations from those around them. They are thus experts in manipulation, scheming, power politics, and cheating others. Demonic persons often become politicians, bankers and other leaders of high finance, journalists, and religious bureaucrats in large religious denominations.

The interrelationship between the *daivika* (divine) and the *asurika* (demonic) individuals is an especially asymmetrical one. This is the case because, due to their trusting nature, *daivika* persons often find themselves incapable of understanding the full extent of evil that the *asurika* persons are capable of. Good persons often automatically assume that everyone else in the world is, likewise, goodhearted like them. The *asurika* persons, on the other hand, have no illusions about the existence of people with evil motivations, since they themselves are such persons! The end result, unfortunately, is that the good are all too often open victims of the evil due to their inherent naiveté.

Those persons who are relatively innocent in nature form the largest group by far, and fall in the middle of the spectrum in between the divine and the demonic groupings. Innocent/commonplace individuals consist of roughly 92% of any given population. Being a relatively malleable group of people, there exists also a broad spectrum of diverse natures to be found among this large group of innocent, common folk, with some segments leaning more toward the divine nature, and others leaning more toward the demonic. Both the divine and the demonic persons attempt to influence the common person, the divine toward the good, and the demonic toward evil. It goes without saying that Sanatana Dharma encourages people to embrace the divine (*daivika*) nature as much as possible, since this is the human nature that is most reflective of the spiritual and of God.

5.3.1 Karma and Reincarnation

Since the popularization of the term "*karma*" in the Western world from the 1960s to the present day, this important metaphysical and ethical concept has, unfortunately, been understood in only the most simplistic and cursory of manners by the majority of Europeans and Americans – including by many scholars, by most self-professed spiritual teachers, as well as by many common spiritual practitioners. Many followers of New Age and pop spirituality have an even more speculative understanding of *karma*, believing that the concept of *karma* is somehow tied to the idea of fate or predetermination. As we will see, the concept of *karma* in no way represents either a "fatalistic" or a "pre-deterministic" view of the cosmos. Rather, it is a logical and ethically rooted science of activity, a metaphysics of action. *Karma* is, in actuality, a principle of radical personal freedom. Given the many misconceptions that abound in the modern mind concerning the nature of *karma*, we will analyze the metaphysical grounding of the principle of *karma*, and the operation of the principles of *karma* and reincarnation upon the illusion-bound *atman* in accordance with the teachings of Sanatana Dharma, or The Eternal Natural Way.

Two of the most important principles of Dharma, as well as two crucial keys to understanding the nature of the soul's sojourn in the material world, are the dual realities of *karma* and reincarnation. Both of these concepts are so mutually dependent upon one another that it is impossible to fully understand one of these concepts without also fully understanding the other. More accurately, *karma* is the direct cause of reincarnation. Reincarnation is dependent upon the antecedent impetus of *karma* for its operation. Despite the fact that much has been written and stated about these dual principles in recent decades, there remain a great deal of misconceptions about how these two principles operate on the part of most spiritual practitioners.

The word "*karma*" is derived from the Sanskrit verb root "*kṛ*", meaning "to do, act, work, perform", etc. We find that the world around us is a world of constant and varied activities. Can we imagine the world without any motion taking place? The wind moves; the Sun rotates in its orbit; around us there is constant growth and movement. Nothing in our world is static. In this most general of senses, then, any action that we engage in is really "*karma*" - from reading this book, to strumming a guitar, to the involuntary beating of our heart, to helping our fellow man.

Of all these different kinds of motion, however, we can clearly distinguish between two different kinds of movement. The first is motion without a person's will being involved. These are actions that just take place of their own accord. For example, right now as you're reading this sentence, your heart is beating, your lungs are expanding and contracting, and your pulse is active. Are you consciously making these activities happen? Of course not. They take place by themselves, of their own accord. So, the first type of actions consists of those actions that take place without the direct involvement of overt consciousness. But it is the second kind of activity that we are most interested in: action in which our conscious will is involved. These are activities in which we make the choice to engage in some sort of activity. In Dharma, it is recognized that there are three ways in which we can engage in action with will: a) in thoughts, b) in words, c) and in deeds.

It is in this second kind of action, action in which our will is involved, that we consciously choose to do something. For example, when we choose to snap our finger, or whistle a tune, we are now choosing to perform a certain action. We are now acting with awareness. Many of these types of actions are free of ethical content. Actions that are performed with awareness, too, can be separated into two distinct categories. There are a) conscious actions that do not contain ethical content of any sort. In other words, actions in which we are not choosing to either harm or benefit another living being. For example, if we choose to simply wave our hand in the air, we are neither choosing to hurt someone, nor to perform a positive act toward someone. Then there are b) actions that do contain ethical content, actions in which we have chosen via our will to either harm or benefit another living entity. For example, if in waving our hand in the air, we are aware that we are giving a signal to an assassin to then shoot someone, we are then morally culpable in the killing of another person. It is when we choose of our own free will to direct our action toward someone with the intent of either maliciousness or beneficence that the Dharmic principle of *karma* becomes operative.

The latter type of activity, action with ethical awareness, in turn, denotes two different concepts: a) Action Per Se: every activity that either occurs or that we consciously perform, as well as b) Resultant Reaction: the natural consequence of each of our individual actions that are performed with ethical content involved (the common notion of *karma*). When we perform conscious actions in which we are specifically choosing to either harm or benefit a living being, we are now performing actions that have ethical-content. These are precisely the type of actions that bear within them the seed of future karmic consequences.

When the meaning that we infuse into our actions is designed either to harm or to help someone, then we are engaging in an action that has ethical content, or specifically ethical meaning. And every time that a human being consciously performs any action that involves either the harm or benefit of either oneself or others, he then sets into motion the retributive law of *karma*. This is the meaning of the term "*karma*" as used in the sense of *karma* as a metaphysically defined retributive principle. This law requires that our ethical-content-actions must be returned to us in kind, and in equal proportion.

Where the concept of *karma* goes from mere activity to being a metaphysical principle is precisely at the moment that our actions have specifically ethical content to them. In other words, when an action is then motivated by either a desire to harm or to benefit another living being. When we choose of our own free will to either harm or benefit another, at that moment we are in the process of making an ethical or moral decision. It is at this point that the impersonal and perfect law of nature known as *karma*, in the more common sense of this word, comes into play.

Every action with ethical-content that we perform - specifically of either ethically good or bad content - necessitates an equal and opposite reaction. There is no ethically willed activity that we are capable of performing, either verbally, mentally or physically, that is devoid of meaning. Every ethically willed act has meaning. Seen from the converse perspective of effect, as opposed to cause, this principle is known among Western philosophers as the Law of Sufficient Reason: that is, the principle that there is no event, no effect, in existence that is without a cause of one form or another, even if the immediate cause is not perceivable to us.

As we engage in either ethical or unethical actions, we are doing two things: 1) we bring into motion the natural law that states that for every action there must be an equal and opposite reaction; thus necessitating a future result as a consequence for our present actions. If we perform positive ethical actions, then we will in the future experience meritoriously positive states of equal proportion. If we perform negative, unethical deeds, then we have secured for ourselves future experiences that will be equally negative. 2) By choosing to perform actions that are either ethically positive or negative, we are choosing at the exact moment of such activities to create our own future states of being. We are choosing to mold our psychophysical state, our mode of consciousness, our future course of action. The principle of *karma* teaches us that we have the power through our own present free-will decisions to literally create who and what we will be in the future. Thus, rather than being a doctrine that teaches the importance of "fate", "predestination", or a type of unalterable "destiny", the principle of *karma* actually teaches us the opposite: That we are radically free beings, with the ability at every given moment to choose to mold ourselves and our individual futures. *Karma* is thus a doctrine of radical freedom.

Karma is ultimately a theory of inherent cosmic balance. Both the physical laws of nature, and the underlying metaphysical laws known as Dharma that form the more subtle basis of even physicality, each seek the return to balance in all states. This is the case, as well, when it comes to the more metaphysical concept of justice, and the attendant *karma* that serves as the enforcing mechanism of justice. It is no mistake that the symbol of justice in Western civilization to this very day is a blindfolded woman holding the scales of balance in her outstretched hand. Justice is balance. For every negative act, there must be a corresponding corrective and punitive measure. For every positive act, likewise, there needs to be a corresponding benevolent motion of reward. This is the nature of justice, and of the most powerful ensurer of justice, which is the Dharmic law of *karma*.

Karmic effects (*karma-phala*, or the "fruits of *karma*") can become manifest either in the same lifetime as the actor (*karmi*), or such effects might take many lifetimes to eventually manifest. Understanding this karmic mechanism, we can see how *karma* serves as the very engine for reincarnation, and how reincarnation can only become operative and properly understood through the workings of *karma*. If you are meant to either suffer the consequences or enjoy the rewards of your present activities in 1,000 years, then that necessitates future births. In this sense, then, both good *karma* and bad *karma* have always been equally considered something to avoid, since both force us to have future lives bound to material illusion. The ultimate goal for the spiritual practitioner on the Vedic path is to transcend all material activities, and thus all *karma*, altogether.

The only way to understand the mechanics and the meaning of reincarnation is to understand the fundamentally distinct natures of body (*deha*) and spirit (*atman*). The body is inherently temporary, imperfect, bound by space and time. The soul, on the other hand, is eternal, perfect in its essence, and transcends both space and time. We are soul. We are *atman*, and our relationship to our bodies has been compared to the relationship between the person and his clothes. While we will temporarily wear a coat, for example, and while others may even be able to identify us because we are wearing our particular coat, we are certainly not the coat with which others identify us. Being different from us, when our coat eventually becomes old are worn out, we throw away our old coat and put on a new one, yet we are not affected by this change. In the *Bhagavad Gita*, reincarnation is described as being a very similar process: "As a person puts on new garments, giving up the old ones, similarly, the soul accepts new material bodies, giving up the old and useless ones" (2:22). Our bodies are temporary and multiple, but our soul is eternal, singular, and constitutes perfect self-identity.

The law of *karma* teaches us that the world is a purposive moral order, where the individual obtains what he desires as a direct manifestation of his own will. Any lesser cosmic retributive mechanism would be unjust. And any seeming injustice in the metaphysical constitution of God's creation would reflect negatively upon the Divine, thus requiring precisely the many unsatisfactory forms of speculation (known as theodicies) used to attempt to explain the existence of suffering that are found throughout the 2800 year history of Euro-American philosophy of religion.

As long as we have not fulfilled our karmic debt by experiencing the reactions to our activities, we are required to remain here, in the realm of material non-self, undergoing the repeated experience of birth, death and rebirth. We remain within the realm of the laws of *karma* until we do experience these reactions. It is as a direct result of our karmic activity that we find ourselves entangled in the non-spiritual realm. We, as eternal soul (*atman*), then find ourselves undergoing repeated transmigration through a string of material bodies - human, animal, insect, plant, demigod (*deva*) and/or demon (*asura*) - until we learn to finally transcend the entire *karma*-producing process altogether, freeing ourselves from the illusion of separation from God, and resituating ourselves in the transcendental, divine abode of God known as Vaikuntha, or "the Realm of No Anxiety".

The goal of life, according to Sanatana Dharma, is to put an eventual end to the perpetual cycle (*samsara*) of births and deaths that form the process of reincarnation, along with the accompanying suffering that we experience as a result of our egoic attachment to the results of our activities, and to eventually transcend this cycle altogether through spiritual liberation (*moksha*).

In the ecstatic state of radical existential freedom known as *moksha*, we are no longer in illusion; therefore we do not act out of false ego; therefore we no longer produce *karma*; therefore we no longer need to reincarnate in a series of material forms designed as vehicles through which we can meet our ultimate spiritual purpose. At liberation, all material name and form (*nama* and *rupa*, respectively) has served its purpose, and can be left behind as we joyfully commence our final journey toward our blissful and eternal spiritual Source.

5.3.2 Karma and Fatalism

Though *karma* does condition and circumscribe the nature of both our present and future experiences, this doctrine is not to be confused with "fatalism," or with the mistaken idea that there is no free will. For, while it is true that we may need to experience some good or bad activity in our future as a result of our present actions, it is imperative that we remember that this future *karma* is the direct consequence of our previous free-will decisions. *Karma* is merely the present effect of which we ourselves were the willing past causes. It is we who freely chose to engage in the very actions that would then necessitate a karmic reaction, and thus color our consciousness either negatively or positively. We freely choose to do an activity which then limits our future freedom within the bounds that we ourselves chose to create for ourselves through our actions.

To give an example: I may choose to commit suicide by jumping off a cliff. That decision was one of my own making. It was a decision that I made freely. Once I have then translated this decision into action by physically leaping off the cliff, then my path is chosen and unalterable. I cannot suddenly say I have changed my mind halfway down and have my descent now miraculously stop! Now that I have committed myself to this action, it must be seen out to its completion. In the same way, once I make the free will, conscious choice to act either benevolently or malevolently toward someone else, then I must face the karmic consequences of my own free-will actions. Thus, I have chosen of my own free will to create a specific future for myself.

The law of *karma* is one of the subtle, yet powerful, intrinsic laws of nature known in Sanskrit as Dharma. This principle of *karma* is "...the law of moral justice and as such it must exist because, otherwise, our intuitive distinction between the ethical and the unethical would be falsified; humankind would be left no incentive to be just and no disincentive to avoid injustice" (Patel, 1991). *Karma* is God's means of ensuring a perfect distribution of just rewards on a universal, temporally operative and equitable scale. Consequently, it is a concept that is inherently and necessarily ethical by its very nature. The goal of Sanatana Dharma and of Yoga, then, is to live one's life in such a way that we not only no longer produce *karma*, but that we use the force of our own conscious activity as a means of transcending *karma*.

This is done, however, not through the renunciation of all actions, but by

160

actually engaging in actions in such a way that we remain unattached to the results. The *Bhagavad Gita* supports this with the following words. "Not by merely abstaining from work can one achieve freedom from reaction, nor by renunciation alone can one attain perfection." (*Bhagavad Gita*, 3:4) As Lord Sri Krishna further explains, it is not mere the actions in themselves that produce *karma*, but it is the especially deeply laid intent behind our actions that are responsible for creating *karma*. Speaking of the outlook of the *yogi*, He says:

> *tyaktva karma-phalasangam nitya-trpto nirashrayah*
> *karmany abhipravrtto'pi naiva kinchit karoti sah*

"Abandoning all attachment to the results of his activities, ever satisfied and independent, he performs no fruitive action, although he is engaged in all kinds of undertakings." (*Bhagavad Gita*, 4:20)

In other words, it is not actions in and of themselves that produce either meritorious or negative reactions. Rather, it is the state of the moral agent's consciousness at the time that the action is performed which determines the nature of that action and the subsequent reaction that will result. Intentionality is the factor that determines the ethical content of any action.

If we can perform our duties in such a state of mind that our mistaken notions of self-interest are not the motivating factor, then we are freed from the results of *karma*. Consequently, the *yogi* tries to avoid two extremes in life. He avoids both the exploitation of God's creation, as well as any attempt at an artificial renunciation of activities. It is the mistaken idea that everything around us exists just for our own enjoyment that binds us to illusion. Such an idea is an outgrowth of an unhealthy state of egoism. On the other hand, though, sometimes in our frustration with the suffering and anxiety we feel in this world, there is the immature temptation to then artificially renounce the things of this world, to try to live like a hermit, or a recluse. This is also an unhealthy attitude to have, since it arises more from a sense of fear than a yearning for spiritual harmony and balance. An attitude of exploitation leads to hedonism. While the path of renunciation leads to fanaticism.

Instead of practicing either of these extreme paths of exploitation or renunciation, we should practice dedication of all our actions to the service of God. This is the path of *bhakti*, or devotional consciousness. As a direct result of this process of conscious dedication "...the consciousness of the individual is changed from material to spiritual, leaving all other factors the same. The activities are performed by the individual as before, but under a spiritual awareness" (Chaturvedi, 1991). By offering his activities to the Transcendent, the *yogi* thereby makes those very actions, themselves, transcendental and therefore free of all binding *karma*.

Such an individual must practice a mental discipline of radical equanimity towards all actions that he both produces and undergoes. He must see, with equal vision (*sama-darshina*), all the dualities of pleasure and pain, happiness and distress, and prosperity and misfortune that he experiences. For the *yogi*, it is understood that such dualistic states are ever changing. Additionally, such dualities come and go of their own accord, like the passing of winter into summer and summer into winter. The *Bhagavad Gita* expresses this truth beautifully in the following way.

> *matra-sparshas tu kaunteya sitoshna-sukha-duhkha-dah*
> *agamapayino 'nityas tams titikshasva bharata*

"O son of Kunti, the nonpermanent appearance of happiness and distress, and their disappearance in due course, are like the appearance and disappearance of winter and summer seasons. They arise from sense perception, O scion of Bharata, and one must learn to tolerate them without being disturbed." (*Bhagavad Gita*, 2:14)

We ultimately have little say in the coming or going of material pleasure and pain. As such is the case, why allow ourselves to be so easily affected by them - either by being pleased or by being disturbed?

It is by practicing such a healthy sense of equipoised detachment, coupled with the cultivation of our inherent state of devotional consciousness (*bhakti*) toward Sri Krishna, that we have the ability to truly exercise our freedom for our highest good. That highest good in life is to dedicate ourselves to the eternal truth, love, wisdom and beauty that is the Divine.

5.3.3 Refuting the Theory of Collective Karma

There is no such thing as collective *karma* in the directly causative sense anywhere in the Vedic world-view or scriptures, but only in the coincidental retributive sense. In other words, there is no such concept as "shared *karma*". Rather, it is possible for an incidental grouping of individuals to experience their individually accrued *karmas* at the same place and time.

By both definition and logical necessity, *karma* is, and can only be, operative on an individual basis, and upon each particular *jiva* (an *atman* who is presently in illusion), in accordance with his free-will works containing ethical content. Thus, each individual is solely responsible for his own actions, and the resultant effects of that action.

However, what does periodically occur is the manifestation of several individual *karmas* occurring simultaneously among several individuals comprising a group of people in such a manner as to make it appear to our vision that several people are experiencing the resultant effects of their individual *karmas* at the same particular place and time. Even if you have a number of individuals all experiencing their own *karma* at the same time and place, the individuals' respective *karmas* would be the result of their own individual actions in previous lives, and not the result of some action they all performed collectively.

Experiencing *karmas* in unison is more an instance of indirect and unrelated correlation of karmic events, and not ever because any group of individuals somehow "shared" *karma*. The idea of "collective *karma*" would directly negate the meaning of free will on the part of the person performing materially motivated action, and consequently producing *karma*, thus rendering the entire Vedic world-view null and void both metaphysically and logically. For this reason, there is no such thing as "shared *karma*".

5.3.4 Is There "Evidence" for Reincarnation and Karma?

The question has often been asked about what evidence there is for the process of reincarnation. To answer this question properly, it depends on what someone means by the term "evidence". Since reincarnation is a metaphysical reality (meta = "beyond"; physical = "material"), and not a material one, it doesn't stand to reason that there can really be scientific empirical "evidence" per se. A non-material, metaphysical reality, or even an intellectually necessary concept, simply cannot be grasped by merely material physical means.

That does not mean, though, that reincarnation cannot be proven. After all, we can know that many other non-material things exist that cannot be proven scientifically or empirically. For example, we all know that we have minds…yet no one can really see a mind. We cannot examine a mind in a microscope, nor can we put a mind in a test-tube. If I were to ask you for "evidence" that you have a mind, you would be very hard-pressed to provide any empirical proof whatsoever.

This is not to say, of course, that a mind's existence cannot be proven. The proof for your mind's existence is that we can infer that you have a mind because you act intelligently: you display the attributes, qualities, and actions of one who has a mind. Therefore, you must have a mind. More, it cannot be "proven" empirically that, if you do indeed possess a mind, that this mind that you possess is a different mind than is possessed by every other being who has a mind. How can we prove that our minds are not all one, and that we instead are all possessed of individual minds? Again, while such a fact can never be proven empirically (we cannot see other people's minds any more than we can see our own!), it can be proven inferentially. In a similar way, reincarnation cannot be proven through scientific experimentation…but it can be proven through inference and logic.

One of the most powerful inferential arguments for upholding the fact of reincarnation is that, without the existence of reincarnation and *karma* (reincarnation and *karma* are inseparable in the philosophical system of Sanatana Dharma; you cannot have one without the other), the existence of human suffering has no satisfactory explanation and no coherent meaning. Logically speaking, we can only explain the meaning of suffering that we observe in the world by inferring the fact of reincarnation and *karma*.

The Western philosopher John Locke (1632-1704) famously proclaimed that all human beings are born as *tabula rasa* (Latin), as blank slates to be written upon only later in life. Clear and common empirical evidence, however, has shown us that Locke was exceedingly wrong in his naïve assessment of inherent human equivalence. In actuality, we are all born with different degrees of talent, intelligence, beauty, aptitudes, desires, temperaments, likes and dislikes, and aspirations. If each of us merely springs into existence at the moment of conception, and did not have a pre-existence before the creation of the present physical form (as is taught by the Abrahamic religions), then how do we explain the fact that people are born so radically different at birth? Very specifically, how do we explain the suffering the some undergo at from the very moment of birth? Some people are born with terrible birth defects (blindness, lacking a limb, developmental disabilities, etc.), while others are born with perfect health. How can a merciful and loving God allow some babies to be born fine and healthy, and others to be born in a terrible state of pain and suffering? The only explanation for suffering that does not make God seem either unjust or impotent or insentient is the concept of reincarnation and *karma*.

Reincarnation teaches us that our present physical birth is not the beginning of our existence, but that we exist eternally. Having God as our source and sustainer, we are eternal beings who have always existed, just as God is an eternal being who has always existed. The birth of each new material body that our eternal spirits inhabit is merely the latest manifestation of our *karma*, which is created by our desire, our free will, and the quality of our consciousness. Some are born in happiness, while others are born in suffering, due to the fulfillment of our own self-created *karma*, and our need to experience the lessons of that specific life.

We see that people are all born with very different capacities, talents, attributes, and personalities. As much as we want to pretend that all human beings are born as completely equal *tabula rasas*, or blank slates, the truth is that none of us are born with equal intrinsic faculties. Some people are born with an inherent talent to be more creative and artistic than others. Some are born more cerebral and intelligent than others. Some are born 7 feet tall and can become famous basketball players, while some are 5 feet tall, and cannot. One person will have perfect eyesight his entire life, while another will need glasses by the age of five. Our very genetic inheritance itself is a manifestation of our personal *karma*. Again, the only logical explanation for why a just and merciful God would allow people to be born with such diverse and unequal qualities is reincarnation and *karma*.

The Abrahamic religions (Judaism, Christianity and Islam) especially find it difficult to explain the reason for suffering and evil.[21] Throughout the two-thousand year history of Christian philosophy, for example, Christian philosophers and theologians have attempted to create innumerable explanations for the existence of suffering - so many, in fact, that these attempts at explanation became a whole category of philosophical argument called "theodicies". None of these attempts, however, have ever

---

[21] Marxism finds it altogether impossible to explain the presence of suffering and evil in the world.

been proven philosophically sustainable, demonstrable or satisfactory. The reason why is precisely because it is impossible to explain the existence of suffering without turning to the concepts of *karma* and reincarna- reincarnation.

Without the soul being an eternal reality that existed before the creation of the material body, there is no explanation whatsoever that can be offered for why a good, merciful, all-knowing and all-powerful God would allow some of His children to be born less than whole. Only the Dharmic path can give an intellectually satisfactory and spiritually comforting explanation for this reality of human suffering.

The concept of reincarnation and *karma* teaches us that with every thought, action and word containing ethical-content that we engage in, we are creating who we are – and who we will be in the future. When we perform actions that are of an ethically positive and good nature, we are directly affecting our own consciousness in such a way as to purify and ennoble who we are. Conversely, when we perform actions that arise from selfishness, egotism, and negativity, we are ensuring that our future only holds darkness and sorrow.

So, the concept of reincarnation and *karma*, ultimately, is a positive and hopeful concept of radical freedom, in which each and every one of us has the ability, moment to moment, to freely create both our destinies and ourselves. With every decision we make today, we are creating our own futures, our own destinies, and our own future lives. Such is the grace and love of God that He gives us the complete freedom either to choose to know Him, or to flee from His face. The choice is ours.

5.4.1 Discerning Spirit from Matter

One of the primary steps on the spiritual path is the attainment of self-realization, beginning with discerning the nature of true self from that which is not self, discerning spirit from matter. The first Yoga that the *Bhagavad Gita* discusses is Jnana-yoga, or the path of just such discernment. This path consists of acquiring the salvific knowledge that will assist us in attaining liberation from the material anxieties, fears and blockages that we so frequently encounter in our day-to-day lives. The term, *jnana* (knowledge), does not refer to a mere academic endeavor, nor to a dry theoretical grasp of truth, but to that living - and life-giving! - spiritual wisdom that will best provide us with a direct understanding of the nature of our true self.

> *raja-vidya raja-guhyam pavitram idam uttamam*
> *pratyaksavagamam dharmyam susukham kartum avyayam*

"This knowledge is the king of sciences," says Sri Krishna in the *Bhagavad Gita*, "the most secret of all secrets. It is the purest knowledge, and because it gives perception of the self by realization, it is the perfection of religion. It is everlasting and it is joyfully performed" (*Bhagavad Gita*, 9:2). Krishna praises the importance and efficacy of this unique form of knowledge throughout the entirety of the *Gita*. In the fourth chapter, for example, He compares the ability of spiritual insight to help us to the power of a blazing fire (4:37). Later, in chapter five, He compares it to the sun lighting up the world with its brilliant effulgence (5:16). Glorifying this divine knowledge again, Krishna says:

> *na hi jnanena sadrsam pavitram iha vidyate*
> *tat svayam yoga-samsiddhah kalenatmani vindati*

"In this world, there is nothing so sublime and pure as transcendental knowledge. Such knowledge is the mature fruit of all Yoga..." (4:38).

Without having a direct experience of this life-freeing knowledge, a knowledge of how to achieve complete liberation from suffering, it is very difficult to make any real and meaningful progress on the spiritual path.

The path of Jnana-yoga consists primarily of having a direct intuitive insight into the dual ontological natures of the 1) true self (*atman*) and 2) that which is not the self (*anatman*), as well as the difference between these two elements. This important distinction between self and non-self is especially seen in the second chapter of the *Bhagavad Gita*. There, Krishna explains the saving knowledge of the differentiation between the self (what He here calls "the existent") and the body, or matter ("the nonexistent"). Krishna says:

> *nasato vidyate bhavo nabhavo vidyate satah*
> *ubhayor api drsto'ntas tv anayos tattva-darshibhih*

"Those who are seers of the truth (*tattva-darshibhih*) have concluded that of the nonexistent there is no endurance, and of the existent there is no cessation. This seers have concluded by studying the nature of both" (2:16)

One of the goals of the system of *jnana* is, therefore, acquiring valid and practical knowledge of the nature of the self in relation to our everyday empirical reality, which is comprised of both the material body we inhabit, in addition to our external environment.

We all know that we have a body. When we look in the mirror every morning to brush our teeth, or when we step on the scale to see what damage last night's meal caused our waistline, we are made immediately aware of that fact! As the above verse explains, though, the body of the individual is temporal and ever changing in its makeup. It is not something that is eternally existent by nature. This fact can be explained in the following way.

Since the body is composed entirely of matter, it necessarily shares in all of the qualities of matter. Everything that is empirically perceivable - that is, everything that we can see, hear, touch, taste, smell or trip over - is composed of material substance (*prakriti*). Matter is by nature something that is temporary. It comes into being, is here for some time, begins to disintegrate, and in time, it disappears. By its very ontological constitution, anything that is material – bricks, walls, chairs, mountains, including even our very own bodies - is then necessarily temporary (*anitya*). All material things are in a constant state of flux, a state of perpetual becoming. They come into being, remain for some time, and eventually are resolved in a state of dissolution. The material body of the eternal true self undergoes birth, a brief state of existence, and finally the experience of death.

While a human being may potentially experience a life-span of as much as one hundred years, when seen in the broader context of infinity, this period of time is actually no longer than the proverbial blink of an eye. Consequently, the corporeal body is "nonexistent" in comparison to the eternal self, which is ever existent. This fact is confirmed by the great Advaita philosopher, Shankara (8th century C.E.), in his commentary on the *Bhagavad Gita*:

The perishables are things which have an end or *anta*. For instance, the idea of reality, associated with things like a mirage, snaps when tested by means of right cognition. This is its 'end'. Likewise, these bodies of the eternal and indeterminable self are as perishable as the bodies seen in a dream or projected by a magician. (Shankara, 1983)

The material body, being of a temporal and consequently imperfect nature, is radically different from the true self, that self for which the body serves as just a temporary vehicle.

The spiritual self, according to the *Bhagavad Gita*, is qualitatively far superior to the physical body, being eternal, indestructible and immeasurable. Krishna states this clearly when He says:

> *avinasi tu tad viddhi yena sarvam idam tatam*
> *vinasham avyayasyasya na kaschit kartum arhati*
> *antavanta ime deha nityasyoktah sharirinah*
> *anasino' prameyasya*

"Know that which pervades the entire body to be indestructible. No one is able to destroy the imperishable soul. Only the body of the indestructible, immeasurable and eternal living being is subject to destruction..." (2:17-18)

The individual soul, the autonomous, monadic unit of consciousness that is the true self, is ontologically anterior and qualitatively superior to the lesser material substance of which the soul's present physical body is composed. "Our very existence is in the atmosphere of nonexistence," according to Bhaktivedanta Swami, "Actually, we are not meant to be threatened by nonexistence. Our existence is eternal. But somehow or other we are put into *asat*. *Asat* refers to that which does not exist" (Bhaktivedanta, 1992). The *atman* is, by analytic contrast, *sat*, or that which cannot but exist, and unceasingly so.

The soul, or true self (*atman*), is by nature transmaterial. Its origin is not matter, but God. Consequently, it does not participate in the enervative nature of matter. The body may undergo all sorts of unpleasant experiences, eventually even death, but the soul is immortal. Since the body is merely a temporary vehicle for the immortal soul, and will eventually perish, the first prerequisite for the *yogi* is comprehending the difference between the body (*deha*) and the true self (*atman*). The aim of Jnana-yoga is to provide the conceptual and analytic groundwork necessary for this understanding, which is absolutely necessary for any meaningful spiritual advancement.

Having now conducted in in-depth examination of Atman, we will now proceed to a deeper understanding of the Vedic conception of the Absolute, or Brahman.

5.5.1 B) God: The Nature of the Absolute.

Let us look at what Sanatana Dharma holds to be the Absolute. The ultimate goal and Absolute of Sanatana Dharma is termed "Brahman" in Sanskrit. Even though it is recognized that there are an unlimited number of names for God,[22] many of which are revealed in the Vedic scriptures, the primary philosophical designation for the Absolute is Brahman. The word "Brahman" itself comes from the Sanskrit verb root *brh*, meaning "to grow". Etymologically, the term means "that which grows" (*brhati*) and "which causes to grow" (*brhmayati*).

---

[22] Among the more well known of these many sacred names for God are included Sriman Narayana, Krishna, Rama, Vishnu and Govinda. The scripture known as the *Sri Vishnu Sahasranama* alone reveals one thousand sacred names of the Divine.

5.5.2 Brahman is not Anthropomorphic "God"

Brahman, as understood by the scriptures of Sanatana Dharma, as well as by the Acharyas (spiritual preceptors) of the Vedanta school, is a very specific conception of the Absolute. This unique conception has not been replicated by any other religion or theological construct on earth, and is exclusive to Sanatana Dharma. Thus to even call this conception of Brahman by the English term "God"[23] is, in a sense, somewhat inelegantly imprecise. This is the case because Brahman does not refer to the anthropomorphic concept of God of the Abrahamic religions. When we speak of Brahman, we are referring neither to the "old man in the sky" concept, nor to the idea of the Absolute as even capable of being vengeful, fearful or engaging in choosing a favorite people from among His creatures. For that matter, Brahman is not a "He" at all, but rather transcends all empirically discernable categories, limitations and dualities.

5.5.3 What is Brahman?

In the *Taittiriya Upanishad* (2.1.1), Brahman is described in the following manner: *"satyam jnanam anantam brahma"*, "Brahman is of the nature of truth, knowledge and infinity." Infinite positive qualities and states have their existence secured solely by virtue of Brahman's very reality. Brahman is a necessary reality, eternal (i.e., beyond the purview of temporality), fully independent, non-contingent, and the source and ground of all things. Brahman is both immanently present in the realm of materiality, interpenetrating the whole of reality as the sustaining essence

---

[23] The term "God" is, in turn, derived from the German word "gott", or the Good.

that gives reality its very structure, meaning and existential being, yet Brahman is simultaneously the transcendent origin of all things. God is thus understood in panentheistic terms. God is simultaneously transcendent and intimately immanent in relation to all things.

5.5.4 Does God Have Attributes?

The question of whether or not God possesses the ability to have qualitative attributes has been an unfortunate point of debate among a number Vedanta philosophers for the last two millennia. As a result of this debate, some philosophers have claimed that Brahman is *nirguna*, or without qualities. Others have claimed that God is wholly *saguna*, or possessed of qualitative attributes. The Vedic *shastras* (scriptures) teach that the Absolute (Brahman) is both equally *nirguna*, meaning without material qualities, and *saguna*, or possessed of transcendent qualities, simultaneously. One aspect is not "lower" or "higher" than the other. Rather, one necessitates the other. If God is ontologically transcendent and antecedent to matter in His being, then it necessarily follows that God is without delimiting or conditioned material qualities and attributes. The Absolute has no material (*prakriti*-conditioned) attributes within the contexts of temporality, sequential causality, enervativeness and spatial extensiveness that constitute the functional make-up of all things material. But the Absolute does have infinite auspicious qualities (*ananta-kalyana-gunaih*) that are wholly transcendent and spiritual in nature. The fact that God cannot even be understood without reference to God's qualities is evocatively demonstrated in the truth that even the very statement that God is *nirguna* in itself is directly stating a quality of Brahman. God is *nirguna*; God is without material qualities, which is itself clearly an attribute.

These spiritual qualities of the Divine are enumerated by the multiple thousands all throughout the Vedic scriptures. In the *Taittiriya Upanishad* (2.1.1), as one of many thousands of examples of the attributes of God delineated throughout the totality of the Vedic scriptures, God is described in the following way: *satyam jnanam anantam brahma*, "God is truth, wisdom and infinity." Thus, God can be both described and recognized in accordance with His natural inherent attributes. The *Sri-Vishnu-Sahasranama*, as another example, is only one of myriad scriptures that are completely dedicated to outlining some of the qualities of the Divine. Accordingly, the many thousands of names of the Absolute all designate various divine attributes of that Absolute: Narayana means "Sustainer of All Beings"; Krishna means "All Attractive"; Vishnu means "All-Pervading", Vasudeva means "One Who Resides in all Things", etc., all of which are transcendent attributes of the Divine. Each one of God's names reveals a specific quality about God.

Indeed, according to the Vedantic principle of *sharira-sharirin*, all of reality that is encompassed within the two Vedantic *tattvas* (philosophical Reals) of Atman and Jagat exist within a purely attributive relationship with the third Vedantic *tattva* of Brahman. By implication, then, all reality consists of nothing more than attributive elements of Brahman. Everything that is either conceivable or perceivable is either directly or indirectly an attribute of the Divine! All of reality is *dharmas* (in the Vaisheshika definition of essential attributive features) of the supreme Dharmin, or possessor of essential attributive features.

In summary, the Absolute (Brahman) is both *nirguna* (meaning that Brahman transcends all material attributes) and *saguna* (meaning that Brahman has infinite auspicious attributes) at one and the same time.

176

5.5.5 The Nature of Brahman

As the primary causal and energetic source-substance of even material reality (*jagat-karana*), Brahman does neither arbitrarily or deterministically will the coming into being of the extra-Brahman metaphysical principles of matter (Jagat) and Atman (individuated consciousness), but rather they are manifest into being as a natural result of the overflowing of Brahman's grandeur, beauty, bliss and love in accordance with His will. Brahman cannot but create abundant good in a similar manner to how Brahman cannot but exist. Both existence and overflowing abundance are as much necessary properties of Brahman as love and nurturing are necessary qualities of any virtuous and loving mother.

5.5.6 God and Determinism

In Vedic cosmogony, interestingly, the Absolute (Brahman) is actually not directly involved in the process of material creation. Rather, individually bound *jivas* (souls) are understood to be causally responsible for instigating the creation of the material cosmos. This is true in two senses. First, the material creation devolves into being from *prakriti*, or prime materiality, as a direct result of individual souls developing illusory ego (*ahamkara*) and consequently coming in contact with that-which-is-not (*maya*, or *prakriti*). Thus, the material world comes into existence at the instigation of illusory ego, as well as to serve as the field of experience for *jivas* to both play out the karmic consequences of their illusory ego, and conversely to eventually liberate themselves from such ego and transcend material creation altogether. Second, the functional process of creation itself is not carried out by the Absolute directly, but is performed by a secondary, powerful being called Brahma, or the Demi-urge in Platonic, Neo-Platonic and Gnostic terms. Brahma (not to be ever confused with Brahman, who is God, or Sriman Narayana) is also a limited, individual, bound *jiva* suffering from illusory ego, just as the rest of living beings in the material cosmos are, but who is empowered by Narayana to construct the material cosmos.

That being said, while functionally this system is operating in accordance with Dharmic (or Natural Law) necessity, the necessary laws of Dharma and the instigating decision to have this system exist is originally located in the free-will agency of God. God is free from all conditionality, and is never determined by anything or anyone outside of His own inherent free will. Free will is one of the essential defining attributes of consciousness itself. Thus, both God (Brahman) and the individual souls (*atman*, or *jiva*) are inborn with free will as an aspect of their very ontological natures.

Baruch Spinoza's (1632-1677) cosmogony, cosmology, ontology and metaphysics, which call for a God who is bound by deterministic laws, are thus wrong on several counts. Spinoza was a pantheist, or someone who believes that the totality of material creation equals God. Vedic spirituality is opposed to pantheism, and is instead panentheist in outlook. Vedic panentheism postulates God as existing both transcendent and previous to material creation, while simultaneously being present within all creation as its sustaining foundation, which is the precise meaning of the term "Narayana" as God's highest name. The will of Narayana is ever free.

5.5.7 Rejection of Pantheism

In brief, pantheism is the general idea that the totality of all individual elemental features of nature, taken as a whole, constitutes the Absolute. There are, of course, many variations of this general idea - some of which posit the primacy of consciousness (which is actually a philosophical impossibility with pantheism), and some of which are more atheistic. There are several immense problems with pantheism that have been pointed out repeatedly by many previous philosophers, and which renders pantheism a philosophically unviable proposition. This is the short list:

1) One of these problems is that it necessarily reduces anything we would wish to call "God" to an entity that would be, not only non-transcendent, but also inferior to, and dependent upon, something that is an ontological effect to which God is the ontological cause. Thus, a) it is an irrational reversal of cause and effect, and b) it renders the philosophically accepted definition of God as an omnicompetent being meaningless since it limits God's unrestrained ability via an inferior force lying in a relationship of ontological dependence upon God.

2) In addition, the theory of pantheism also eliminates all of the functional and inherent attributes that make God precisely God. Since the Absolute whole that is God would be dependent upon the integration of the numerically infinite parts of nature, this would mean a) God is a physical (and thus limited and imperfect) being, b) God cannot be omniscient, since it cannot be determined what is the inter-connective force connecting each individual part of nature together to each other, thus serving as the inter-communicative bridge necessary for omnisciency to be operative, c) it would eliminate God's omnipresence for the same reason as (b), d) it would eliminate God's omnipotence since the maximal

scope of God's power would be severely limited to the maximal scope of nature's power (which **is** very limited and finite), and to the finite number of individual existents creating the whole, e) it would eliminate freedom of will (along with conscience, personhood, phenomenological scope, compassion, etc.) from God's power, thus making God's decisions as arbitrary and bound by causality as are nature's decisions.

The teachings of Sanatana Dharma on the meaning of nature, and of our connectedness to her, is much more spiritually satisfying, as well as philosophically supportable, than anything that pantheism can offer. In Sanatana Dharma, nature is seen as a living manifestation of one of God's primary energies, both infused with the ordering principles of Dharma, and reflecting Dharma in her essence and function. Thus, when we as beings whose true essence is that of consciousness cooperate with nature, we are cooperating with Dharma. And when we cooperate with Dharma, we are cooperating with God - who is the transcendental source of both Dharma and nature.

Thus, God, Dharma, Nature, and all individual units of consciousness (*atmans*) are all perfectly and harmoniously integrated in an ontological and functional hierarchy in such a manner that nothing is taken away from any one element, thus potentially leading to unnecessary philosophical contradictions. Panentheism, then, is a vastly more philosophically sound way of understanding the nature of God in relationship with the material universe than pantheism.

5.5.8 Brahman as the Source

One can say that Brahman Himself indirectly constitutes the essential building material of all reality, being the antecedent primeval ontological substance from whence all things, both perceivable and conceivable, proceed. There is no *ex nihilo* creation in Sanatana Dharma, or creation from nothingness, as is postulated in the Genesis account of creation. Brahman does not create from nothing, but from the reality of His own being in the form of His material energy, *prakriti*, or Jagat. Brahman is, in Aristotelian terms, both the Material Cause as well as the Efficient Cause of creation. Thus, while it would be correct to say that God is creation (the panentheist perspective, which sees God as the source of all reality), it would be incorrect to make the converse statement that the creation is God (the pantheist view, which says that the world is the source of God).

5.5.9 The Final Goal and the Final Cause

As the source of Dharma, the metaphysical ordering principles inherent in the design of the cosmos, Brahman can be viewed as the Formal Cause. But in addition, as the final goal of all reality, Brahman is also the Final Cause. Being the ontological source of all reality, Brahman is the only substantial real that truly exists, all other metaphysical categories being either a) contingent transformations of Brahman, having their very being subsisting in attributive dependence upon Brahman, or else b) illusory in nature. These views about the nature of Brahman are in general keeping with the philosophical teachings of both the Advaita and the Vishishta-Advaita schools of Vedanta.

All reality has its source in Brahman. All reality has its grounding sustenance in Brahman. It is in Brahman that all reality has its ultimate repose. Sanatana Dharma, specifically, is consciously and exclusively aiming toward this reality termed Brahman.

5.5.10 Proving God's Existence

How can we have certainty that God, or any proposed metaphysical entity or phenomenon, is real? More to the point, is it possible to prove God's existence? Would such proof have actual meaning to us? There are several consideration that we must take into account to fully understand the philosophical implications of this question itself.

First, the very notion of "proof" for something that exists outside of time, space, causality and even material physicality is an interesting problem in and of itself. It is not logically possible to "prove" the existence of something that is trans-empirical. The mind, as one of many examples, is not a physical "thing" that we can detect with the senses, and thus "prove". We cannot see, feel, hear, taste or smell our own mind, or the mind of even our closest friend. But despite this lack of empirical proof, we know that both our friend and we have minds. Indeed, we know intuitively that to deny that we have a mind would be the utmost absurdity, since it takes the existence of a mind to even deny the existence of a mind. We know that we ourselves have a mind because we have the ability to detect the activities on the mind internally, and not through the senses.

The tougher problem is, how do we prove that our best friend actually has a mind since, being situated as a person who is necessarily separate from our friend's subjective perceptual experience, we cannot know that our friend has a mind by using our own internal sense to detect his mind? The fact that our friend has a mind is not any more empirically demonstrable than the fact that we have one; but more, we cannot even use our own personal experience (*anubhava*) as a means of detection. In the case of proving the existence of a non-empirically detected mind in another person, we can infer that the other person has a mind, if only because our best friend exhibits all of the symptoms that are universally acknowledged as being the attributes of mind. What the senses cannot empirically detect, then, the intellect can often just as accurately infer.

Thus, we need to understand, first, that the normative and popular definition of "proof" does not necessarily even apply to phenomena that are not physical. The senses cannot detect something that is beyond the capability of the senses. That the senses cannot detect such objects, however, is not sufficient grounds for claiming that such objects to not in fact exist, what to speak of claiming that such trans-empirical objects necessarily *cannot* exist, as atheists do attempt to claim. Empiricism is highly limited and imperfect.

Second, the intellectual approach to proving the existence of God, soul, Dharma, and other metaphysical objects also leaves much to be desired as a meaningful mechanism of "proof". This is the reason why. Let us say that we could, in fact, come up with a logical proof for God's existence that was so simple and economic in its design that it could be stated in the form of one sentence, yet so powerful in its validity that even the most virulent atheist on earth, upon seeing this logical proof, had to admit immediately that, yes, there is a God after all. The next question that needs to be asked by any intelligent thinker after seeing that God can be logically proven is the following: So what?

In other words, even if a former atheist now accepts *intellectually* that God is, indeed, an existent thing, that mere intellectual acceptance in and of itself does not necessarily mean that the now 'converted' atheist will consequently do something of spiritual significance with this knowledge. If the person was, for example, a self-centered miscreant before believing in God, he could still very easily chose to be a self-centered miscreant even after now believing in God. There is an over-abundance of "religious" miscreants in the world! Thus, the atheist may have undergone a philosophical/intellectual acceptance of God's existence without also undergoing a personal transformation as a direct result of that acceptance.

Where does this leave us? The ultimate proof for the existence of God or of anything that is a metaphysical existent (our own soul, gods and goddesses, spirits, etc.) is our own direct experience of these things. Moreover, this must be an experience that not only fulfills the function of proof, but that is simultaneously positively transformative in nature.

The only way to have such a transformative spiritual experience is through patient, systematic and expertly guided spiritual practice. This means specifically a) a daily meditation practice, b) the consistent deepening of virtue within oneself, c) contemplation and absorption of the wisdom of such sacred texts as the *Bhagavad Gita*, and d) all cultivated under the loving guidance of an authentic and highly qualified *guru*. This practice also needs to be accompanied with four internal qualities that the spiritual practitioner must already posses to some degree, and be willing to cultivate to their maximal extent: 1) sincerity, 2) humility, 3) openness to Truth, 4) a deep yearning to know that Truth. The most meaningful proof of the sweetness of honey is to taste honey. In the same way, the only truly personally impactful means of proving the existence of God to oneself is to taste deeply of the sweetness of God's reality.

5.6.1 C) The Material Cosmos

Vedic Cosmology: The Tripartite Universe and Multiverses

According to Sanatana Dharma, each universe consists of three distinct levels of being, sometimes called three planetary systems (*triloka*). These three planetary systems are: a) Bhu: the middle plane that human beings are situated within, b) Svarga: a higher plane of heavenly beings, occupied by the gods and goddesses (*devas* and *devis*), and finally c) Patala: a lower, hellish plane of demonic beings (*asuras*). This tripartite system should be quite familiar to most people even today since almost all of the historically more recent religions borrowed their derivative concepts of earth, "Heaven" and "Hell" from this original Vedic cosmology.

As a result of our individual *karma* and re-incarnation, we have the ability to traverse throughout this tripartite universe from one lifetime to another, sometimes being in the heavenly realms, sometimes the earthly realms, and periodically the hellish plane. Wherever we happen to find ourselves within the three planetary systems in any given lifetime, that visit is necessarily temporary, since upon our death, we go on to other lifetimes in other places. In the case of advance *yogis*, *siddhas* (perfected mystics) and the *devas/devis*, on the other hand, they often have the ability to travel relatively easily from one plane of existence to another at will.

All three of these planes are situated firmly within the material cosmos. Thus material joys and pleasures that are experienced even in the heavenly plane are temporary in nature. As Sri Krishna explains in the *Bhagavad Gita*, the goal is to transcend the material world entirely, and to gain entry into the transcendental and eternal Kingdom of God (Vaikuntha).

Thinking that true and lasting happiness can be found anywhere within the material realm is an illusion. "From the highest realm in the material world down to the lowest, all are places of misery wherein repeated birth and death occur. But one who attains to My divine abode, O Arjuna, shall never take birth again." (*Bhagavad Gita*, 8.16) Thus, the goal of Sanatana Dharma is the transcending of all materiality, including all three realms within the material universe.

In addition to the universe being a tripartite structure, the Vedic scriptures also explain to us that ours is not the only material universe in existence. Rather, there is an almost infinite number of material universes, some physically larger than ours and some smaller. Indeed, it is clearly stated that, as God exhales, millions of universes are created. He then expands Himself into each one of these new universes as their invisible sustaining medium. As He inhales, millions of universes are annihilated. In the same way that our universe is filled with so many species, each of which is comprised of an uncountable number of unique individuals, each of the other universes in existence are likewise teeming with living entities. Such is the immensity and grandeur of the power of God's material energy (*apara-prakriti* or *maya-shakti*), which is itself actually considered to be inferior to both the marginal energy (*tatashtha-shakti*) of God, which is synonymous with the realm of *atmans*, and His spiritual energy (*para-prakriti* or *chit-shakti*). These three primary energies of God correspond to the Tri-tattvas, the three primary Vedic deities, and the three paths in the following way:

Para-prakriti = Brahman = Narayana > Vaishnava

Tatashtha-shakti = Atman = Shiva > Shaiva

Apara-prakriti = Jagat = Shakti Devi > Shakta

5.6.2 The Three Gunas: The Metaphysical Grounding of Physical Reality

"Deluded by the three gunas, the whole world does not know Me who am above the *gunas* and inexhaustible. This divine energy of Mine, consisting of the three *gunas* of material nature, is difficult to overcome. But those who have surrendered unto Me can easily cross beyond it." (*Bhagavad Gita*, 7.13-14)

The empirical reality that we perceive around us is composed of matter, known in Sanskrit as Jagat, or *prakriti*. Whether we are referring to the buildings we reside in, the many possessions we strive for, or the very bodies with which we identify so intimately, all objects are composed of the *prakriti*, or the prime material energy, of God. Of the many qualities that are discernible in *prakriti*, the essential feature encountered is that of transience. Matter is in a constant state of flux, a continual cycle of becoming, being and dissolution. Thus everything that we perceive around us, though seemingly stable, ultimately is destined to cease existing. *Prakriti*, herself, is not a purely undifferentiated field of substance. *Prakriti* consists of a substratum of three different modes, each one dependent upon the other two for their mutual existence and proper functioning. These three modes of *prakriti*, or material energy, are also known as the three *gunas*, which in Sanskrit (the ancient sacred language of Sanatana Dharma) means "qualities" or "modes."

In the two verses from the *Bhagavad Gita* that are quoted above, Sri

Krishna (the last full incarnation of God, who walked the earth 5200 years ago) gives Arjuna a glimpse into the nature and power of the three *gunas* of which *prakriti*, or prime matter, is composed. This triad of material modes consists of 1) *sattva* (positivity, goodness, and wholesomeness), 2) *rajas* (passion, energy, and movement) and 3) *tamas* (negativity, lethargy, darkness, and ignorance). These three aspects of material energy exist as the very core of all empirical material phenomena. They can be seen as being three different modes in the spectrum of the one primary material substance. They represent the unitary material substance in three different, yet completely interdependent, frequencies or states. Every aspect of material phenomena that we perceive around us - including our own body, mind and intellect - is composed of a combination of these three *gunas*, with one or the other of these three *gunas* predominating. Thus everything in the material world, including us, is affected by the interplay of the *gunas*. We will now briefly examine the primary characteristics of each of the three *gunas*.

We will begin this exploration of the *gunas* by examining the *guna* that the *Bhagavad Gita* considers to be the highest quality: *sattva*. *Sattva* can be translated as "goodness." This *guna* denotes such qualities as purity, brightness and essence. It is also light - both in the luster of its radiance and in terms of its actual weight in terms of physics. Thus, individuals who are of a spiritual, clean (both physically and mentally), intellectual and peaceful nature are said to be living a sattvic existence; they are residing in goodness. *Sattva* is the quality most sought by all spiritual practitioners.

The next *guna* is *rajas*. *Rajas* denotes activity and movement. It is the mediator between the other two *gunas*, as well as their empowerer. For without the kinetic assistance of *rajas*, neither *sattva* nor *tamas* can act. It is *rajas* which motivates the individual to labor and that inspires work. Those persons in whom *rajas* predominates tend to be of a fiery and passionate disposition. While a certain degree of *rajas* is always necessary in order to facilitate any sort of activity, too much of this quality makes one restless, thus hampering meditation and other forms of disciplined spiritual pursuits.

When the material energy (*prakriti*), through the medium of *rajas*, becomes turned to its lowest frequency, it is then known as *tamas*. *Tamas* has the characteristics of dullness, ignorance and inertia. It is a dark mode, both intrinsically and in the resultant consequences it brings about. Due to its heavy, weighted nature, it provides stability and forms the very foundation of matter. *Tamas* is the source of obstacles, resistance and obstructions. *Tamas* brings about cessation. Those who are of a tamasic nature tend toward lethargy, procrastination and self-destructive behavior. It is the end point of the descent and devolution of *prakriti*. It is, thus, the very antithesis of *sattva*. Those wishing to make any sort of spiritual progress must thoroughly avoid tamasic tendencies.

These three interdependent strands of the material substance are different aspects of the same energy, which in turn is under the full control of the Supreme Godhead (Narayana). *Sattva* is the finest frequency that *prakriti* adopts. *Rajas* is the intermediate catalytic energy source. *Tamas* is the resting place, the dullest mode of material energy. The qualitative hierarchy of the three *gunas* can be visually represented in this way:

THE THREE GUNAS

Sattva = goodness

Rajas = energy to act

Tamas = lethargy

The practitioner of Yoga seeks to ultimately transcend these three *gunas* by a process of gradual progressive ascent. This ascent occurs in several stages. The first stage is to determine which of the three *gunas* presently predominates one's life, thought and actions. If it is determined that either *rajas* or *tamas* is the strongest influence in one's life, then the next step is to rid oneself of these negative influences. This is done by leading as sattvic a life as possible. There are several lifestyle choices that are recommended in order to make one's life more sattvic. This sattvic program includes the following:

The Sattvic Program

1) Practicing the philosophy and disciplines of Yoga on a daily basis. This includes following the ethical virtues taught in the path of Yoga spirituality (such as non-violence, not stealing, not lying, sexual activity only within the context of marriage, etc.), as well as the *asanas*, or psychophysical exercises of Yoga.

2) Always seek cleanliness and purity in all of your thoughts, words, body and actions. Always be pure in mind. This means focusing your awareness always upon the highest Truth, and never allowing your mind to become a cesspool of pornographic or dark thoughts. You become like that upon which you meditate. Always use your words to state the truth, especially by compassionately teaching Dharma to others to the best of your own capacity. Keep your body clean by bathing each and every

morning. Make sure your activities in the world elevate you spirituality, rather than degrade you.

3) Having a purely vegetarian, healthy and organic diet. A purely sattvic diet is lacto-vegetarian, that is, avoidance of all meat, fish and eggs (dairy products such as milk, yogurt and cheese are acceptable). Such a diet will increase one's health, stamina, and intelligence, and bring about peace of mind.

4) Ridding one's senses and mind of all negative, violent and disturbing thoughts and images. This is done, for example, by avoiding violent and negative entertainment, ridding oneself of feelings of vengeance and hatred, and filling one's mind with thoughts of God instead. The music we hear also affects our consciousness. We want to avoid music that is charged with explicitly sexual (tamasic) or violent (rajasic) lyrics, such as all "rap" "black metal", and "hip-hop" music.

5) Meditating daily. In order to have a sattvic existence, we need to purify and still the mind. This is best achieved by having a daily practice of meditation and prayer. The most powerful form of meditation is a practice that focuses on the names of God. "**Aum Namo Narayanaya**" is the most powerful and purifying of all *mantras*. Meditate on these names of God daily.

6) Associating with others who are also leading a sattvic lifestyle. We are all consciously and unconsciously influenced by the nature of the company we keep. If we associate with tamasic or rajasic people, we in turn become tamasic or rajasic. But if we associate with those who are sattvic by nature, then we cannot help but be positively influenced by them.

Avoid the company of bad people, and seek the company of the good.

By strictly and enthusiastically following this Sattvic Program, we can gradually transform our consciousness from one of self-destructiveness into one of positive spiritual attainment. For more information on how to live a sattvic lifestyle, refer to my book *The Sanatana Dharma Study Guide*, which is the companion guide to this book.

As Krishna explains in the *Bhagavad Gita*, or "Song of God," the position in which we presently find ourselves as human beings is a state of self-imposed separation from the loving will of God. Rather than recognizing our true ontological nature as beings who exist in an eternal, loving relationship with the Absolute, we have instead become subject to the illusion of separation from God. As long as we are under this false assumption of separation from God, we will be under the binding influence of these respective *gunas*. Upon consciously and freely surrendering to Sri Krishna, however, we then reclaim the ability to transcend the *gunas* altogether, and to achieve a state of radical freedom from all material influences, sufferings and illusions. This state of spiritual liberation is known as *moksha*, Freedom, a state in which we have full knowledge of our true selves, complete personal fulfillment and bliss beyond compare.

Chapter 6 Ethics: Walking the Talk

6.1.1 The Virtue-Ethics System of Sanatana Dharma

In our attempt to know and to live Truth, it is crucially important to try to live as ethical a life as possible. For the Dharmi (follower of Dharma), the Good, the True, the Real, the Beautiful, the Eternal, and the Absolute, in the highest metaphysical sense, are all one and the same. Thus, one cannot know the Absolute unless one also knows the Good. And one cannot know the Good unless one also *is* good.

There is no religious or philosophical system in the world that doesn't hold some position on ethics. This is the case even for so-called Ethical Relativists who hold the position that ethical norms are ultimately only a matter of personal preference or dictated by the particular situation at hand. Even this shortsighted claim, however, represents a position on ethics. The realm of ethics, stated very simply, centers upon the question of what constitutes good versus bad behavior on the part of human beings. In the tradition of Sanatana Dharma, specifically, this question is answered in a unique way that beautifully balances the often opposing concerns of a) transcendently-originated moral absolutism and cosmic/social justice, with b) the common sense logic and rational practicality that are inherent elements of the Dharmic way of life.

The goal of the Dharmi is to always follow the good course of action in any given situation. The nature of goodness itself is seen as being ultimately rooted in, and as being a reflection of, the Divine. Thus, good in this world, both in the form of Goodness itself as a metaphysical reality and in the form of good actions, has its origins in Transcendent reality...in the very essential nature of the Divine.

Generally speaking, the Good is separated into two different categories: a) good as a virtue, and b) good in action. Goodness as an inherent virtue of the living being has its origin in the very soul (*atman*) of each living being. The goal of the spiritual seeker is to make the inherent goodness of our internal soul manifest in the external world for all to see and bene-fit from. To perfectly manifest our own soul's inherent goodness is synonymous with being an enlightened, liberated being, and reflecting that inner state outward for the world to benefit. Goodness in action, on the other hand, consists of the day-to-day, free will decisions that we need to make in always seeking the higher path in how we treat others. These good behaviors in action are the ethical and moral principles that we must each follow as we are on the road to full self-realization and God-consciousness.

There are a variety of practical ethical principles, imperatives, and laws that we find in Dharma. Many of these ancient Dharmic laws are found in the guidebooks of Dharma known as the *Dharma Shastras*, including the *Manava Dharma Shastra* and the *Vishnu Smriti*. Of these many laws, ten of the most important are listed in the traditional "Yamas" and "Ni-yamas", or proscriptions and prescriptions, respectively. These are the ten ethical principles of Dharma, with a brief commentary.

6.1.2 Ten Ethical Principles of Dharma

Five Yamas - Proscriptions

• Ahimsa (non-violence)

Ahimsa is one of the most important of the ethical proscriptions. Contrary to the false notion that Vedic spirituality believes is passivism, the principle of *ahimsa* does not support passivism or a lack of will to defend oneself. On the contrary, we are called upon to be strong and courageous warriors for our people, our nation, and for Dharma. However, the principle of *ahimsa* does insist that we are to be as maximally non-violent in our minds and in our hearts as is possible, even as we defend Truth, and especially in how we treat our fellow Dharmis and all innocent living beings around us.

• Satya (truthfulness)

For followers of Dharma, Truth is much more than merely the opposite of a lie. Rather, Truth is seen as being one of the infinite, positive attributes of the Divine. Truthfulness is followed both in our attempt to always tell the truth, but more, also in that we are meant to manifest Truth (God) in our everyday lives in all of our thoughts, words and actions. In practicing the telling of truth verbal, we are manifesting the highest Truth spiritually.

• Asteya (non-stealing)

All property, up to and including the very Earth herself, ultimately belongs to the Supreme. To not steal means both to not take from others, as well as to acknowledge who is the ultimate owner of all things. Theft is the direct result of suffering from the illusion that we are in lack. For those who are devoted to God, we know that the soul can never lack, and that the very source and owner of all reality is none other than our very best friend.

• Brahmacharya (sexual continence)

Sexuality is one of the most powerful natural forces found in living beings. We must have fidelity to the Good in how we relate to others sexually, never exploiting others for selfish pleasure, but always reflecting the pure and healthy love that is God's gift to us. What this means in concrete terms is that sexuality only finds its ultimate fulfillment within the context of a loving marriage between a man and a woman.

• Aparigraha (non-covetousness)

It is in transcending the ugly impulse of greed that we overcome the illusion of the egoic self. To be non-covetous is to realize that wealth, material goods and property alone are not sufficient to give us the lasting fulfillment and happiness that we seek. Rather, it is in living within our means, pursuing a life of simple living and high thinking, that we find both material fulfillment and spiritual enlightenment.

Five Niyamas - Prescriptions

• Shaucha (purity)

Purity consists of both scrupulous external hygiene, and internal cleanliness of mind. The former is achieved by bathing, brushing one's teeth, etc., every day without fail. The latter is accomplished by allowing only good, pure, positive and spiritual thoughts to flourish in our minds, and by conversely not allowing the opposite - evil, impure, negative and materialistic thoughts - to dominate our minds.

• Santosha (contentment)
Discontent is the root of all immoral and unethical actions. It is because
we are discontent that we feel the false necessity to exploit and harm
others. When we are content, we approach the world as God's kingdom,
rather than a mere playground for our own selfish exploitation. As is true
of all the Yamas and Niyamas, contentment is a quality that can be cultivated by daily spiritual practice.

• Tapas (austerity)
Tapas is choosing to challenge ourselves each day to take the path that
will make ourselves stronger, rather than weaker. It means taking the
stairs up to our apartment rather than the elevator whenever we can. It
means walking the four blocks to the store rather than driving. It means
pushing ourselves toward excellence, increased strength and health, and
personal growth whenever we see the opportunity to do so arise in our
day-to-day lives. It means always choosing that path that will further elevate us in our personal life.

• Svadhyaya (self-education)
Svadhyaya includes both the daily self-analysis that is such a crucial exercise in our spiritual journey, as well as daily study of the wisdom of the
Dharmic scriptures, such as the *Bhagavad Gita*, *Yoga Sutras*, *Narada Bhakti
Sutras, Srimad Bhagavatam,* and the *Upanishads*. In addition, self-education
occurs when we study the teachings and writings of our own *guru* (spiritual teacher).

• Ishvara-Pranidhana (devotion to the Divine)

The daily cultivation of devotional consciousness (*bhakti*) is the ultimate path to knowing the Divine, because devotion is the very opposite of selfishness. In selfishness, we merely try to take from the world around us. In devotion, we give of ourselves, and in love, back to our Source, which is God, and to all other living beings. Devotion to the Divine can be practiced by meditation upon such Holy Name *mantras* as "Aum Namo Narayanaya", by conducting simple but meaningful *puja* ceremonies in one's own home, or by serving God directly by supporting those authentic *gurus* who teach the world the path of liberation by supporting such *gurus* either with one's volunteer service (*seva*) or charitable donations.

In addition to the Yamas and Niyamas, there are twelve primary qualities that every follower of Dharma should cultivate in themselves.

1. Humility
2. Simplicity
3. Devotion
4. Compassion
5. Loyalty
6. Wisdom
7. Equanimity
8. Balance
9. Excellence
10. Discernment
11. Strength
12. Courage

There is no spiritual progress without the prerequisite practice of conscious and concerted ethical development. To be a Dharmi means, by definition, to be a wholly virtuous person. By sincerely and strictly following the Yamas and Niyamas, as well as cultivating the above twelve indispensible virtues in your life, you will begin the process of manifesting the innate virtue necessary to fully open yourself to God's presence and grace, and realizing the ultimate reality of your true spiritual self.

6.2.1 A Comparative Analysis of Dharmic Ethics and the Judeo-Christian Ten Commandments

In this section of the book (6.2.1–6.2.8), we do a comparative analysis of the Vedic view of ethics versus the Abrahamic view by contrasting the ten principles of Yama-Niyama against the Ten Commandments.

The theological claim for the existence and efficacy of a divinely revealed set of norms for ethical human behavior has been proffered by every major world religion. Moreover, the notion that there can be a trans-rational basis for ideal human behavior, in addition to being universally acknowledged, is also one of the most consistently ancient beliefs commonly held by the faithful of every religious tradition. The practical result of such a belief in the importance of spiritually motivated morality has been the repeated codification of specific and diverse sets of moral proscriptions and prescriptions on the part of each individual religion.

Despite the fact that moral certitude is a common goal of every religion, however, there has historically been a great deal of diversity of codes of morality, often with individual rules and commandments of one religion standing in mutually opposing positions to the rules and commandments of other religions. Religions are not the same. Consequently, history has witnessed immense difference of opinion between religions on the question of which specific religion's moral code is the correct moral code. Without necessarily venturing in this section of the book to settle the argument of which, if any, religion's moral code is actually of divine origin, we will see that the moral codes presented by Sanatana Dharma and the Judeo-Christian Decalogue tradition are different in content. They are, in fact, different not only in substance, but they are quite different in their individual approaches to what even constitutes the underlying foundational enterprise of ethics.

6.2.2 Diversity of Ethical Systems

While there are arguably a number of discernable similarities between some ethical rules upheld by several of the world's many religions (for example, murder, incest and theft are universally held moral wrongs), we also find that there is a great deal of dissimilarity between particularly held codes of ethics. When we do even the most rudimentary comparative analysis of the major world religions' diverse ethical systems, we immediately see that there is some considerable disagreement between them on the question of what is a morally good action versus what is a morally objectionable action. In some religions, for example, it is considered an immoral act to drink alcohol (Sanatana Dharma, Islam, Evangelical Christianity). In other religions, by contrast, alcohol is considered to be just fine from a moral perspective (Judaism, Catholicism, Unitarianism). For some faiths, the killing of animals to eat meat is an ethically prohibited activity (Sanatana Dharma, Jainism, and traditional Buddhism). In other religions, killing animals is an ethically neutral activity (Islam and Christianity). In some religions it is considered morally legitimate to periodically kill members of another religion merely for the shear act of being members of a different religion. Historically, the Abrahamic religions of Judaism, Christianity and Islam have all been culpable in supporting such a view to greater or lesser degrees. For most of the other religions of our world – especially the Dharmic religions of Sanatana Dharma, Buddhism and Jainism - on the other hand, to kill someone simply because they practice a different faith from one's own would be considered demonic (*asurika*), and has never been an activity that these religions have historically engaged in. These differences in moral codes are, in turn, tied closely to the historically developed ethnic, linguistic and paradigmatic differences that we see in the overall world-views of our world's many culturally distinct geographic regions.

6.2.3 Differences Between Dharmic and Judeo-Christian World-views

While there are several distinct similarities between the world-views of Dharmic civilization, with its foundation in the religions of Sanatana Dharma, Buddhism and Jainism, and the overall world-view of the Abrahamic Judeo-Christian tradition, these similarities are far outweighed by the significant differences between them. The similarities tend to be of a more superficial and formal level. These similarities include the primacy of a spiritual world-view, the belief in a unitive and transcendent ground of being, and the centrality of a moral outlook in general. The differences, however, are much more pronounced and specific. Moreover, they are grounded in completely divergent views and approaches to the ontological reality of the human person.

Sanatana Dharma views the human person as being primarily composed of consciousness-substance (*chaitanya*)– termed very specifically *atman* in

Sanskrit when referring to the individual unit of consciousness (often translated into the English language by the word "soul"). *Atman* is onto-logically antecedent, causally non-contingent in relation to matter, and qualitatively superior to matter. For the greater Abrahamic Judeo-Christian tradition, on the other hand, the human person is seen to be a necessarily co-existent matrix of consciousness (spirit, or soul), physical body and personality. The precise degree to which primacy is according to one or another of these elements of the human person varies in ac-cordance with whether one speaks of the Jewish, Christian or Islamic perspectives, and further, whether one is referring to a specific school of thought in either of these traditions.

The Judeo-Christian worldview has traditionally stressed religious prac-tice as a more socially manifest phenomenon. Spirituality, for them, is more of a collectivist community concern. The primary motivating fac-tors for living a moral life include a) pleasing God / fear of God, b) becoming a better person, c) creating a society in which the rule of law and ethical concern for others are sovereign, d) avoidance of divine retri-bution and punishment. Morality is seen in terms of exteriority of behavioral norms, goals, and empirically observable consequences. Vir-tues, for the Judeo-Christian denominations, are qualities to be cultivated and acquired from our external behavior, and not to be made manifest as a direct result of the inherent presence of virtue subsisting in the very essence of the living being. Moral behavior, for the Abrahamists, is a temporally derived phenomenon.

The Sanatana Dharma world-view, on the other hand, has always stressed religious practice as a process of interiorization, and manifesting natural qualities that lay hidden within the human person as an inherent aspect of the soul. Moral behavior, for Sanatana Dharmis, is an essentially derived phenomenon. Religion is seen as a process of interiority, a process of self-realization, rather than merely self-improvement. Given the above outlined Dharmic position on the nature self, the human person is seen, in his deepest atmic essence, as being inherently spiritual, good and virtuous by his very ontological nature. Via the process of leading an ethical life, coupled with the systematic practice of Yoga ("unity with the Divine") and meditation, one's essentially virtuous interior attributes are brought to exterior manifestation. Virtues, for Sanatana Dharma, are qualities to be rediscovered as aspects already present in the soul, and not merely as acquisitions to be gained by the soul from any external source.

Epistemologically, Judeo-Christian theology can be said to primarily stress Biblical revelation, coupled with theology, dialectic, and discursive deductive reasoning. The traditional philosophical trends found in Sanatana Dharma, on the other hand, put more of an epistemological emphasis on a) non-mediated intuitive insight and introspection, intimately coupled with b) the modalities of logical reasoning, and c) scriptural authority of the *Vedas*.

6.2.4 Inherent Virtue Ethics and Proscribed Ethics

Two fundamental observable distinctions in the realm of general ethics are a) Virtue Ethics, and b) Proscribed Ethics. For the former, the inner qualities of the individual are seen as being of preeminent importance. In this view, moral laws exist in order to foster positive internal qualities. For Proscribed Ethics, on the other hand, the functional externalities of moral laws, formal adherence to the precise minutia of each rule and regulation, is seen as the primary goal of ethics. As is the case for most non-Judeo-Christian religions, and many of the natural religions of the ancient world, Sanatana Dharma upholds a form of Virtue Ethics. For Sanatana Dharma, social morality and ethical laws are seen as a means to an end. That end is to discover and reclaim the inherent goodness of the unencumbered Self (*atman*), which in turn serves as the very basis of social morality and ethical laws. As a result of this Virtue Ethics approach, the proscriptions and prescriptions of Sanatana Dharma are seen as existing in order to serve the higher purpose of self-realization, as well as to serve as an externalized behavioral model for the eventual manifestation of the internal qualities of the soul.

6.2.5 Shruti Versus Smriti

The scriptures of the Judeo-Christian tradition (whether the Torah of Judaism, or the "Old" and "New" Testament of Christianity) are viewed as a unified set of scriptures, a continuous divine canon of literature, revealed incrementally throughout human history. Thus for both Jews and Christians, the Ten Commandments, as found in the Book of Exodus, are considered to be the authoritative pronouncements of their god, made temporally manifest within the context of space/time. For Sanatana Dharma, on the other hand, scripture is seen as both pre-existing temporal and spatial reality, and not being existent-dependent upon any audible receiver (i.e., human beings). Rather, scripture, or *Veda*, is considered to be *apaurusheya*; that is, scripture transcends all materiality, is eternally manifest, is infallible, and is not dependent upon its own revelation for justification of its validity - as is true for God as well.

Vedic scripture is of two qualitatively conterminous forms: *Shruti*, or scripture that is directly heard, and which is infallible, authorless and eternal by nature, and *Smriti*, or scripture that is remembered, and is thus also infallible, authorless and eternal by nature but the veracity of which is more dependent upon human remembrance of its sacred content. While many moral codes are to be found in the *Shruti* canon, the vast bulk of ethical codes is found in the latter category of *Smriti*. The primary law books for Sanatana Dharma are a collection of scriptures called the *Dharma Shastras*, and are considered part of the *Smriti* canon. Written by a variety of individual sages and philosophers, the genre of sacred literature known as the *Dharma Shastras* has served as general guidebooks for Sanatana Dharma morality, law and jurisprudence for over 2500 years. The British even employed the authority of one of these works, the *Manu Smriti*, as a guide to formulating the colonial legal system of India during British rule. At no point, however, did orthodox Dharmis (followers of Sanatana Dharma) consider the moral rules of the *Manu Smriti* to be the very last word on Vedic morality, universally binding upon all Dharmis for all times of history. Rather than being written in stone, the applicability of the rules and laws found in the *Manu Smriti* were considered fluid and dependent upon time, rational cogency, and culture given the fact that it was only one text of many constituting the *Dharma Shastra* literature.

6.2.6 Ten Principles of Yoga

While numerous lists of ethical codes are to be found in many different scriptures of Sanatana Dharma, possibly the most influential code of behavior for Dharmis has historically been the Ten Principles of Yoga.[24]

---

[24] These ten principles are mentioned, among other places, in the *Yoga Sutras* of

These ten principles are divided into a) *Yama*, or five proscriptive rules of behavior, and b) *Niyama*, or five prescriptive rules. The Ten Principles are the following:

Yamas

    a) Non-violence

    b) Truthfulness

    c) Non-stealing

    d) Sexual restraint

    e) Non-attachment.

Niyamas

    a) Contentment

    b) Discipline/austerity

    c) Study of Hindu scriptures

    d) Devotion to God

    e) Cleanliness

While there is certainly some slight, superficial overlap between the Ten Principles of Sanatana Dharma and the Ten Commandments of the Judeo-Christian tradition, these very few similarities are greatly overshadowed by the distinct differences. The Ten Principles are quite different from the Ten Commandments in both content and purpose.

Patanjali, 2.30,32.

6.2.7 Comparative Analysis of the Ten Commandments and the Ten Principles

The Decalogue consists of the following ten pronouncements, found in Exodus 20: 1-17: [25]

1. You shall not have any gods before me.
2. You shall not carve idols for yourselves in the shape of anything in the sky above or on the earth below or in the waters beneath the earth.
3. You shall not take the name of the lord, your god, in vain.
4. Remember to keep holy the Sabbath day.
5. Honor your father and your mother.
6. You shall not kill.
7. You shall not commit adultery.
8. You shall not steal.
9. You shall not bear false witness against your neighbor.
10. You shall not covet your neighbor's house.

As can be readily seen, the general emphasis in the Ten Principles of Sanatana Dharma is geared toward self-transformation. These yogic principles are focused on revealing the true spiritual nature of the inner person. The Ten Commandments, on the other hand, are more externally oriented. They focus on proper social conduct. While the Ten Principles are mystical and spiritually subjective in content, the Ten Commandments are more social and legalistic in content. More, each set of rules contains codes of conduct that are parochial and sect-dependent in nature. For the Ten Principles, for example, the importance of studying Vedic scripture is upheld. This code would certainly not pertain to a follower of either Judaism or Christianity, who do not subscribe to the

---

[25] There are three versions of the Decalogue mentioned in the Torah (or Hebrew Scriptures). All are different. They are found in Exodus 20:2-17, Exodus 34:12-26, and Deuteronomy 5:6-21. The version in Exodus 20 is by far the most commonly cited today.

spiritual authority of Vedic scriptures. Conversely, keeping the Sabbath holy would hold no significant meaning to a Sanatana Dharmi, Buddhist or Jain, since the latter religions have a different cosmogony from that portrayed in the Book of Genesis. Thus, traditional Sanatana Dharmis would not uphold the Decalogue as authoritative, and the Ten Principles are not accepted as being divinely inspired by either Jews or Christians.

6.2.8 Decalogue and Dialog

Despite the many similarities that are found among the world's many diverse religious traditions, the fact that these religions nonetheless remain distinct and unique traditions cannot be overlooked. In the pluralistic democratic society that we live under in the Western world, religious differences must be respected and protected by law. Only by respecting the religious differences of minority religions such as Sanatana Dharma, Buddhism, Jainism, Sikhism, Taoism, and others, as well as protecting such minority religions' right to practice their respective religions, can we ensure the freedom of religious belief and practice for all.

This ends the section of the book comparing the Ten Principles of Sanatana Dharma with the Ten Commandments of the Old Testament.

6.3.1 The Twelve Qualities of a Dharmi

Sanatana Dharma is a philosophy that boldly encourages human beings to strive to become maximally noble and excellent in all their thoughts, words and behavior. Our goal is nothing less than achieving the perfection of spirit, intellect, mind, emotions, virtue, beauty and health. The following is a list of twelve inner virtues that every follower of Sanatana

Dharma (Dharmis) should try to cultivate in themselves. This is the distilled essence of the qualities of noble human behavior as revealed in the Vedic scriptures.

1. Humility
2. Simplicity
3. Devotion
4. Compassion
5. Loyalty
6. Wisdom
7. Equanimity
8. Balance
9. Excellence
10. Discernment
11. Strength
12. Courage

It is by consciously manifesting these twelve Vedic virtues in our lives that we can eventually become *arya-manushya*, noble human beings, and perfect both our worldly life, and our spiritual existence.

6.4.1 The Four Jewels (Chatur-Ratna)

In addition to the ethical precepts found in the Ten Principles, and the virtuous qualities outlined in the Twelve Qualities, there are four specific jewels that are necessary for any spiritual practitioner. These are known as the Four Jewels, or *chutur-ratna*.

Humility (*dainya*)

Simplicity (*saralata*)

Devotion (*bhakti*)

Compassion (*karuna*)

These four qualities are a causally linked sequence with humility leading to simplicity, simplicity fostering devotion, and devotion giving birth to compassion.

6.5.1 Honoring Life: The Principles of Vegetarianism

One of the most important of the Ten Principles is *ahimsa*, or non-violence. Non-violence, in turn, is especially practiced by the observing of a lacto-vegetarian diet, a diet that excludes all meat, fish and eggs, but that includes dairy products, such as milk, cheese, ghee, yogurt, etc.

The ancient Sanatana Dharmic diet of vegetarianism has recently been gaining a great deal of popularity throughout the world, both as a diet and as a way of life. Influenced by a number of different factors, millions of people worldwide have been increasingly turning to this ancient vegetarian lifestyle. In the United States alone, there are an estimated twenty-five million people who consider themselves vegetarians. Their reasons for turning to the vegetarian diet are almost as diverse as are the individuals themselves. As medical data continually streams in linking meat-eating with a number of illnesses, such as cancer and heart disease, many have chosen to renounce meat for health reasons. While others have decided to become vegetarians for primarily ethical and moral concerns. As the animal rights movement continues to gain momentum, many are beginning to recognize the natural link between fighting to alleviate the suffering of animals in laboratories and hunting ranges, and our refusal to consume their tortured bodies in our kitchens.

Another concern of vegetarians is the adverse impact upon our environment due to the wasteful policies of the meat industry. Consequently, a large number of environmental organizations have adopted vegetarianism into their agendas. Despite the fact that vegetarianism has gained a great deal of recent popularity, however, it still remains a little understood phenomenon to some. What is even less known is the truly ancient and spiritual roots of the vegetarian philosophy. In the following section of the book, we will explore the philosophy of vegetarianism from the ancient Vedic perspective.

One of the central tenets of Sanatana Dharma philosophy is the concept of *ahimsa*, or non-violence. While many ethical systems purport to espouse some form of non-violent ethic or another, what makes the Vedic practice of *ahimsa* radically unique from other systems is the universal scope of its concern. For most ethical schools of thought, the concept of ethical concern extends no further than the human race. The criteria for whether or not a being is worthy of being the object of compassion is determined by the species of the being involved. For Dharmis (followers of Sanatana Dharma), on the other hand, all living creatures are worthy of respect, compassion and ethical concern, regardless of whether they are human or non-human. Dharmic ethics are all encompassing, and thus consistent.

The general Western consensus is that humans are completely justified in their periodically harsh treatment of animals, both theologically and philosophically. From the Christian philosophical perspective, it has been claimed that animals are of an inferior order of being in comparison to humans. This being the apparent case in the minds of Christians, it is considered to be perfectly permissible for humans to kill animals for consumption, for experimentation, for their furs, or for any other purpose they deem appropriate. Animals were, after all, supposedly created by a loving and compassionate God - so the Biblical argument goes - for our own parochial human needs. Animals are seen as being mere means to an end. That end is the gratification and satisfaction of human desires. Thus, all non-human living beings have no inherent value as ends in themselves, but only acquire a minimum sense of value as objects for our use.

Indeed, the Abrahamic god seems to have confirmed this functionalist relationship between human and non-human animal in the Bible: "God blessed them saying: 'be fertile and multiply; fill the earth and subdue it. Have dominion over the fish of the sea, the birds in the air, and all the living creatures that move on the earth.'" (Genesis 1:28) One representative of this distinctly anthropocentric outlook was Thomas Aquinas, the great synthesizer of Aristotelian philosophy and Christian dogma. He has written that, "...irrational creatures have no fellowship with human life, which is regulated by reason. Hence friendship with irrational creatures is impossible...". (*Summa Theologica*) Thus stands the traditional Christian argument in favor of man's continued exploitation and killing of animals.

If one examines these opinions with a deeper philosophical scrutiny and from the perspective of the Dharma concept of *ahimsa*, however, their many flaws are quickly revealed. First of all, while it is apparent that God gave us a superior position over animals in the hierarchy of being, this higher status does not automatically give us the right to kill other life-forms simply for our selfish ends. Mere superiority over another sentient being can never be interpreted as a license for abusing a less capable being, or a class of such beings. The contemporary philosopher Bernard Rollin confirms this in his work *Animal Rights and Human Morality*, "Even if man has been placed by God at the peak of the Great Chain of Being, or even in command of it, it does not follow that the creatures beneath him many be treated in any way he sees fit." If it were the case that superior beings have the right to exploit supposedly inferior ones, then it would be morally permissible for one human to enslave and victimize another. An intellectually or physically more powerful man could justifiably kill another, weaker man. Physically weaker women and children would be at the mercy of stronger, aggressive men. Indeed, the entire moral order - which is based on the premise that ethical means, and not merely brute force, should be used to achieve ends - would collapse.

Moreover, the Sanatana Dharma position is that if we are, indeed, superior to other life-forms, we should clearly exhibit that superior nature in precisely the manner of our actions towards them. It is the very height of irrationality, says Sanatana Dharma, to claim that our inherent intellectual and ethical superiority over other beings gives us license to then act in unthinking and immoral ways towards these less capable beings. Overall, then, the traditional Christian philosophical arguments against compassion towards animals simply do not stand up to close scrutiny.

Two other, somewhat more sophisticated, arguments that are used to justify the unwarranted killing of animals are as follows. First, animals are incapable of thinking rationally. Therefore, they are not worthy of the same ethical consideration that humans are. Only a being who is able to formulate (or at least understand) ethical principles via the process of discursive reasoning is eligible to be considered a moral agent, and therefore a moral object. The second argument is that only beings that are capable of communicating through language are to be deemed worthy of moral consideration. Let us now explore these anti-*ahimsa* arguments in more depth.

While seemingly valid arguments at a first glance, from the Sanatana Dharma perspective these two opinions are revealed to be exceedingly flawed. If we were to hypothetically accept these two criteria as being valid, namely that only living beings who exhibit the abilities to think rationally and to communicate verbally were worthy of being treated morally, it would then follow that several categories of human beings would also consequently lie outside the bounds of moral consideration. Human infants, for example, would not pass these criteria for ethical inclusion. Infants are incapable of either thinking rationally or of speaking. Does this fact, then, give us the right to kill human infants at will? According to the flawed standard of judging who is worthy of moral treatment that is outlined above, the answer would have to be yes. The argument for *ahimsa* can be further developed.

For the defender of Abrahamic anthropocentric ethics may then attempt to rebut that while a human infant may be presently incapable of rational thought and speech, he is still categorically - and solely - worthy of our ethical treatment because there lies within this human infant at least the potential for these two faculties. Given time, the infant will eventually (and hopefully) think rationally and be capable of human speech. The new, broadened, standard for a being having inclusion within the scope of ethical concern would then be the possession of at least the potential for rational thought and language, even if their actual fruition has not yet occurred.

This anti-*ahimsa* argument, however, presents yet another problem for the proponent of a "humans only" ethical concern. For there are several categories of human beings who do not possess even this minimal potential. For example, what of a mute person who is simultaneously suffering from severe mental retardation and who will, consequently, never truly have even this potential? What of someone's mute mom or dad who may be suffering from irreversible Alzheimer's disease, and who has thus lost this potential? Again, following the logical chain of thought contained in the anti-*ahimsa* argument, these human individuals would fall completely outside the scope of moral concern. The contemporary philosopher and bioethicist Peter Singer goes so far as to say that, "Whatever the test we propose as a means of separating human from non-human animals, it is plain that if all non-human animals are going to fail it, some humans will fail as well." (*In Defense of Animals*) In order to be consistent with his arguments, someone who opposes the concept of *ahimsa* would be forced to treat these people in the same terrible manner in which he treats animals: he would have a right to kill them at will. Obviously, however, no spiritual or religious person, even if they were an Abrahamist, would want to support such a conclusion.

The problem with these anti-*ahimsa* arguments is that they are using the right criteria for the wrong argument. The dual abilities to think rationally and to speak are, indeed, correct standards for judging whether or not a being can be a moral agent, that is, whether or not a being is capable of comprehending and being accountable for its actions. Most human beings fall under this category. However, being a) a **moral agent**, and being b) an **object of moral concern** are two completely different things. Agreeing with this criteria, Bernard Rollin writes, "It is easy to see, of course, why rationality would be important for a being to be considered a moral agent, that is, a being whose actions and intentions can be assessed as right and wrong, good or bad...but it is, of course, not obvious that one must be capable of being a moral agent before one can be considered an object of moral concern." This point having been firmly established, then, exactly what would be the proper criterion for deciding which living beings will or will not be included within the range of moral concern?

For Sanatana Dharma, to be a proper object of moral concern, all that is required is that a being is sentient (*ajada*), that is, that it be a living being capable of experiencing feeling, and thus pain. All living beings, regardless of their physical form, are *atman*, or individual units of consciousness, in their innermost essence. The attributes of *atman* are *sat*, *chit* and *ananda*, or being, knowledge and bliss, respectively. The *atman* is the ultimate experiencer (*drashtur* or *bhoktur*) of all that occurs to the body, either good or bad. That being the case, causing any suffering to any living being is considered to be the greatest offense. If any being is capable of experiencing pain, regardless of what species that being is a member of, it is immoral to needlessly inflict pain upon that being.

That a being is unable to express itself rationally only tells us that we will not be able to engage in a philosophical dialectic with it or have a conversation with it about the latest fashion trends. But, by registering such a clearly and universally recognizable verbal sign of suffering as a scream when we abuse it, torture it or try to kill it, a conscious being is pleading with us to cease its suffering. The entire realm of living beings thus falls within the scope of moral concern, and not just human beings. It is in keeping with this ethic of valuing all life that thoughtful Dharmis follow a strict vegetarian diet, a diet which seeks to reduce suffering to its minimal level.

6.5.2 Vegetarianism for a Better World

There are actually many reasons for becoming a vegetarian. Vegetarianism makes sense from every possible perspective.

Health - Vegetarians have been shown to live longer, as well as suffer much less from such health problems as cancer, heart-disease and other illnesses. Contrary to popular belief, meat foods are not a necessary component of the human diet. In fact, evolutionarily and biologically, humans are not designed to be carnivores. Our teeth and intestinal structures are best suited for an herbivorous (vegetarian) diet.

Economic - A cow has to be fed up to 16 pounds of grain in order to produce only one pound of beef. If this grain were to be fed directly to human beings, world starvation could be eliminated. In addition, the meat industry is one of the most heavily federally subsidized industries in America. Your tax dollars are being wasted supporting an industry that produces an inefficient and unhealthy product.

Environmental - Central and South American rain forests are being decimated at the alarming rate of 2.5 acres per second. Much of this destruction is occurring in order to provide grazing land for beef cattle. Every burger we eat represents a tree mowed down in a rain forest. Also, the meat industry has been repeatedly cited as one of the major industries responsible for massive pollution, including the dumping of noxious wastes into our nation's water supplies.

Ethical - To kill or give pain to any living creature, especially when such actions are unnecessary and not in self-defense, is morally unjustified. Like you and I, animals are sentient living beings, and have been proven to be capable of feeling pain and suffering. Animals, like humans, cry out if cut; they scream if killed; they mourn if separated from those they love. God created animals, not for us to torture and gobble up thoughtlessly, but to cooperate with, learn from and protect. If we are, indeed, vastly superior to animals in both our ethical development and in our sense of justice, should we not perhaps behave as such?

Spiritual - Most of the world's varied religious traditions are opposed to creating unnecessary suffering. The two most important qualities that the spiritual path attempts to instill in its adherents are wisdom and compassion. These qualities are impossible to develop as long as we engage in violence of any sort. However insignificant or distant an act of violence may appear to us (such as the killing and eating of animals), it nonetheless contributes to an overall social attitude of justifying violence. Violent minds lead to violent lifestyles. In such a state of consciousness, it is impossible to make any serious advancement on the spiritual path.

These, and many other considerations, make it quite clear that the vegetarian alternative is a lifestyle that is both reasonable and healthy for your body, mind and soul. If you want to enjoy the full experience of what it means to follow the Vedic lifestyle, I would strong suggest that you consider making the healthy transition to vegetarianism.

6.5.3 Vedic Etiquette (Shishtachara)

A very important aspect of observing an ethical Vedic lifestyle consists of Vedic etiquette. In Sanatana Dharma, the principle of proper etiquette is not merely a matter of courtesy and conscientious social behavior. Nor is Vedic etiquette a manifestation of superannuated and fastidious custom. Rather, Vedic etiquette is considered to be a set of revealed behavioral norms that are spiritual in origin, and that are just as important as ethical and moral conduct. Etiquette is considered to be the manifestation of eternal ethical principles translated into the realm of social interaction and relationship. Vedic etiquette is the Dharma of human interaction. Thus, to go against Vedic etiquette does not merely mean that one is un-cultured, but that one is decidedly unspiritual. To break etiquette norms in a Vedic context leads to negative *karma*; and depending upon whom one offends in not observing Vedic etiquette, it can lead to extremely bad *karma* indeed!

The willful breaking of Vedic etiquette is termed *aparadha* in Sanskrit, or "offence". To commit an *aparadha* is to perform an activity the results of which are literally the very opposite of *sadhana* (disciplined spiritual prac-tice). Rather than making spiritual advancement and progressing toward the goal of liberation, the person who has committed *aparadha* has dam-aged himself spiritually, and regresses to a very low point of spiritual development.

Vedic etiquette is a system of helpful guidelines designed to ensure max-imally healthy human interactions in light of the differing relationships that pertain between different types of people, situated on different hier-archical levels, in any given Vedic community. As was discussed previously (sections 5.2.1 and 5.2.2), each and every individual person is situated somewhere in a natural hierarchy that is determined by their spiritual status, coupled with their individual psychophysical nature. Given that people are not equal, the guidelines of Vedic etiquette teach us how to relate to different persons in accordance with the specific area that they have earned within the vertical hierarchical spectrum.

The Three Relationships: Community means relationship, and relationship means healthy and appropriate reciprocation. How we are meant to interact and reciprocate with individuals will differ in accordance with the degree of stature they inhabit in relation to our own. There are three different types of relationships that we experience with others that determine how we reciprocate with people. A) Any being who is greater than us must be offered full respect, reverence and obeisances. B) Any being who is on our same level must be treated as an equal and a friend. C) Any being who is below us must be treated with compassion and empathy. When the dynamic interplay of these three levels of relationship is harmoniously upheld in society, all concerned are benefited. Such interrelationships foster humility, learning, growth, camaraderie, mentorship, compassion and social cohesion.

General Guidelines of Vedic Etiquette

Vedic etiquette is a vast field that would constitute a small book on its own. So we will only be covering a small number of these principles. The following are a few of the most important rules of etiquette that followers of Sanatana Dharma observe. For a more in-depth list of principles of Vedic etiquette, refer to the companion book *The Sanatana Dharma Study Guide*.

<u>Guest-Host Etiquette</u>: Another important principle of etiquette that is found throughout the Dharmic world (including pre-Christian Europe)[26] involved the respectful treatment of guests to one's home. The guest must always be treated with the utmost hospitality. He is offered respect and courtesy, as well as whatever comforts and accommodations the host can afford. The guest is never insulted in one's home. To break this rule of etiquette unnecessarily is to welcome great inauspiciousness to the home.

<u>Sadhu Etiquette</u>: One of the most important aspects of Vedic etiquette is shown in how the sage (*sadhu*) is treated by society in general, and how the disciple treats the *guru* specifically. The saintly person – whether we are speaking of a *guru*, *rishi*, *sadhu*, *yogi* or any other exalted spiritual being – is considered to be the most valuable member of any culturally developed human civilization.[27] This is the case because the sage provides the greatest model for the citizens by upholding the highest spiritual, moral and civilizational standards in his own personal behavior. More, the very presence of the sage emanates a dynamically diffusive auspiciousness throughout his surroundings that helps to elevate the very atmosphere of any place he inhabits. For these reasons, the sage has always earned the very highest praise, reverence and respect that a civilized society could afford. Throughout the totality of Vedic culture, for example, whenever the sage would choose to grace the royal palace with his presence, the

---

[26] The principle of hospitality toward the guest and the traveler was known in ancient Greece, for example, as *xenia*, the patron god of which is Zeus himself.
[27] The importance of this particular social virtue does, of course, bring into question just how culturally developed most modern societies actually are given the fact that there are very few cultures today that still extend any degree of social respect to their living sages and authentic spiritual teachers.

king himself would stand with hands folded in humble respect toward the sage!

Likewise, the *guru*, who is considered by the disciple to be the greatest of sages, is given more respect than any other person in society. In the famous *Guru-Stotram*, as one of hundreds of examples, the following is stated:

Gurur-Brahma Gurur-Vishnu Gurur-Devo Maheshwarah
Guru-sakshat Para-Brahma tasmai Sri Gurave Namah

"The *guru* himself is revered as if he is Brahma (the creator), Vishnu (the sustainer) and Shiva (the destroyer). He is treated in the same manner as the Supreme Absolute is treated. My reverential salutations to that glorious teacher." (*Guru-Stotram*, 3)

In keeping with the teachings of the scriptures, we are to treat the *guru* with the following etiquette.

The *guru* is never to be treated as a pal, a colleague or an equal. This is one of the greatest offenses (*aparadha*) that any person can commit. The *guru* is he who opens widely for us the window to liberation – and must be treated as such.

When the *guru* is in the process of instructing, the disciple tries not to interrupt unnecessarily, but to appreciate each and every word the *guru* utters. The disciple must listen to the *guru* with the utmost attention and respect. It is *guru-vani*, the divine words of the *guru*, which will lead us to wisdom and liberation. It is in listening to such sacred words that we learn and grow, and not by trying to show how much we think we know.

The disciple avoids sitting on the same physical level as the *guru* (and certainly never above!), and whenever possible sits at a lower level at the *guru's* feet. Truth descends from above, in a vertical fashion, from the heavenly realm coming down to the earthly plane, and not from the level of horizontal imperfection. As the visible teacher and personification of the very truth we claim to seek, the *guru* must always be understood by all students, and by society in general, to be always existing in a plane that is situated "above".

We always refer to the *guru* with the most respectful and accurate title that approximates his spiritual station. If the *guru* is a Swami, for example, then minimally we refer to him as "Swami Maharaja". If he is an Acharya, then we call him minimally "Acharyaji". Other acceptable titles for the spiritual master are "Gurudeva", "Guruji", etc. We never refer to our *guru* by his pre-spiritual name (the name he was known by previous to his initiation by his own *guru*).

Familial Etiquette: Children must show respect toward their parents, grandparents and all elders. The husband must view his wife as the incarnation of the Earth goddess, and the wife must see her husband as the incarnation of the King of Heaven (Indra). One's ancestors must be deeply revered, propitiated with offerings of food, and asked to share their wisdom, guidance and blessings with one's family. Reverence for one's ancestors is one of the most important practices in Sanatana Dharma.

Etiquette Toward Sacred Objects:

Any objects that are considered sacred, such as copies of the *Shastras*

224

(Vedic scriptures) or the books written by our *guru*, *japa-mala* (beads used for reciting *mantras* in meditation), images of the Divine, implements that are used in *puja* or any other sacred ceremony, etc. are seen as being invested with the power of God. Therefore, they need to be treated with special care and reverence. By developing such reverence toward that which associated with God, we cultivate devotion toward God. Such items should, for example, never be taken into the bathroom, put directly on the floor, handled with unclean hands, put in a dirty place, tossed across the room, or in any other way handled roughly. One should never write in the margins of a sacred text.

Etiquette Toward Sacred Places:

When we enter into temples, *ashramas*, sacred groves and grottos, the *guru's* residence or any sacred space, we are to observe the greatest reverence. All such places are called *tirthas*, or places of pilgrimage. Such necessary reverence includes taking our shoes off before entering a sacred place; maintaining a quiet volume of our voice; never partaking of alcohol, drugs, tobacco, or eating meat either during our visit or immediately beforehand; and focusing our full concentration on our immediate spiritual goal while visiting the sacred place. Areas that are exclusively dedicated to serving God are like open portals to the spiritual realm.

If all the above-mentioned guidelines of Vedic etiquette are observed with diligence and devotion, the result will be health, prosperity and the blessings of the gods. Such observances are an integral part of any healthy *sadhana* program.

Third Wave

- Socio-Historical Grounding

Chapter 7 Comparing Religious Traditions

7.1.1 Sanatana Dharma and Buddhism

Whenever Westerners see a statue or other image of the Buddha, we often see him meditating in full lotus position, known in Yoga as *padma-asana*. We know, of course, that this is also the traditional position in which *yogis* engage in meditation. Even in an intuitive sense, then, people do understand that there is a deep connection between Sanatana Dharma and Buddhism. In the following section, we will briefly cover some of the similarities and differences between Sanatana Dharma and Buddhism.

There is, indeed, a very deep connection between the two paths. Buddhism took its birth from Sanatana Dharma in the sixth century BCE. From a comparative historical perspective, the relationship between Sanatana Dharma and Buddhism is somewhat equivalent to the causal relationship of Judaism and Christianity. We know that originally Christianity started as an innovative reformation attempt within Judaism, but then it eventually became its own independent religion. In a parallel manner, Buddhism originated as a path within the context of the Vedic tradition. It was only several centuries after the passing of the Buddha himself that Buddhism then emerged as an independent religion. It actually took much longer for Buddhism to break away from its parent religion than it took for Christianity to do so. For the first several hundred years of its existence, then, the teachings of the Buddha were considered to be a part of Sanatana Dharma.

Gautama Siddhartha, the Buddha, himself was known to have actually been a Sanatana Dharmi, a strict follower of the Vedic way. He was born a follower of the Vedic tradition. He was a Vedic prince and a member of the Shakya clan, a Vedic tribe in North India. He practiced Sanatana Dharma all of his life, and he died as a Sanatana Dharmi. The Buddha himself never proclaimed that he was renouncing Sanatana Dharma, and at no point did he claim that he was starting a new religion. The Buddha, in other words, was himself not a "Buddhist" in the sectarian sense of this term.

The similarities between Sanatana Dharma and Buddhism are many. General Buddhist philosophy, cosmology and practices were very similar to those of Sanatana Dharma. The further back we go in history, the more similar the two traditions were. If we examine the Buddha's original teachings as they are found in the Pali cannon, which is the original language of the earliest layer of Buddhist sacred texts, we find that those teachings were very similar to what we find in the Vedic *Upanishads*.

The concept of Dharma - a belief in Natural Law, the Natural Way - is central both to Sanatana Dharma and to Buddha Dharma. Indeed, the very heart of Buddhism to this very day consists of the Three Jewels (Tri-ratna) of Buddha/Dharma/Sangha. Another similarity is the concept of the tripartite structure of the universe. According to both Sanatana Dharma and Buddhism (and many other ancient spiritual traditions), the universe consists of a) **Bhu**: the middle plane that human beings are situated within, in addition to b) **Svarga**: a higher plane of heavenly beings, occupied by the gods and goddesses (*devas* and *devis*), and finally c) **Pata-la**: a lower, hellish plane of demonic beings (*asuras*). As a result of *karma* and re-incarnation, we have the ability to traverse throughout this tripartite universe from one lifetime to another.

We know that the Buddha practiced both Yoga and meditation, which are foundational practices of Sanatana Dharma. Yoga and meditation are central to both Sanatana Dharma and Buddhism to this day. One of the most advanced and unique forms of Buddhist yoga is found in Tibet very specifically. There are *asanas* that are found in Tibetan Buddhist Yoga that were also found previously in the Vedic tradition of Hatha Yoga. We know that the individuals who served as the Buddha's teachers were Vedic *yogis* and *gurus*. Buddhist ritual *puja* and *yajna* (fire ceremony) are to this day extremely similar to the *puja* and *yajna* found in Sanatana Dharma. How the monks of both traditions dress is very similar, with shaved head, ochre robes, and meditation beads worn around the neck or wrist. Often if one were to see a Vedic monk and a Buddhist monk at the same time, there would be little difference in their appearance. Ethics as well, for example the ethics of *ahimsa*, or non-violence, is central to both traditions. There are literally hundreds of additional similarities between the traditions of Sanatana Dharma and Buddhism.

We need to understand, however, that there is a vast distinction between who the Buddha was and what the he actually taught, versus what we witness today as a contemporary Buddhism that has undergone 2500 years of transformation and change. There is a radical difference between the Buddha and contemporary Buddhism in the same manner that there is a radical difference between Jesus and contemporary post-Nicene Christianity. There is a radical difference between Jesus the person, and what he taught and how he acted, versus the concretized institution that has developed for two thousand years known as Christianity. Jesus and Christianity are not synonymous.

In the same way, Buddha and contemporary Buddhism are not synonymous. We know that the original teachings of the Buddha were actually synonymous with Sanatana Dharma. Strictly speaking, we could say that it was a bare bones version of Sanatana Dharma. However, Buddhism at it exists presently has changed throughout its history quite dramatically since the time of the Buddha. There have been alterations in original, paleo-Buddhism that are now accepted as mainstream Buddhist teachings, but which nonetheless are dogmas the Buddha himself did not teach. We know this by examining the original Pali canon of Buddhism.

Despite the fact that Buddhism has become extremely popular in the Western world in recent decades, most Western Buddhist practitioners tend to lack a very in-depth knowledge about what Buddhist philosophy actually teaches. Almost once a month, for example, I will encounter a person who will tell me that they have recently decided to become Buddhist. My response to them usually will be, "Oh that's wonderful. So you're an Atheist then?" To which they will respond, "Oh no, no, I believe in God. I want to know God. That's what I'm actually trying to achieve." I'll then explain to them, "But you do know that Buddhism is officially Atheist? Buddhism does not believe in God and they're very strict about that philosophical assertion." When I ask the new Buddhist this, the person will either admit that they did not know that contemporary Buddhism is officially an atheist religion, or else they will state, "Oh I know. I read that, but that doesn't matter. I still choose to believe in God." Next I will ask the person, "Well okay, then you don't believe in the concept of your own soul, that you are an eternal being who will have perpetual existence?" To which the new convert to Buddhism will more often than not reply, "Of course I believe in the soul!" "But you do understand that Buddhism denies the existence of any permanent soul?", I will then continue to ask, "You understand that Buddhism, from the Dalai Lama on down to most knowledgeable lay-practitioners, are very strict about this doctrine that there is no permanent self? Contemporary Buddhists will very proudly proclaim that they do not believe in any Divine being, or God, and that they do not believe that there is any permanent self." Of course, the answer that I will usually get from the American Buddhist is "Well, I know, I understand this is Buddhist doctrine; and that may be what the Dali Lama chooses to believe...*but I believe in an eternal soul!*" Thus we tend to witness an inherent philosophical confusion on the part of many Western converts to Buddhism.

More, this confusion points to an unsurpassable contradiction that we witness in contemporary Buddhist philosophy. On the one hand, it is a natural human desire to want to know the Divine, and to yearn for spiritual liberation. However, we also understand intuitively that it is impossible to know the Divine if there is no Divine, and it is impossible to achieve liberation if there is no actual conscious being to be liberated.

Now this is the question. How did we get from this wonderful enlightened sage known as the Buddha, who taught the practice of Dharma, Yoga and meditation as the path to liberation (*nirvana*), to what we have today in the form of a contemporary Buddhism that is extolling a philosophy that is demonstrably different from the Buddha's original teachings?

Within the context of history we have seen that religions do change over time. We have seen that what was originally pure, in time, necessarily becomes impure, and that this is a degenerative principle that is operative regardless of the spiritual teaching in question. The nature of religion is such that there will be always be a pure being who appears on the world scene; it can be either a Buddha, a Jesus, a Prabhupada, or any other pure spiritual being whom we can think of. A being will appear who has had his own profound mystical experience that has transformed him from a mere human being to a transcendent Master. As a result of that profound change in him, others who then encounter that being will begin to also feel that change start to affect them as well. The sage's disciples learn as much as they can from that person. But then the sage eventually dies. Even enlightened spiritual beings have to eventually leave their bodies.

What we consequently witnessed in such perennial scenarios is that, as time goes on, and generation after generation of spiritual practitioners has elapsed, the original followers of that great sage are no longer alive. As more time elapses, first five, then ten generations has gone by, with the religion having become more institutionally powerful and politically oriented, more theologically and philosophically divided, with each passing generation. It is an axiomatic constant that over time religions change.

Institutions will change. Religions as institutions will become corrupt. There is no question that they will. What true spiritual practitioners hold onto, however, is the spirit of the original sage. What we hold onto is the original spirit of the *rishis*, a Buddha, a Jesus, a Prabhupada, and what it is that these great sages actually taught. This is precisely why many today make a distinction between religion and spirituality. The same process of philosophical enervation eventually happened with Buddhism as well.

There were three Buddhist councils that took place within the first few hundred years after the Buddha's passing. The first Buddhist council was a conference that took place very soon after the passing away of the Buddha himself, his *pari-nirvana*, or final enlightenment. In that council,

the sacred scriptures of Buddhism were collected. This became the Tripi-
taka, or what is called the Three Baskets of sacred Buddhist literature.
The second council was not quite as noteworthy. Basically they had a
second Buddhist council to resolve a dispute about whether monks
should be handling money.

It was with the third council that Buddhism as it was known up to that
time radically changed. The third council was convened under the emperor Ashoka (circa 304-232 BCE) in India. The emperor Ashoka is
usually depicted by historical revisionist scholars as a heroic figure due to
the fact that he was the person who initially institutionalized Buddhism in
a form very close to what we have today.

Truthfully, for those who understand the necessity of not tampering with
authentic spiritual traditions, Ashoka was actually a villain in world religious history. His actions in relation to Buddhism were parallel to the
Roman emperor Constantine's actions toward the original path taught by
Jesus. The abiding damage that Constantine did to Christianity in his attempt to rigidly institutionalize it, and in his sometimes-violent
suppression of dissenting Christian voices, was originally witnessed in the
similar damage that Ashoka ravaged upon Buddhism five hundred years
earlier. Ashoka himself was a Vedic king who became a follower of Buddhism at a certain point because he was tired of the violence of war that
he had witnessed in his life as a monarch. This newly peaceful military
man decided to take up the teachings of the Buddha and to then convene
a council of some of the most important Buddhist leaders of that time.

At that time there were many diverse schools of thought on what the
Buddha taught. Most Buddhists up until this point still believed in a posi-

tive Absolute and in the existence of *atman,* or a true and eternal self. Most Buddhists did believe in a metaphysical reality beyond the empirical and intellectual realms. However, not all Buddhists agreed. The purpose of this infamous Buddhist council was purportedly to reconcile all the various philosophical disagreements that existed in the Buddhist community. Those Buddhists who did believe in *atman* and who believed in a positive Absolute were afterwards suppressed, and in some cases quite violently so. Ashoka is known to have even sent his soldiers to several monasteries on a few occasions to burn them to the ground because they disagreed with the new and rigidly institutionalized dogma that Ashoka had forced upon the Buddhist Sangha (community).

Ashoka essentially formed the institution of Buddhism as we have it today, and all other dissenting schools of thought were subsequently suppressed. That was the first major alteration of paleo-Buddhism that Ashoka was responsible for. The second of his actions that was designed to solidify this dramatic change in post-Third Council Buddhism was that he sent Buddhist monks and missionaries throughout the entire world, including many parts of Europe, to spread his new version of Buddha Dharma. We know for a fact that Buddhist monks sent by Ashoka reached as far West as Greece and the Roman republic. We also know that they reached as far as Egypt and that, in fact, there was a Buddhist community in Alexandria that existed for hundreds of years up until approximately the fourth century when it was finally violently suppressed by the nascent Christian rulers of Egypt.

Let us now look deeper into what the Buddha actually taught, and then examine some of the post-Third Council distortions that crept into Buddhism, and that are still mistakenly accepted as authentic Buddhism to this day. I mentioned earlier that the Buddha himself had taught a bare bones, minimalist, version of Sanatana Dharma. The Buddha himself was actually not very interested in speaking overtly about metaphysical subject matters. Often, when people approached him and asked him such questions as, "What is your opinion about God? What is the nature of ultimate self? What is the nature of anything that transcends materiality?", his answer would almost invariably be that he did not wish to discuss such transcendent subjects. His reasoning for avoiding such topics was the following.

Spiritually, according to the Buddha, we presently find ourselves in an emergency situation. We understand that we are beings who are currently experiencing suffering. We need to alleviate that suffering. We need *nirvana*, or spiritual emancipation. In the Pali literature it describes an example that he gave to illustrate the nature of our spiritual emergency. If you find yourself in a field and are suddenly hit by an arrow, you have two distinct choices. You can look at the arrow and try to speculate about the arrow. "Oh who shot this arrow? What direction could it have come from? What is the arrow made out of?" Or you can save yourself and try to remove the arrow as quickly as possible. Thus, the Buddha's concern was a very immediate one. His goal was not theological speculation, philosophical wrangling, nor debating what is the nature of God, but his was a very simple goal. We are suffering. How do we cease that suffering? According to the Buddha, we suffer because we desire. Why do we desire? We desire because we have ego.

One of the doctrines of the Buddha, as well as of Sanatana Dharma in general, is that of dependant origination, or *pratitya samutpada*. *Pratitya samutpada* teaches that everything that exists is dependent upon some-

236

thing else, which is in turn dependent upon something else, *ad infinitum*. The goal of life is to understand the causally dependent, and therefore temporal, nature of this world, and to thus take shelter of the atemporal. To become awakened to the atemporal reality is to have achieved *nirvana*, enlightenment. This is the gist of the teachings of the Buddha. At no point did he deny that there is an Absolute. He did not deny the existence of an eternal self. He simply did not wish to talk about such metaphysical matters, and he even provided his own explanation for why this was the case.

Hundreds of years after the Buddha's remarkable life, several philosophical propositions ended up becoming a part of Buddhism that were not reflective of what the Buddha himself actually taught, but which are now accepted as standard Buddhist philosophy. Two of these dogmas were the idea that there is no permanent self, and that there is no Absolute. A third departure from the Buddha's original teachings was created by a famous Buddhist philosopher Nagarjuna, who lived roughly 150-250 AD.

Nagarjuna came up with a very interesting doctrine termed *shunyata* in Sanskrit, or "nothingness". *Shunyata* was a teaching originated by Nagarjuna, which then in turn became the official teaching of most of Mahayana Buddhism. The idea of *shunyata* is that there is no Absolute other than nothingness. According to Nagarjuna, if we were to analyze anything around us that is either perceptual or conceptual, including the components and constituents of materiality, and even our own thoughts, we can ultimately break all things down, reducing them to the point where we find nothingness. This was the teaching of Nagarjuna. This in turn, became the primary teaching of much of contemporary Buddhism, and especially the Mahayana branch of Buddhism. So Buddhism as it exists today has several doctrines that the Buddha himself did not actually originate or teach, including the ideas that there is no self, that there is no God and that ultimate reality is nothingness.

We will now explore how the original and authentic teachings of the Buddha fit into a more Vedic context, and how we can understand these teachings both spiritually and practically in such a manner that we can then incorporate the positive Vedic teachings of the Buddha into our spiritual practice.

The teachings of the Buddha are what I have termed a *via negativa*. This is Latin for a negative path, a negative way. Negative in this sense does not mean bad, but rather a path of negation. To further elaborate, when we want to actively explore the constitutional makeup of reality, there are one of two approaches that we can take. The first approach is the path of negation, which attempts to grasp what is reality not. "Reality is not this", "reality is not that", is a *via negativa*, or a path of negation. In Vedantic terminology, such a path of negation is referred to as *neti-neti*, or "Not this. Not that." The next route naturally following from this is the path of *via positiva*, or the path of positively establishing what reality is.

The teachings of the Buddha are very simply a *via negativa*. He tells us what reality is not. This fact is reflected in some of the central teachings of the Buddha, for example in the concept of *anitya*, the principle that nothing material is eternal, that everything is temporary. Everything that we see around us, according to the principle of *anitya*, is in flux. Things may seem permanent to our empirical vision, but they are not. The chair that a person is sitting on has enough permanency to it that he can sit on it safely. However, the very same chair that the person is sitting on is also imperceptibly changing at every moment. All the atoms are changing. It is disintegrating in such a manner that the very chair that the person is sitting on currently will not be here in several hundred years. All buildings eventually will disappear. Our own bodies eventually disintegrate. All matter is impermanent.

Everything that we can point to goes through this process of constant change. As a result of this, we know that there is nothing permanent in material reality. In this way, what the Buddha teaches us is what Truth is not. Truth is not merely the physical world. Truth is not merely the physical body. Truth is not even the temporary thoughts of the mind or intellect. Truth is nothing that we can point to that is impermanent. By thus analyzing the reality around us, and by analyzing even our own selves in this way, and understanding this distinction between that permanent reality that we are seeking versus that which is not permanent, we can then negate that which is illusory in nature. This *via negativa* path is, in a nutshell, what the Buddha taught.

There is, however, a difficulty that arises when we employ a *via negativa* to the exclusion of any positive grasp of reality. When we go through this entire process of negating reality, and grasping that all material reality is temporary - that the body is temporary, the mind is temporary, the intellect is temporary, the ego is temporary, and everything material is temporary - once we have negated all perceptual and conceptual reality, what then do we have left? Unfortunately, these are the areas of philosophical concern on which the Buddha was purposefully silent. The Buddha's teachings were primarily concerned with what reality is not.

What is there, then, that is permanent? What are the positive qualities of the soul? What are we as eternal beings? What are we positively? Both the Buddha himself, and certainly contemporary Buddhism, do not address these questions in any satisfying way. The Buddha chose not to address these questions, and contemporary Buddhism is incapable of addressing these questions.

The practical distinction between Buddhism and Sanatana Dharma is the following. While Buddhist teachings only brings us to the neutral point of knowing what both we and our material reality are not, Sanatana Dharma offers the further stage of directly and positively addressing the metaphysical issues that form the very foundation of the illusory reality that Buddhism negates. The entire spectrum of philosophical concern in the Vedic system includes conclusive knowledge of the nature of the positive Absolute (Brahman), the eternal self (*atman*), the attributes (*visheshas*) of both Brahman and *atman*, in addition to addressing the illusory nature of temporal material reality (Jagat). Sanatana Dharma is a *via positiva* that presents the whole picture of reality.

Sanatana Dharma is actually in complete agreement with the Buddha's original, pre-Third Council and pre-Nagarjuna teachings. Sanatana Dharma agrees with everything that he taught. The only difference is that the Buddha purposefully only went to a certain point and chose not to venture beyond that point. On those topics upon which the Buddha chose to be silent, the *Upanishads*, the *Bhagavad Gita*, and the rest of the scriptures of Sanatana Dharma are anything but silent.

7.2.1 Jesus: The Dharma Master

We all understand just how rare it is to find an authentic jewel. If you are walking down the typical sidewalk, it is not a very common occurrence to look down and see a precious jewel merely sitting there waiting for you to pick it up. It is a very rare occurrence. In the same way, to find gold is also a very rare thing. That is why prospectors will traditionally go to very secluded areas, repeatedly shaking dirt and mud through their prospector's pan until they finally find that one little gem, that one little piece of actual gold. The prospector knows that so rare an occurrence is this find, that it is a cause for celebration.

Even more rare in this world than finding a jewel, or finding gold, or finding anything of very great and rare value is to find an individual who is a pure devotee of God. Such a sage is an individual who lives his life is such a way that God is vividly present, manifest within that person. Some people will venture to traverse the world in their quest to find such a liberated being. There are many different names for these sorts of beings. In the Vedic tradition such an individual is known as a *guru*, or a *rishi*, or a *sadhu*, a person who has the ability to reveal the truth to others because they themselves have seen the truth. In the Buddhist tradition they are called a Buddha, one who is awakened. They are also called the Bodhisattva, one who manifests goodness in his very being. In the Western world we call them saints, or sages, or enlightened beings. There are many names for these beings in many different traditions of the world. Jesus was one such enlightened and empowered being, and he is the person whom we will be discussing in this section of the book.

In the last two thousand years there have been many differing images of

Jesus, and many different perspectives on the significance of the personality of Jesus. Many people have been killed, and many people have killed, in the name of Jesus. Many monolithic church institutions have been built in the name of Jesus. Many civilizations and peoples have been destroyed in the name of Jesus. Thus, when we speak about this one being known as Jesus, there have been so many different perspectives on this one being; and interestingly, this fact in itself actually reveals to a significant degree the very power of that great personality.

There is a tremendous amount of confusion on the part of the average person about who Jesus is. What I will be writing about in this section of the book is the nature of the personality of Jesus from the Dharma perspective, from the perspective of Truth, and not merely the perspective of sectarianism, denominationalism, theology, Christology, or subjective opinion. We will explore Jesus as he was and as he is.

In traditional Christianity, Jesus is considered to be both perfect man and perfect God. He is wholly and simultaneously each. In actuality, there is some truth to this assertion. From the Dharma perspective Jesus was a human being. He was a being just like any one of us. The major difference between Jesus and us, however, is that he chose to perfect himself in such a manner that he ceased to be merely human. He perfected himself in such a manner that he rid himself of ego, hate, anger, lust and greed. He purged and freed himself from all of these lesser flaws that so many of us as human beings manifest in our daily lives, and then conversely, he positively filled himself with God's love. What Jesus ended up becoming in his own being was quite literally a human manifestation of God's Love.

In Sanatana Dharma it is taught that such transcending of illusory ego, coupled with manifesting God's love in our lives, is the goal of life for each of us. We live in this world so that we too can perfect ourselves spiritually. When we talk about perfecting ourselves, we are not speaking in a mere quantitative sense, as in a type of spiritual Olympics. Rather, spiritual perfection is qualitative in nature. We are all meant, like Jesus, to perfect ourselves, to rid ourselves of false ego and selfishness, and to instead become as selfless as a Jesus. We are called upon to achieve this Christ-like state of spiritual perfection. When, like the great *guru* Jesus, we finally have the ability to fill ourselves with God's love and grace, we then become a living vehicle for that love and grace.

The following story illustrates the path that was followed by Jesus, and which we are also meant to follow, of emptying ourselves of illusory ego and filling ourselves with God's grace. Lord Krishna is often depicted playing a flute. Once, Radharani approached him and asked Him: "Oh! Krishna, this flute is so fortunate that it is constantly in your company. It is touching your lips and you are blowing your Divine breath through it. What has this flute done that it should earn such grace from You?" And this is how Krishna responded to Radharani's question. Very simply, Sri Krishna said: "This flute has emptied itself." It emptied itself. What does this mean? If you have a stick of wood that does not have an empty portion dug through it, then it cannot serve as a flute. The flute quite literally had to empty itself such that it could then serve God's purpose. We too are meant to be a vehicle of God's grace in just the same way. We are meant to empty ourselves of our own selfishness self-interest. When we do empty ourselves in just this manner, we then find that we are not actually empty. We discover that we are then filled with God.

Such was the nature and path of Jesus, as all great *gurus* before him. He was a being who was so filled with God's grace that when a person looked upon him, they did see a human being with a head, with arms, with legs, and with a body, who had to sleep, drink water, and who had to eat. But at the same time they were also seeing God. This was the case because, Jesus' will and God's will were one. Thus when 2000 years ago, people looked upon Jesus, many had the intelligence to know that they were also observing God's grace manifest in a perfected human being. They were observing what in Sanatana Dharma is termed an *avesha-avatara*, or a human being who was a direct manifestation of God's power. This esoteric teaching was lost as the original teachings of Jesus become institutionalized and Abrahamized with the later marriage of the church with the Roman state apparatus.

How did the original Dharmic teachings of Jesus revert to the Abrahamic model after his passing? *Because it is always easier for human beings to worship than it is for them to follow.* It is easier to take a divine sage like Jesus and to merely place him upon an altar, rather than attempt to follow in his footsteps and to become like him. To follow in the footsteps of Jesus and to become like Jesus is certainly difficult. However, this is precisely what Jesus wanted of his sincere followers.

In this regard, the Gospels are very illuminating, because they contain the actual words and actions of Jesus. In the Gospel of John 10:30, Jesus makes the statement that, "I and the Father are one." In contemporary Christian theology, this passage is misinterpreted to mean that Jesus is God, and that we are thus meant to simply worship Jesus from afar. In actuality, the tradition of Sanatana Dharma understands that this statement is pointing to the concept of Jesus empting himself of ego and filling himself with the grace of God. More, this verse also demonstrates how we too are meant to follow in Jesus' path of self-surrender (*prapatti*) in such a manner that eventually we too can one day declare that, "I and the Father are one."

We all know the illustrative story of the wealthy man who approached Jesus wanting to become his disciple. Jesus told the rich man that he could become a follower, but only if he agreed to take all of his wealth, give it to the poor, and with no material possession left, follow in the footsteps of Jesus. With this request, the man shrunk away and said that he could not. Jesus walked away from the man. Afterwards his disciples asked him why did he did this. And Jesus said to his disciples that it is easier for a camel to fit through the eye of a needle than for a rich man to get into heaven. Interestingly, this rich man had faith in Jesus. He believed everything that Jesus was saying. Indeed, he "accepted Jesus as his Lord and Savior", as televangelists love to repeatedly harangue their flock to do. This man did accept Jesus as his Lord and Savior...and yet Jesus rejected him. This man had faith...but Jesus rejected him. Why? It was because he could not follow. Again, to simply worship Jesus from afar is simply not enough. We are meant to follow directly in Jesus' footsteps.

This is how Jesus himself explains the importance of spiritual practice in Matthew, 16:24-26. "Then Jesus said to his disciples, 'If anyone would come after me, he must deny himself and take up this cross and follow me.'" Jesus explains that "...he must deny himself". We are meant to deny our lower self, the illusory self, that which we think we are, but which is not our true essence. According to the authentic teachings of Jesus as recorded in the Gospel of Matthew, to follow Jesus means to deny this lower self, to deny the illusory ego and take up his cross. It is only when we have the ability understand Jesus as a perfected *guru*, as a teacher, that suddenly Jesus's teaching and life begin to make full sense to us. Through the Vedic world-view, we can understand Jesus in a more vivid way, in such a way that actually touches us and has meaning for us.

Jesus was a person who found himself understanding the highest, realizing the highest, wanting to teach the highest in an Abrahamic culture that could barely even understand the lowest. An intelligent teacher teaches in accordance with his audience. It is a display of true compassion to teach in accordance with what one's audience can understand. If a teacher has a class of first graders, that teacher would not be showing compassion by teaching those students lessons that can only be understood in the third year of college. A true teacher teaches in accordance with his audience's capacity to understand. Jesus was a true teacher, and taught in accordance with this principle. Jesus often taught in parables. The reason why he taught in parables is because his teaching was not for everyone. Rather, it was especially designed for those individuals who had the ability to not just listen, but to truly understand, to not just see, but to have clear transcendental vision (*tattva-darshana*).

This dual method of teaching that Jesus employed is clearly explained in the Gospel of Mark, 4:33-34. "With many similar parables Jesus spoke the Word to them, the crowds that followed him, and as much as they could understand. He did not say anything to them without using a parable, but when he was alone with his own disciples he explained everything." Thus, he had a simpler message for the less noble, Abrahamic masses, and a higher message for those who had the ability to fully understand. Earlier in Mark, 4:10-11, Jesus actually confirms this in his own words: "The secret of the kingdom of God has been given to you.

But to those on the outside everything is said in parables so they may be ever seeing, but never perceiving, and ever hearing, but never understanding." It is understood in Sanatana Dharma that for the true teacher, the highest teachings are given only to those individuals who have the ability to not just listen, but to truly understand the deeper esoteric purport of the teacher's words.

Jesus was not a Christian. Jesus was a Dharma Master. The original teachings of Jesus are synonymous with the teachings of Sanatana Dharma. They are echoes of such earlier works as the *Bhagavad Gita* and the *Upanishads*, as well as the divine utterances that were revealed from the lips of all the great *rishis, yogis*, and *gurus* of the Vedic tradition. Like Sanatana Dharma, Jesus taught that the nature of reality lies within. The Kingdom of God is neither a geographic entity, nor is it situated only at a certain time in history. The Kingdom of God is a transcendent reality that lies within. The true nature of that Kingdom is self-luminous. Our very selves (*atman*) are reflective of that light of the Kingdom of God. The Kingdom of God is known as Vaikuntha in the Sanskrit language, the "realm of no anxiety" of Sriman Narayana. In this and many other ways, Jesus proved himself to have been a pure follower of Sanatana Dharma."

There are several beautiful verses from the Gospels that help us to understand the authentic teachings of Jesus in this refreshing new light. For example, in Luke, 17:20-21, there is the following story. "One day the Pharisees asked Jesus, 'When will the kingdom of God begin?' Jesus replied, 'The Kingdom of God isn't ushered in with visible signs. You won't be able to say, 'It has begun here in this place or there in that part of the country.' For the Kingdom of God is within you.'" More, in Matthew, 5:14-16. Jesus tells his disciples: "You are the light of the world. A city set on a hill cannot be hidden. Let your light shine before men in such a way that they may see your good works, and glorify your Father who is in heaven."

Before we can begin any process of spiritual attainment, we have to first understand what is the nature of our true self. We need to understand that, indeed, as Jesus proclaimed, "The Kingdom of God is within you." (Luke 17:21) Every positive acquirement that we are searching for externally, including happiness, prosperity, goodness and beauty, all of these objects of our search in actuality lay within. There is a hidden treasure laying deep within the heart of every living being, and that hidden treasure is our own soul, which in itself is a partial manifestation of God, a part and parcel, a small spark of the Divine.

Another practice that Jesus taught is the concept of devotion to God. There is a specific incident, among many, that is illustrative of Jesus' approach to devotional consciousness. This beautiful story is found in the Gospel of Mark 12:41-44. "Jesus sat down opposite the area where the offerings were placed for the temple and watched the crowd putting their donations into the temple treasury. Many rich people threw in large amounts, but a poor widow came and put two very small copper coins in, worth only a fraction of a penny. Calling to his disciples, Jesus said 'I tell you the truth this poor widow has put more into the treasury than all the others. They all gave out of their wealth, but she out of her poverty put in everything, all she had to live on.'"

Such is the nature of devotion to God, that spiritual growth is not viewed merely in terms of quantity, but in the quality of one's actions. It is not

248

how much you give that determines one's spiritual depth. Rather, it is the sincerity, the humility, the love and the devotion with which you give that is the crucial spiritual factor. This is how we know God, not by making a big show, not by externals, but through love and self-surrender. Why was this widow glorified by Jesus? She was not glorified because she was poor, as many shortsighted Liberation Theologians would claim. There are plenty of poor people who have no love. She was glorified because she gave to God out of love. Such devotional consciousness is called *bhakti* in the Vedic tradition.

Finally, we also find in the teachings of Jesus the highest conclusion of the *Bhagavad Gita* itself, which is called *prapatti* in Sanskrit - or self-surrender to God. It is taught in the *Bhagavad Gita*, in the philosophy of Yoga spirituality, and in Sanatana Dharma in general that the very highest spiritual path designed to reveal the truth is the path of surrender (*prapatti-marga*) to that truth, the path of surrender to God. Jesus himself exhibits the perfect example of self-surrender in Mark, 14:36 when he is about to be crucified by the envious Abrahamists. Jesus prays to God and states, "Abba, Father, all things are possible for you. Please take this cup away from me. Nevertheless not what I will, but may your will be done."

Such a consciousness of surrender is the example that Jesus has gifted to us all. Towards the end of his ministry, he understood that the very people whom he was trying to teach the very highest of spiritual ideals to could scarcely even understand what he had tried to share with them, and that they were going to kill him. Knowing this, it was not Jesus' choice to die at the hands of the ignorant masses. In fact, he asked God to kindly take this away such a burden. However, "...not what I will, but may your will be done." This is the nature of surrender.

We find a parallel to Jesus' teaching on self-surrender in the *Bhagavad Gita*. In the eighteenth chapter of the *Bhagavad Gita*, Krishna finally says to Arjuna,

> *Sarva-dharman parityajya mam ekam sharanam vraja
> aham tvam sarva-papebhyo mokshayishyami ma shucaha.*"

"Abandon all lesser varieties of religiosity and simply surrender unto Me. I shall deliver you from all negative reactions. Do not fear." (*Bhagavad Gita*, 18:66)

This is the highest path for any true saint or sage, regardless of where they are situated historically or geographically, regardless of whether it is a Jesus, or a Buddha, a great *yogi*, a *rishi* or a sage of any authentic Dharma tradition. If we want to embrace truth in a living way, we must surrender to that Truth. Jesus showed us this as he hung on the Cross.

We are all destined to surrender to God in different ways. Again, Jesus was the *guru*; thus he wanted to give us a very vivid example. We are not all meant to necessarily die on a cross. But we are all called upon to also surrender, to "pick up our own cross" in ways that will be different for different people. But, ultimately, we are meant to surrender if we are to know that Truth. This is a teaching that is not meant for everyone, but only for those few who truly can hear, only for those who truly can see. The eyes see, but the soul understands.

7.3.1 Sanatana Dharma and Islam

In its relatively short, and decidedly Abrahamic-centric, history, a wide
variety of academic terms have arisen from within the discipline known
as Religious Studies in the expressed order of assisting the field to more
ably grasp the structure and outlook of various religious sects and institutions. One pair of such terms that we encounter are the concepts of
"Expansive" versus "Contractive". It is important to note that these two
words are used by scholars, not with the intent of ascribing a superiority
status to any one particular sect or religious phenomenon over another,
or of denigrating any particular religious belief system, but with the aim
of rationally understanding the functional and attitudinal aspects of differing religious institutions. In the following section, I will illustrate the
two very different religious traditions: Sanatana Dharma and Islam by
using the terms Expansive and Contractive.

Before we begin, however, it is important to first explain the difference
between these two academic terms. An expansive religion is one that
tends toward social and philosophical inclusiveness. Overall, such spiritual paths tend to be both tolerant of internal differences of opinion, as
well as open to positive contributions from outside the institutional
bounds of the faith. Generally, they seek to embrace the social, political
and philosophical realities that exist outside the sectarian confines of the
religion. Expansive religions are inherently open, classically liberal, accepting and rooted in the ancient.

By marked contrast, a contractive religion is exclusivist in nature. Members of contractive sects tend to view themselves as being thoroughly
separated from non-believers by virtue of their own espousal of the "one

and only true faith". Unlike expansive religions, contractive faiths tend to be highly suspicious of both internal dissent, as well as of perceived external challenges. Consequently, such faiths will often suppress any attempts at reform, change and renewal from within, and will repeatedly wage both ideological and martial war against other faiths that they consider to be at odds with their own rigidly cherished notions of truth. Such faiths are reactionary and historically more recent (i.e., no more than two-thousand to four-thousand years old).

7.3.2 Sanatana Dharma: Inclusiveness, Tolerance, Compassion

It has been argued by numerous scholars and practitioners that the religion of Sanatana Dharma is radically expansive by nature. This expansiveness can be seen, first, in the realm of traditional Vedic philosophical and theological thought. The six schools of Vedic philosophy (Shad-Darshanas), while completely united in their assessment and acceptance of the basic philosophical foundations of Sanatana Dharma, are also seemingly diverse in their respective approaches (*upaya*) to *moksha*, or the ultimate spiritual attainment of liberation. For example, while the Samkhya school of Vedic philosophy posits a dualistic ontology, juxtaposing the two distinct elements of *purusha* (spirit) and *prakriti* (matter), the school of Advaita Vedanta contrarily sees reality in purely monistic terms. For Shankara's Advaita, there is only one substance in reality: Brahman, or unbounded consciousness.

For Vedanta, on the one hand, ritual is generally viewed as being merely a collection of symbolic rites, the efficacy of which is negligible in contrast with the attainment of *brahma-vidya*, or the knowing of Brahman; but for the Mimamsa school of Vedic philosophy, ritual in accordance with Vedic injunction is the highest religio-philosophical activity that can be performed by human beings. Despite the diversity and freedom of opinion that has existed both within and between these many schools of Vedic thought, these schools have all peacefully co-existed for thousands of years, preferring to do battle in the realm of civil academic debate rather than on the bloody battlefields of supposed holy wars.

In keeping with this respect for diversity of opinion and thought, dozens of various traditions and schools of thought have arisen within the tolerant framework of Vedic culture, all united in a mutual respect of the Vedic literature as the highest epistemological authority for all Vedic schools. So open-minded has the Vedic outlook traditionally been that it has sometimes been mistakenly asserted by some Western academic observers of Sanatana Dharma that whatever an individual's particular belief, concern or practice may be, there is (or at least has at one time been) a branch of Sanatana Dharma that embraces it. While this claim is certainly a vast exaggeration on the part of some outside observers, the existence of such a claim does at least point to the fact that Sanatana Dharma is, indeed, a religion of tolerance, diversity and expansion.

The atmosphere of tolerance traditionally encouraged by Sanatana Dharma is dramatically seen in how Sanatana Dharma has historically dealt with heterodox religious and philosophical movements that later arose within the context of the Dharmic religio-cultural milieu. The religions of Buddhism, Jainism and Sikhism are three religions that originated as direct offshoots from Sanatana Dharma. Both Buddhism and Jainism began as ascetically oriented movements within mainstream Sanatana Dharma in the fifth century B.C.E. Sikhism, which was founded by the great Guru Nanak in the fifteenth century C.E., was an attempt to synthesize the profound philosophical insights of Sanatana Dharma with the zealous martial spirit of Islam. While all three of these heterodox Dharmic movements were founded as schools of thought within the greater rubric of Vedic culture, in time all three began to view themselves as religions distinct from the Vedic world-view.

Despite several major philosophical and religious differences between these three later Dharmic sects and Sanatana Dharma, however, most of the contention between these religions has remained on a purely philosophical level. At no time in South Asian history did there occur such instances of persecution and bigotry between these religions as was witnessed in the Inquisition, the Crusades or the witch-hunts so well known in the sad history of Abrahamic religious expression. Consequently, while it is certainly true that no religion falls perfectly into either the expansive or the contractive category, it is rather safe to say that Sanatana Dharma has overwhelmingly displayed more expansive characteristics throughout its long history than not.

7.3.3 Islam Means Submission

With the above caveat about the dangers of generalizing in mind, we will now explore a more contractive religion. Unlike the tolerance observed throughout the long and very illustrative history of Sanatana Dharma, the relatively new religion of Islam demands that its adherents follow a very rigidified code of beliefs, attitudes and practices. Every Muslim, for example, is required to uphold six religious beliefs. Muslims must believe: a) that there is only one true god, whose name is Allah, b) in the existence of a vast repertoire of semi-divine beings called angels, c) in a specific number of recognized prophets (ranging from Abraham to Muhammad, and including Jesus and Moses) who were purportedly sent by Allah to reveal his commandments upon humanity, d) in the revelations given by Allah to these specific prophets, e) in a final Day of Judgment in which all beings will either join Allah in his paradise or else perish eternally in hell, and f) in the doctrine of predestination (the idea that Allah has already preordained who will be saved and who will perish).

In addition to these six obligatory beliefs, it is required that each Muslim performs five practical religious duties, known as the Five Pillars of Islam. These are: 1) confession of the faith ("There is no god but Allah, and Muhammad is his prophet"), 2) prayers five times daily, 3) fasting during the month of Ramadan, 4) Almsgiving, and 5) the Hajj pilgrimage to Mecca. All people who do not follow these commands of Allah are traditionally considered by Muslims to be unbelievers, and are subsequently subject to conversion to the "one true faith" of Islam, or else subjugation or death.

In Islamic theo-political theory, the non-Muslim world is divided into two broad categories: a) Dhimmis, or people of "the book", and b) Heathens, or subhuman non-believers. The Dhimmis - Jews and Christians - are considered to be people of the Covenant because they are followers of the earlier revelations of the prophets Moses and Jesus, respectively. Dhimmis were therefore historically given relatively elevated protective status in the Islamic world. Despite this special treatment by Islamic rulers, however, Judaism and Christianity are still considered by Muslims to be religions that fall far short of being the true religion. Thus, Dhimmis are always under due pressure to convert to Islam.

Followers of all other religions that lay outside of the Judeo-Christian-

Islamic world-view, however, are looked upon as "heathens" by the Islamic religious law. Such "heathens" include Buddhists, Taoists, Sanatana Dharmis, Shintoists, Pagans, and the followers of all earth-centered indigenous religions. "Heathens", up until the last few hundred years, were considered third class citizens in Islamic societies, and were subject to forced conversion, special taxation and often severe persecution. The temples and sacred relics of such "heathens" were systematically destroyed; their priests, saints and sages were killed, and their histories rewritten by Islamic scholars. Indeed, according to the Qur'an itself: "Punish the unbelievers with garments of fire, hooked iron rods, boiling water; melt their skin and bellies." (22.19) Islam is considered by more liberal Muslims as being the most legitimate of all religions, and by its conservative elements as being the only true religion, all other forms of religious expression being but pale imitations of the "glory of Islam".

Not only do Muslims look upon non-Muslim religions with a very high degree of suspicion, but internal dissent is also rarely tolerated in Islam. Heterodox movements within Islam, such as the Shias, Druze and Alawites, are considered heretical, and their respective followers have historically been persecuted and killed by the majority Sunnis. In addition, strict Islamic societies are usually guided by the Sharia, the rigid code of religious laws and rules that governs the life and behavior of all Muslims. The strict demands placed upon believers, coupled with a lesser degree of tolerance than is exhibited in more expansive religions, make for a convincing argument that Islam would be considered a contractive religion by most objective academic observers.

It is crucial that the many varied and diverse religions of the world be studied, as much as is feasible, on their own terms, and from an objective perspective. Like all the many attempts that have arisen from the field of Religious Studies to analyze and categorize faith systems, the Expansive/Contractive definition is but an attempt to better understand the differences between the many diverse religions of the world. These terms are certainly helpful pointers to a general understanding of the specific religions under observation, but they are not designed to be perfect instruments in making such assessments. It is my hope that these two terms have assisted the reader somewhat in gaining a more objectively focused glimpse into the psychological, philosophical and social distinctions that exist between two very different, and in many ways thoroughly juxtaposed, world-views, that of Sanatana Dharma and Islam.

7.4.1 The Abrahamic World-view Versus the Dharmic World-view

Dharma represents cultural normality, psychological health, and living in concert with reality. Dharma has historically been the norm in human behavior and inter-relational dynamics. The birth of the Abrahamic world-view (circa 1800 BCE) marked a stark and very distinct break from this long-standing reality. The Abrahamic world-view (i.e., Judaism/Christianity/Islam/Marxism) posits itself as very consciously and purposefully juxtaposed to the world-view of Dharma. Abrahamism has historically viewed itself as inherently incompatible with Dharma, and as Dharma's polar opposite. In *The Dangers of Monotheism in the Age of Globalization*, Jean-Pierre Lehmann contrasts the Dharmic and Abrahamic ideologies. Speaking specifically within the context of ancient Greco-Roman Paganism versus the new Abrahamic Christian movement, Lehmann describes the conflict in the following way:

> The great pre-Christian civilizations of Greece and
> Rome had no religious wars and had a far healthier view
> of their frolicking gods and goddesses than the intole
> rant monotheistic Christianity that later came to domi
> nate Europe.

Abrahamism represents an artificial imposition on reality, an attempt to build a manmade (*paurusheya*) ladder to the Transcendent by consciously rejecting the very principles and culture of Transcendence itself.

7.4.2 The Abrahamic World-View

Judaism, Christianity and Islam are historically referred to as the "Abrahamic" religions because all three religions trace their origins to the prophet Abraham (circa 1812 BCE - 1637 BCE), and can thus be seen to be quite similar in many aspects of their respective outlooks. While some very important theological and ritual distinctions can be seen between them all, nonetheless Judaism, Christianity and Islam share a common world-view, psychological make-up, and guiding ethos.

All three religions share a great deal in common, including the following ten shared elements (to name only a few):

> 1. Acceptance of the teachings of the Old Testament proph
> ets (in addition to the OT prophets, Christianity also accepts
> Jesus. Islam, in addition to the OT prophets and Jesus, also ac
> cepts Muhammad).

> 2. Biblical anthropomorphic monotheism.

> 3. A profound sense of religious exclusivity.

> 4. The belief that theirs is the sole true faith, and that any other
> faith is necessarily a blasphemous affront.

258

5. The acceptance of violence, terror and aggressive missionary tactics to spread their religion.

6. A common sense of being at a war to the death, both figura tively and literally with the "Pagan" world (i.e., the Dharmic world).

7. The centrality of prayer to commune with the divine, and the exclusion of meditation.

8. A belief in the existence of angels, the devil, demonic spirits, etc.

9. All Abrahamic faiths teach the bodily resurrection, the Final Judgment, the post-natal creation of the soul (as opposed to the soul's pre-existence), the binding effects of sin, etc.

10. The importance of one specific day of the week set aside for prayer and rest. For Jews – Saturday. For most Christians - Sun day. For Muslims – Friday.

These are only a few of the elements of the Abrahamic world-view, of which Pauline Christianity is an integral part.

Below is a small list of differences between Dharmic and the Abrahamic world-views.

The Dharmic and Abrahamic World-views

DHARMA	ABRAHAMISM
Pro-Nature	Anti-Nature
Tolerant	Intolerant
Integrative	Conflictual
Inclusivistic	Exclusivistic
Not Patriarchal	Patriarchal
Divinity is Masculine/Feminine	Divinity is Exclusively Masculine
Qualitative Values	Quantitative Values
Cyclical	Linear
Panentheistic Monotheism	Anthropomorphic Monotheism
Compassion	Justice
Mercy	Law
Natural	Artificial
Art	Science
Omnisentiency	Homosentiency
Ethno-Pluralism	Ethno-Chauvinism
Beauty Revered	Beauty Feared
Women Respected	Women Oppressed
Vegetarian	Carnivorous
Rational	Emotional
Organic	Synthetic
Virtue	Morality
Acknowledgement of Lesser Divinities	El-Yahweh Only
Peaceful	Warlike
Non-imperialistic	Imperialistic
Philosophical	Dogmatic
Literate	Non-literate
Pre-denominational	Denominational

The contrast between these two opposing world-views is dramatic and as unbridgeable as night and day, evil and good, truth and untruth.

7.5.1 2000 Year Genocide Against Dharma

At one time in the not too distant past, most of humanity understood and attempted to live in accordance with Dharma. Consequently, people prospered, were healthier, happier, more satisfied, and lived in greater spiritual and material abundance than we do even today. Dharma sustained meaningful civilization, and prompted people to pursue peace, tolerance, nobility, excellence, wisdom, goodness, and Truth in all that they did and in all that they aspired for. Up until 2000 years ago, the concept of Dharma was universally held to be the highest standard of both civilized human behavior, as well as a healthy and balanced ordering of complex societal dynamics.

The word "Dharma" (Natural Law) is a term that has ordinarily been associated with the philosophical systems of Asia. This is an inaccurate linkage. In this work, I have been using the term "Dharma" in the more accurately defined universal and philosophical sense. The present global Dharma Movement consists not only of those Asian traditions that have always consciously identified themselves with the specific Sanskrit term "Dharma", such as Sanatana Dharma, Buddhism, Jainism, and Sikhism, but also with all those ancient spiritual cultures that have historically identified themselves with the world-view and ethos of Dharmic civilization and values under a vast myriad of alternate names. Some of these traditionally Dharmic cultures include (in addition to the historic traditions of South Asia) the majority of pre-Christian and pre-Abrahamic cultures, spiritual traditions, and civilizations on earth, such as Greco-Roman; Druidic; Asatruar; Taoist; Confucianist; Shintoist; Zoroastrian; Egyptian; Native American; Mayan; Incan; Reconstructionist Pagan; and many others. Some of these ancient Dharmic cultures are still thriving today. Many others have been forced to near extinction by centuries of unrelenting persecution, genocide, and wholesale mass conversion of their populations by the aggressive Abramahic religions originating from the interminably violent Middle East. Sadly, most individual Dharmic cultures of the world have been forced to extinction outright by the in-human barbarism of anti-Dharmic, Abrahamic forces. Some of these now extinct cultures include the traditional Celtic, Nordic, Persian, Berber, and Native American cultures, among many hundreds of others.

Up till 2000 years ago, the Dharmic world-view was by far the predominant world-view of most of humanity. This was the case until the radically anti-human and anti-nature Abrahamic ideology suddenly burst upon the world scene two millennia ago with a evangelical fury, religiously-inspired violence, and zealous civilization-destroying vengeance the likes of which the civilized world had never seen previously. Never before had the multiple ancient and noble pre-Christian cultures of the world ever experienced such massive destruction, death, persecution, forced conversion, spiritual genocide and cultural annihilation performed in the name of religion as it witnessed at the hands of the new, Abrahamic world-view that had arrived, seemingly out of nowhere, onto the world stage. It was in the wake of this never before experienced juggernaut of Biblically inspired destruction that the light of Dharma began to swiftly wane, and that Reality as it was known up till then was turned literally on its head. With the rapid ascent of the Abrahamic onslaught came the counter-proportional descent of Dharmic civilization as once great and noble cultures became the mysterious archeological ruins, the sources of incomprehensible "myth", and the dusty works of ancient literature uncomprehendingly dissected by our present day scholars.

Abrahamism, in retrospect, consists of a quadrangle of artificially constructed, new movements that all fall under the general term "Abrahamic", named after the infamous founder of religious exclusivity, Abraham. These four anti-nature ideologies are 1) Judaism, 2) Christianity, 3) Islam, and 4) Marxism. Whether we speak of Judeo-Christian "holy wars" and Inquisitions, or the bloody and unending Islamic jihads against perceived "infidels", or the genocide of over 100 million people in the name of Marxist revolution, all four of these Abrahamic movements have been responsible for more destruction, loss of life, and social anarchy than all other philosophical systems, religions, and ideologies in world history combined. The Abrahamic onslaught has been an unparalleled juggernaut of destruction.

More, while all four ideologies have remained seemingly divided by dogmatic, sectarian concerns, all Abrahamic movements have been fanatically united in both their origin, and in their shared aim of annihilating their perceived enemy of Dharma from the earth, and seeking sole domination of world power for themselves alone. Dharma and Abrahamism are exact opposites in every way. Dharma and Abrahamism stand for two radically opposed visions for humanity's future, the former standing for nature, peace, and tolerance, the latter standing in respective juxtaposition for artificiality, aggression, and fanaticism. They are the only two real ideological poles of significance throughout the history of the last two thousand years, with all lesser world-views and ideologies being ultimately subsumed under one or another of these two poles.

More, Dharma and Abrahamism are the only two meaningful ideological choices for individual human beings today. Unfortunately, for the duration of this Two-Thousand Year War, Dharma has been on the losing end as Abrahamism has continuously succeeded in its unrivalled ascendancy.

The purpose of this section is to tell the almost unknown story of the systematic destruction of Reality, and the sanity, happiness, and joy that were attendant upon that venerable Reality. What I call the "Two-Thousand Year War" is the history of the near death of Dharma. Another purpose of this section has been to serve as a clarion reminder - an antidote to our long-suffering collective amnesia - of what it means to truly have lives, and to have a society, that is based upon the very best of what nature has to offer us, and of what God has lovingly gifted us with.

Contrary to the false scenario that materialist historical revisionists have attempted to convince us of, there was indeed a time when people were happy, when government truly represented the people, and when society functioned in accordance with compassion, tolerance, and mutual concern. Such is the concept of the Dharma Nation (*dharma-rashtra*), the ideal of government that represents the political instantiation of Dharmic principles. In addition to exploring the philosophy, history and spiritual rewards of the Dharma experience, this book itself has been intended to serve as a programmatic guide for restoring Dharma to prominence as a positive global force in today's world. This is the manifesto for an ascendant Dharma.

Dharma is an eternal phenomenon, originating from the Divine will of the Absolute, and serving as the sustaining foundation of all reality.

Dharma was at one time the guiding principle of the planet. Dharma shall again serve to guide us all back to global sanity in the immediate future. Dharma is again ascending.

7.5.2 Twelve-Hundred Years of Battering

Sanatana Dharma is a religion that has faced over 1200 years of brutal battering and horrendous persecution at the hands of adherents of the Abrahamic religions - specifically Islam and Christianity. First, the Islamic conquerors attempted to quite literally physically annihilate Dharma – killing as many as 100 million Vedic followers, burning our libraries and sacred institutions of learning to the ground, denying us our right to worship, making us third-class citizens in our own nations, and destroying almost every single Vedic temple in North India and anywhere else they imposed their rule. Then the British came. When the British Raj was established, the Christian-inspired British did not attempt to physically annihilate Sanatana Dharma as the Muslims had earlier endeavored to do. Rather, the British Empire attempted a more genteel and sophisticated intellectual/cultural/spiritual annihilation of what remained of Vedic culture. The followers of Sanatana Dharma have been dealing with the negative effects of this less violent form of genocide to this very day.

As a direct result of this millennium-long persecution, we have a Sanatana Dharma that today finds itself only now beginning to arise from the smoldering ashes of this 1200 Year Holocaust. Sanatana Dharma is only now beginning to reconstruct itself from the ground up as an authentic, *shastra*-based Vedic tradition, to rid itself of all non-Dharmic influences over its philosophy and culture, and to begin finally to reassert itself again onto the world-stage.

What we find today is not a Sanatana Dharma that is at the height of its full strength and development, but a Sanatana Dharma is today only in the first few decades of an ongoing process of reconstructing itself. The valiant efforts of several recent Vedic spiritual leaders, such as Bhaktivedanta Swami Prabhupada, Maharishi Mahesh Yogi, Vedacharya Vamadeva Shastri (Dr. David Frawley), and others, have been of incalculable help in this regard. This present book itself - *Sanatana Dharma: The Eternal Natural Way* - is an integral part of that crucial philosophical reconstruction. This book is designed and destined to help lead the way to a state of global Vedic Restoration.

Chapter 8: Sanatana Dharma Today

8.1.1 The Current Global Crisis

It is no exaggeration to state that we are living in some of the most troubling times in recent memory. This is especially the case in the United States. Despite being the wealthiest and arguably most powerful nation the world has ever known, Americans are experiencing a collective state of pessimism about the future that has not been known since at least the Great Depression, if not as long ago as possibly even the Civil War. The real question is: what are the factual roots of the current economic and psychological crisis that we are facing? And more, what is its solution?

America seems to be seriously adrift. On the surface level, the peripheral symptoms of this crisis point to severe economic, social, political, and even environmental concerns. The deeper problem, however, is one of a decades long, continually increasing existential angst in the hearts and the minds of the people, even in the midst of an artificially constructed culture exclusively devoted to a seemingly unending commercial frenzy, entertainment-fueled escapism, and the rabid pursuit of self-pleasure at the expense of self-realization.

America has been a wealthy nation economically, but an impoverished nation spiritually. And now, more than at any other time in her history, the people of America are beginning to experience the dire cost of living a hedonistic "high life" devoid of a life of high spiritual aspirations. The present crisis of modernity has been aptly summed up by the Vedic writer Dr. Subhash Kak in the following way.

> Modernity, calling on all 'others' to assimilate to the supposedly higher, apparently secular and 'modern' value system represented by the West, amounted to thinly veiled pressure to abandon var ious indigenous traditions and convert to the supposedly univer sal notions of modernity. In other words, modernity expected and demanded unidirectional assimilation to alien lego-cultural norms and models, and a stepping outside of one's own inhe rited traditions… While modernity was, at one level, not con cerned about religion, it expected the modern world citizen to be of a secular disposition, thus seeking to prescribe one particular religious perspective as appropriate for modernity. (*The Assault on Tradition*)

A life devoid of Dharma – or the natural spiritual way - is a life lived without peace. And without peace, who can be happy?

Times of crises, however, are often also times of opportunity. They are a gift from God meant to help us contemplate the deeper meaning of our lives, and to reorder our life-style in accordance with His will and with His Dharma. Let us use these dangerous times to reassess what is truly of importance to us in the bigger, spiritual picture. Let us re-embrace an ideal spiritual culture wherein our material needs are all accounted for, but without needlessly neglecting the spiritual dimension of life.

Such a balanced culture is precisely what the concept of Dharma is de- signed to offer us. Imagine, if you will, a world in which all can enjoy both abundant prosperity and inner spiritual fulfillment. A world in which both social justice and social liberty can coexist. A world in which children have good reason to hope and parents have good reason to be secure in the future of their children. Such is the vision of Dharma. As is apparent to all people possessed of spiritual vision, the only alternative to such a Dharma scenario is a nihilistic nightmare. May God grant us the wisdom to embrace the vision.

Sanatana Dharma is the most personally expansive and psychologically empowering religion on earth. It is a path that teaches its followers to be fearless, dedicated, focused, strong, assertive, self-controlled, virtuous, self-reliant, and to strive for excellence in all endeavors. This, however, is only the case when Dharma is actually followed and practiced.

8.1.2 Dharma and Spiritual Empowerment

It is only by embracing the daily practice of Dharma that we can begin to access the full potential that we all have lying within. Through steadfast practice of the remarkable techniques of Yoga, meditation, *puja* (ceremonial ritual), and *bhakti* (devotional consciousness), all of which are at the very heart of Vedic spirituality, God has provided us with powerfully effective tools by which we can perfect ourselves and manifest unparalleled excellence in our lives. By practicing a strict regimen of Vedic *sadhana* (disciplined practice), we can achieve our utmost potential physically, emotionally, mentally, intellectually, and spiritually. It is by practicing, and witnessing the direct results, of these Dharmic disciplines that we can develop the self-confidence, healthy assertiveness, fearlessness, inner peace, and self-control that are the hallmark of any healthy and well-balanced person. It is no longer enough merely to call ourselves spiritual, to be merely nominal-spiritualists anymore; it is incumbent upon us all to actually practice Sanatana Dharma if we are to experience firsthand what it means to live a life that is empowered by the grace of God, and to know that in Dharma all things are possible.

Sanatana Dharma is a religion of the possible. It is a tradition that teaches us that anything and everything we can dream is attainable. In Sanatana

Dharma, we are radically free to perform any positive task, to reach out boldly toward any constructive goal, to achieve any dream that our imaginations can reveal. Dharma frees us from the bonds of ignorance and fear that bind us, and gives mighty wings to realize our inner yearning for peace, joy, and unlimited freedom.

Ours has historically been a religion that has fostered Possibility-Thinking. Sanatana Dharma is a religion that reflects the very essence of the diverse and infinite possibilities that the universe has to offer us. The infinitely expansive range of thinking, feeling, and experiential possibilities that the Dharmic world-view offers is without limit. The Possibility-Thinking that Dharma encourages is one reason why we find so many amazing stories, wondrous deeds, and heroic feats in our scriptures that would otherwise defy our common-day imagination. Only in Sanatana Dharma do we find such stories as Lord Shiva having the ability to fearlessly drink deadly poison from an ocean of milk and yet not die; or stories of the divine Sage Narada freely traversing the length and breadth of the universe at will in his unending mission to share God's love with all sentient beings; or the story of Hanuman bravely leaping to Lanka in a single monumental bound to seek out the imprisoned Sita, the beloved consort of Lord Rama. The one thing that these and so many thousands of similar sacred stories tell us in the boldest of voices is that there is no challenge in this world that cannot be overcome in the service of the Divine. There is no possibility that is beyond us.

The scriptures (*shastras*) and history of Sanatana Dharma are replete with the examples of many thousands of brave men and women who understood the principle of embracing the oceanic potential of Possibility-Thinking. Numerous sages, *rishis*, *yogis*, kings and queens, and leaders of the Vedic people throughout our history have shown us what can be accomplished when we know that all things are possible, and that we can achieve anything in God's service. Chanakya had the determination to drive the Greeks out of Vedic South Asia. Shankara used the power of resolute focus to revive Sanatana Dharma when it was threatened with extinction. Ramanuja possessed the determined will to revive pure *bhakti* (devotional consciousness) throughout the length and breadth of South Asia. Shivaji Maharaja had the fearless fortitude necessary to route the mighty and seemingly invincible Abrahamic Moghul Empire, and to reestablish the Dharma Nation as a viable military-political entity. Vivekananda showed us that Sanatana Dharma is not merely the possession of "India", but can be realized as the future pre-eminent world-view of the entire globe. Prabhupada showed us that Americans and Europeans and East Asians and Russians and the peoples of the entire world can – and will - enthusiastically embrace pure and authentic Sanatana Dharma in their millions.

Dharma, when practiced, provides us with *moksha* – radical existential freedom, and liberation from all the worldly impediments that bind us. Such is the nature of the radical freedom of *moksha* that we find ourselves without the limiting bounds that so affect those who have not yet tasted the nectar of *brahma-vidya* (God-realization). As servants of Dharma and devotees of God, we naturally find that our lives can be lived without limits. When we experience the spiritual revolution in our lives that the Dharma lifestyle can grant us, our possibilities are then endless. By God's grace, there is nothing we cannot accomplish.

8.1.3 Dharma Ascending

The concept of Dharma, or "Natural Law", is predicated upon the recognized need for the organic and munificent spiritualization of culture and of all human concern, as well as the manifestation of the highest potentials attainable by the human person. Dharma views the natural world as an inseparable extension of the Divine, and thus sees God's presence in all facets of creation. The overflowing of Dharma is nothing less than God's mercy and grace as they are manifest in His natural creation. Thus, unlike the artificial and materialistically secular ideologies that have created the atheistic world order of secular modernity, Dharma seeks, not to create an artificial and concocted order, but rather it seeks to reinstate the world to its original and natural order as designed by its Creator. Dharma is the basis and origin of all natural law, of the most natural and healthy way of living, and serves as the very ordering foundation of nature herself. To live in accordance with nature is to live a Dharmic lifestyle. And to live a Dharma lifestyle is to live in the peace, health, contentment, and happiness that God intended us all to enjoy. All of humanity understood the importance of the principle of Dharma at one time. Now having seen our world brought to the brink of ecological devastation, cultural degeneration, and civilizational annihilation, millions are beginning to recognize the critical imperative of reviving and reinstating Dharmic values in our world once again.

8.2.1 Sanatana Dharma and the New Age Movement

As a phenomenon that has gained notable attention and acceptance in the last four decades or so, the New Age movement has been very influential in the popular mind. The history and origin of this essentially

American movement is an especially convoluted one. While several discordant historical trends have contributed to the development of this world view, the main spiritual source for the New Age movement - both since the 1960's, and including its pre-Sixties antecedents - has been the periodic influx of spiritual and philosophical ideas, as well as practices, derived directly from the ancient tradition of Sanatana Dharma (The Eternal Natural Way). Sadly, most of the elements borrowed by the New Age movement from the Vedic tradition have been stolen with very little credit given to the original source, and have often been disrespectfully warped for purely financial reasons.

The modern New Age movement had its origins in the explosive interest in achieving maximal human potential and personal spiritual development that was witnessed in the turbulent 1960's America. Today, included among many of the more infamous New Age leaders are Rajneesh/Osho, H. W. L. Poonja ("Papaji"), Deepak Chopra, Eckhart Tolle, Marianne Williamson, J. Z. Knight, and...Oprah Winfrey. As a social phenomenon, this spiritual movement claims to seek both personal and planetary transformation. Personal transformation, most New Age theoreticians would say, will then lead necessarily to eventual global transformation.

While this movement has gained great notoriety in recent years, however, the core basis of this new movement's ideas are nothing new. Many scholars have, in fact, described New Age ideas as a modern, watered-down revival of esoteric and mystical religion traditions rooted in humanity's ancient past, often presented in rather disguised, commercialized and muddled interpretations especially designed for a more self-involved and philosophically lethargic American audience. Indeed, the greatest single contributor of philosophical concepts and practices to the American New Age movement has been something neither American nor new, i.e., the ancient transformative tradition of Sanatana Dharma and Yoga spirituality.

The very heavy borrowing from Sanatana Dharma on the part of New Age spirituality is evident both historically and in more contemporary observations. Historically, there were several 19th Century antecedents of the New Age movement. These include a) the Theosophical Society, b) the New Thought Movement, and c) the arrival of Swami Vivekananda in America. In addition, the 20th Century Luciferian ideologies of a) Aleister Crowley and b) Alice Bailey have had a tremendous, if surreptitious, influence on the world-view of the modern New Age movement.

The Theosophical Society of H.P. Blavatsky was founded in 1875, and was dedicated to transforming the world through spiritualism and mysticism. The Society openly derived much of its philosophical outlook from the "religions of Asia", specifically Sanatana Dharma and Buddhism. The source of supposed knowledge for Theosophists was derived from the mysterious and elusive "Mahatmas" ("Great Souls" in Sanskrit), who purportedly lived in the Himalayas. The second leader of the Theosophical Society, Annie Besant, herself moved to India and was one of the instrumental founders of India's independence movement. Ms. Besant further "Hinduized" the Society by stressing the importance of Yoga and Sanatana Dharma as the foundations of all human spiritual endeavor.

The New Thought movement - which inspired such 19th century Christian movements as Christian Science and Unity - was also very receptive to religious currents emanating from Vedic sources. Such important New

Thought writers as Mary Baker Eddy and Charles Filmore quoted the *Upanishads* and believed in such Vedic concept as *karma*, reincarnation, meditation and spiritual healing. The New Thought movement, in turn, owed much of its theology to the ideas of the New England Transcendentalists, such as Henry David Thoreau and Ralph Waldo Emerson, who where directly influenced by the *Upanishads* and the *Bhagavad Gita*. About the *Bhagavad Gita's* immense influence in his life, Thoreau has written, "In the morning I bathe my intellect in the stupendous and cosmogonal philosophy of the *Bhagavad Gita*, in comparison with which our modern world and its literature seem puny and trivial".

Finally, the famous 1893 arrival of Swami Vivekananda, and the subsequent growth of his Vedanta Society in America, helped communicate Dharmic and yogic spiritual thought to an eager American audience in a more explicit form. Previous to Vivekananda's arrival in the U.S., Yoga was more of a philosophical concept than a practical path. With the arrival of this great Indian *yogi*, who shrewdly diluted the traditional teachings of Vedic spirituality in order to appeal to a modern Western audience, Americans now began to practice the meditational and spiritual techniques of Yoga in the thousands.

Building upon these 19th Century foundations, the contemporary New Age movement as we know it today began its modern facelift in the 1960's. Though other trends certainly contributed significantly to this development, including transpersonal psychology, neo-pagan revivalism, Wicca, Luciferianism, and occultism, it was the new influx of Vedic-inspired spiritual traditions that was most responsible for the movement's subsequent development and practices.

Due to changes in the immigration laws in 1965, Asian spiritual teachers (*gurus*) found entering the U.S. much less of a challenge. During this time, many esteemed Hindu *gurus* (along with many clear fakes) began traveling about America on lecture tours, including Maharishi Mahesh Yogi, Bhaktivedanta Swami Prabhupada, Swami Rama, Swami Muktananda, Swami Vishnu-Devananda, and Swami Satchidananda. Consequently, many Vedic-based religious movements began to find new and eager adherents in America. Some of these Sanatana Dharma traditions included the schools of Vedanta, Tantra, Vaishnavism and various Advaitic (monist) teachings. The initial contributions of these different Vedic schools of thought to New Age thinking was immense, even if the actual teachings of these schools eventually ended up being severely watered down, plagiarized and warped by most New Age leaders.

The initial Vedic contributions to modern New Ageism included both philosophical and practical contributions. While New Agers currently believe in such concepts as: the interdependence of all life, non-violence, concern for the Earth's environment, and tolerance for diverse viewpoints, such ideas served as the very foundation of the Sanatana Dharma view of reality for millennia before the New Age movement was born. It was the ancient Vedic philosophical heritage that first helped formulate these concepts coherently in the minds of many nascent New Agers.

Other New Age ideas that received strong philosophical support from the Vedic religion included the belief in reincarnation and *karma*, the efficacy of ritual, and the need for compassion towards animals. Indeed, the latter trend within the New Age movement is quite in keeping with the vegetarian and non-violent ethic taught by all Dharmic spiritual traditions (specifically Sanatana Dharma, Buddhism and Jainism).

The most important component that the New Age movement stole from Vedic spirituality, however, is the scientific practice of meditation. Every tradition of Dharmic religion teaches one form of meditation or another. Perhaps the most important proponent of meditation in the U.S. has been the Maharishi Mahesh Yogi, the founder of the Transcendental Meditation movement. Other forms of meditation introduced from the tradition of Sanatana Dharma include *mantra*-meditation, visualization and *karma yoga*. As a result of this influx of Vedic meditational techniques, the practice of meditation has now become an integral part of the American and European New Age landscape. The traditional Vedic approach to meditation has always been to use meditation as a sacred tool for achieving transcendence and enlightenment. The New Age degeneration of meditation has resulted in a more materially and psychologically oriented attempt to simply relieve people of the stress and anxiety that our modern culture has exacerbated to an almost infinite degree.

While it is true that some of the beliefs and practices of the New Age movement can also be traced to other sources, it is quite apparent that the movement owes a great deal of its ideas, as well as its historical development, to the much older tradition of Sanatana Dharma and Yoga spirituality.

Unfortunately, even in the face of the above incontrovertible facts linking the origins of much New Age belief and practice directly to the Vedic tradition, many followers of the New Age movement remain ignorant of this important source of their most important ideas. This divorce from its Vedic roots has thus rendered the New Age movement without a clearly systematized world-view. Consequently, what started as a movement that had enormous potential to introduce authentic Dharmic philosophy to the modern West has, instead, degenerated into a shallow and narcissistic culture of self-help and self-absorption.

Too many Americans have now settled for what I call "Spirituality Lite". This is a very recent and unrooted attachment to faddish spiritual approaches that is more designed to create the appearance of spiritual depth, rather than actually being reflective of any serious form of spiritual inquiry.

Many baseless New Age trends such as the so-called "Law of Attraction", "the Secret", "Indigo Children" and other very recent wishful-thinking concoctions are more reflective of a type of spiritual egotism and selfishness than an actual yearning to know and serve the eternal Truth. This shallow and fluffy "spirituality" consists of the repetition of such pop pseudo-spiritual sayings as *"we are all one"*, *"don't judge"*, *"everyone has their own truth"*, *"luv 'n light"*, *"I'm not religious; I'm spiritual"*, etc., rather than any actual exhibitions of discursive and philosophical thought. Modern American New Ageism is based upon emotional sentiment rather than philosophical thought.

New Ageism has also led to a complete non-understanding of the traditional role of the guru. This is seen in 1) the childish pronouncement that *"I am my own guru"*, rather than any sincere attempt to humbly seek guidance from a true Master and to align with a real lineage of *gurus*; 2) becoming cultish groupies of fraudulent and unknowledgeable "satsang" leaders who are themselves relatively new to spirituality, rather than deeply exploring the ancient and authentic traditions that such fraudulent teachers have stolen their material from; 3) and following such fake modern *"avataras"* as Adi Da, Sai Baba and Swami Nithyananda.

The undercurrent of New Age pop "spirituality" is all too often nothing more than narcissistic self-centeredness, consumerism and wishful thinking. This recent "Oprah-fication" of spirituality has led to zero spiritual enlightenment on the part of any of its groupies, and has only increased people's muddled confusion about the true nature of authentic spirituality. Our world is not better off as a result of the self-indulgent and anti-intellectual spiritual illusions promulgated by the New Age movement. Instead, the people's deep yearning for authentic spiritual experience only increases with each passing day.

A deeply meaningful and authentic spirituality is only to be found in the most ancient, historically rooted and venerable traditions. If you truly wish to understand and experience self-realization, God-consciousness and actual enlightenment, seek the teachings of the most ancient of sages by delving deeply into their writings. Take shelter of such sacred scriptures as the *Bhagavad Gita*, *Srimad Bhagavatam*, and the *Upanishads*. Go directly to the source literature, the scriptures, and not to the latest releases of Oprah's Book Club or the New York Times best sellers list. Learn with deep humility and patience at the feet of the very few authentic spiritual masters alive today (again, read the scriptures to know what is a true *guru*).

The time has now arrived to re-embrace the authentic approach to spirituality. It is in sincerity, humility, self-discipline, dedication, and devotion to Truth that we know Truth. The spiritual journey rewards us in direct proportion to how much respectful attendance we give to it. If you are to truly know God, practice the path as if there is nothing else you could ever desire more.

If one wants to truly know Truth, the prerequisite for this gift is self-surrender at the very feet of Truth with sincerity, humility, openness and yearning. One must consciously follow an ancient, authentic and authorized spiritual path designed and proven to help transcend one's false ego in order to know Truth. Sanatana Dharma, the Eternal Natural Way, is just such a path. To know Truth means to surrender to Truth. Anything less than honest dedication to Truth is merely cheating ourselves in the name of spiritual attainment.

8.3.1 Bridging the Gap: Indian Hindus and Western Dharmis

With over one-billion adherents globally, the ancient religion of Sanatana Dharma represents the third largest religion on earth, with Christianity being the largest, and Islam the second largest. Despite its timelessness and size, Sanatana Dharma is not a monolithic religion. It is not the religion of any one specific nation, ethnicity, race, or language group. Rather, it is a universal religion that finds adherents originating from every national and ethnic group on earth. In addition to the existence of Indian Hindus, there are British Dharmis, Russian Dharmis, Danish Dharmis, German Dharmis, Irish Dharmis, Italian Dharmis, Spanish Dharmis, and Dharmis representing every ethnicity in the world today.

The overall Sanatana Dharma community in America and many parts of Europe can be easily categorized into several demographic groupings, the most broad of which constitutes what I have termed: a) the Indian Hindu community, and b) the community of "Hidden Dharmis."

For over two decades now, I have pointed to the problem that exists between these two sections of the Dharma family that leads to an unfortunate disconnect between the two, and the crucial importance of bridging the gap between these two intimately related Sanatana Dharma communities. As one of the few Vedic *gurus* who has worked very closely with both communities over the decades, these have been my observations:

8.3.2 A) Indian Hindus

Strengths: The Indian Hindu community tends to be culturally Vedic. They consciously identify with the tradition of Sanatana Dharma, they maintain many important cultural traditions, they build and support Hindu temples, etc. And for all this they should be commended and thanked.

Weaknesses: Where Indian Hindus are severely lacking, however, is when it comes to the actual practice of Sanatana Dharma, Yoga and meditation, as well as the proper philosophical understanding of Sanatana Dharma. Most Indian Hindus simply do not practice Sanatana Dharma as a yogic *sadhana* (spiritual discipline) at all. Neither do many of them take the time to actually educate themselves on what Sanatana Dharma actually teaches. When it comes to the actual practice and understanding of the religion of Sanatana Dharma...the non-Indian Dharmis often have the advantage.

8.3.3 B) 'Hidden Dharmis'

<u>Definition</u>: The people whom I term "Hidden Dharmis" constitute the tens of millions of individuals in the West who a) practice Yoga, b) practice meditation, c) believe in the principles of *karma* and reincarnation, d) are vegetarian, e) look to such Vedic scriptures as the *Bhagavad Gita* for wisdom and guidance, f) and who possibly even have a *guru* as their spiritual teacher; but who, despite practicing all the essential elements of Sanatana Dharma in their daily lives, have not had the added advantage of consciously identifying themselves as adherents of this unique and welcoming spiritual tradition.

<u>Strengths</u>: The non-Indian Dharmis practice Yoga and meditation zealously; they learn Sanskrit; study the *Bhagavad Gita*, the *Yoga Sutras*, and the *Upanishads*; they will pay hundreds of dollars to attend seminars on Vedanta; they bring with them the enthusiasm and wide-eyed optimism for practice that is often ascribed to a new "convert" of any religion; and thus when it comes to practicing Sanatana Dharma, few can compare to the seriousness of the Western Dharmis.

<u>Weaknesses</u>: These very same non-Indian Yoga / Dharma practitioners, on the other hand, have little sense of identity with the tradition of Sanatana Dharma. They have a hard time calling themselves " Dharmis", or sometimes even "followers of Sanatana Dharma". Such non-Indians attempt to appropriate the practice Sanatana Dharma without then taking the next important and logical step of consciously identifying themselves with the tradition they have so obviously adopted in everything but name. They would rather identify themselves as "New Age" or "none-of-the-above" or almost anything else, rather than be honest about the fact

that they are, indeed, **Dharmis**. Thus, I call the Western *yogis* the community of "Hidden Dharmis".

What, of course, needs to happen is that both communities need to come together and to learn from one another. What one community is lacking, the other one very obviously possesses.

The Western *yogis* need to know that without consciously embracing and identifying with the ancient tradition that they have chosen to practice, they are actually disrespecting their very own practice. They remain unnecessarily spiritual orphans, when there is a family of one billion members eager to embrace them. Indian Hindus, conversely, need to learn that it is no longer enough to be a nominal Hindu – to merely call oneself "Hindu" - but that it is crucial to begin to make the practice and proper understanding of Dharma central to their lives. The Indians need to begin practicing Yoga, daily meditation, *yamas* and *niyamas*, and to begin studying the scriptures thoroughly. Hindu temples need to cease being merely buildings in which ceremony and cultural identity prevail, and become instead what they were historically designed to be: spiritual institutions alive with the joy of Yoga, the power of the stillness of meditation, and the learning of the wisdom of the scriptures. Without bringing Sanatana Dharma to life in this dynamic way, merely calling oneself "Hindu" is meaningless.

The gap between the two communities of Indian Hindus and "Hidden Dharmis" in America and Europe needs to be bridged. It is up to the leaders of both communities to make this newfound unity a reality. It is time for spiritually minded Yoga teachers to begin bringing their students to Sanatana Dharma temples in the cities where they live to show them the beauty and majesty of the tradition they have chosen to practice. And when these non-Indian *yogis* do visit, it is the duty of Indian Hindus to make them feel that they are part of the family. Because we are.

Together, as one, united Sanatana Dharma community - Indians and Americans, Nepalis and British, Sri Lankans and Australians - let us endeavor to exhibit in our own personal lives and actions the spiritual qualities that form the very essence of Sanatana Dharma, and to work tirelessly together to preserve our common spiritual heritage for all future generations.

8.4.1 Does Sanatana Dharma Have a Future in America?

The mutual histories of both Sanatana Dharma and of the United States of America have been intimately intertwined for the last two centuries. Though the two cultures have been so different from one another in many important ways, the profound and continuing influence of the world's most ancient spiritual culture on one of the earth's youngest nations cannot be denied. Dharma culture, ideas, philosophy, spirituality, and practices have found an eager audience in America since at least the early 19th Century. While today, in the dawn of the 21st Century, Vedic influence has continued to mold the American cultural psyche in many ways, surprisingly, Sanatana Dharma finds itself increasingly in danger of becoming assimilated into the greater American mainstream, and of losing its own sense of identity as a unique and vibrant religious tradition. Many important elements of Sanatana Dharma have certainly had a powerful presence in the making of American history and culture. The question now is whether or not Sanatana Dharma itself has a secure place in America's future.

8.4.2 Turning East: America Discovers Dharma

The Vedic presence in America is longstanding and deeply pervasive. The first instances of these influences can be seen in the writings of several important 19th Century American intellectuals. Ralph Waldo Emerson (1803-1882) and Henry David Thoreau (1817-1862), two of the most important writers and philosophers of the New England Transcendentalist movement, were quite vocal in their admiration of Sanatana Dharma, the *Bhagavad Gita*, and Upanishadic philosophy. Having first read the famous *Bhagavad Gita* in 1832, Emerson wrote the following about his profound experience with this most important of Hindu scriptures:

> It was the first of books; it was as if an empire spoke to us, nothing small or unworthy, but large, serene, consistent, the voice of an old intelligence which in another age and climate had pondered over and thus disposed of the same questions which exercise us.

Thoreau, too, inspired by his first reading of the *Bhagavad Gita*, wrote the following about his admiration for Sanatana Dharma:

> Beside the vast and cosmogonal philosophy of the Bhagvat-Geeta, even our Shaksespeare seems some times youthfully green... *Ex oriente lux* [Light from the East] may still be the motto of scholars, for the Western world has not yet derived from the East all the light which it is destined to derive thence.

Similarly, many other important figures of 19th Century America bathed themselves in the "Light from the East", and incorporated many elements of Sanatana Dharma for their own purposes.

Many of these American intellectuals borrowed liberally from Sanatana Dharma, but often without giving proper credit and acknowledgement of their dependence upon Sanatana Dharma. Mary Baker Eddy, the founder of the Christian Science Church, is known to have derived much of her theology from her readings of the *Upanishads*. Helena Petrovna Blavatsky, the founder of the Theosophical Society, was likewise wholly dependent upon her knowledge of Sanatana Dharma for the formulation of her world-view and teachings.

8.4.3 The Light of the East Comes West

While many of 19th Century America's leading intellectuals, writers, theologians and artists turned to Vedic South Asia for wisdom and insight, it was not until "the East" itself came to America that Sanatana Dharma truly gained widespread appreciation and acclaim. Without doubt, the most significant 19th Century event responsible for America's deep admiration of Sanatana Dharma was the momentous arrival of Swami Vivekananda on American shores in 1893.

A Hindu *sannyasi* (monk) steeped in both knowledge of Vedic truth, as well as Western philosophy and religion, Vivekananda was, without doubt, one of Sanatana Dharma's greatest heroes and ambassadors to the nascent global civilization of modernity. Previous to Vivekananda's arrival in the U.S., all American intellectuals' knowledge of Sanatana Dharma was absent the important element of a living Dharmi voice. Americans had up till now experienced a Dharma devoid of Dharmis, a theoretical Vedanta without the breathing presence of a Vedanta Acharya, a Yoga without living *yogis*. Vivekananda's historic speech before Chicago's World Parliament of Religions in 1893 is the first instance in American history of a living representative of Sanatana Dharma being allowed to represent Sanatana Dharma in its own voice, on its own terms, and from its own intrinsic perspective. Sanatana Dharma, as beautifully portrayed by Swami Vivekananda, set ablaze in the American imagination an interest in Vedic philosophy and religion the likes of which America had not seen previously.

Swami Vivekananda was one of the greatest heroes and ambassadors of Sanatana Dharma to the West. It would be very difficult to overestimate the extremely important and positive impact that he had in the furtherance of the cause of Vedic renaissance. Swami Vivekananda will always be remembered throughout history for his courage, strength and determination to have the entire world understand the greatness of Sanatana Dharma.

Along with the neo-Vedanta of Vivekananda, early 20th Century America witnessed a dramatic growth of interest in such elements of Sanatana Dharma as Yoga, meditation, and *bhakti* (devotional Yoga). Such appeal was sparked by the presence of yet more Vedic teachers who came to the States in the first few decades after Vivekananda's momentous speaking tours. These historic figures include: Premananda Bharati and Swami Yogananda.

Without doubt, however, the explosive interest in Sanatana Dharma that we are witnessing today owes its antecedent momentum to the 1960s. In the '60s, America witnessed several concurrent trends that starkly marked the spiked growth of Sanatana Dharma in the West. In the mid-sixties, immigration policy was altered so as to allow the influx of hundreds of thousands of new arrivals from India. This is a trend that has continued

288

today, and has resulted in the presence of roughly two million people of South Asian origin currently living in the United States. Along with their hopes of sharing in the relative prosperity of the American Dream, many of these Hindu arrivals have brought with them important sacred elements of their precious Vedic heritage.

The most important development that began in the 1960s, however, was the beginning of the influx of dozens and hundreds more living representatives of Santana Dharma. *Gurus*, *swamis*, *yogis* and *acharyas* from South Asia arrived in America, many of whom started movements that would ultimately be responsible for introducing tens of millions of Americans and Europeans to a taste of Sanatana Dharma. Such latter-day Vivekanandas included: Maharishi Mahesh Yogi, Sri Swami Rama, Srila Bhaktivedanta Swami Prabhupada, Swami Satchidananda, Swami Jyotir Mayananda, Swami Vishnu-devananda, and many others too numerous to mention. America witnessed the explosive growth of things Vedic in the 1960s.

Today, in 2015, we are witnessing the mainstreaming of Sanatana Dharma. NRI[28] success in America has become legendary, with the Indian Hindu community now representing the most financially successful minority community in the nation. Over 900 traditional Hindu temples have been built in America, with another 20 or so being built every year. In the post-911 geopolitical scene we are seeing dramatically increasing rapprochement between India and the U.S. in the War on Terror, as well as on economic, military and political cooperation - a trend that can only increase the admiration of the general American public toward both In-

---

[28] So-called "Non-Resident Indians".

dia and Sanatana Dharma.

Most significantly, however, many of the most important elements of Sanatana Dharma have been gaining increasing acceptance and popularity with a very large number of Americans. In 2015, roughly 20 million Americans are practicing Yoga. In multiple polls of American religious beliefs and attitudes, up to 25% of Americans believe in reincarnation. In a recent poll conducted by the Pew Forum on Religion and Public Life, it was revealed that 28% of American Catholic adults believe in the principle of reincarnation. Tens of millions of Americans meditate. Over 20 million are vegetarian. Almost half the population has turned to alternative health systems, such as Ayurveda, herbal medicine and massage - all of which are originally Vedic-based health modalities. Looking at the widespread acceptance of these many elements of Sanatana Dharma, it would seem that we are almost experiencing a "Dharma-ization" of the American cultural milieu!

8.4.4 Vivid Examples of American Dharmis

While admittedly, the vast majority of these Americans tend to be interested exclusively in the various practical and physically healthy elements of Sanatana Dharma, to the exclusion of overt Vedic identification, many Americans have also openly and proudly embraced Sanatana Dharma itself as their own newly embraced religious tradition. Indeed, many have become respected authorities and globally recognized spokespersons for the tradition. David Frawley, Steven Knapp, Georg Feuerstein, Vrindavan Parker, and I myself represent only several of the many better-known American converts to Sanatana Dharma. *Hinduism Today* magazine, by far the highest quality and most widely circulated periodical on Sanatana

Dharma on earth today, was founded and is staffed primarily by American converts to Sanatana Dharma.

8.4.5 Taking the Cross out of the Crossroads

Still, despite the increasing popularity in America of many isolated elements and practices of Sanatana Dharma, most Americans are more interested in the immediate benefits of these useful individual facets of Sanatana Dharma than they are in Sanatana Dharma itself. Americans are interested in Yoga *asanas* (physical postures), but are not as interested in become self-realized *yogis*. They are interested in meditation for its calming effects, but not necessarily as a means to achieve *samadhi*. They are primarily interested in the many goodies that Sanatana Dharma has to offer, but without taking the next logical step of becoming conscious Dharmis, or in many cases without even acknowledging the purely Vedic origins of the many practices that they have derived so much benefit from.

Thus, while many useful aspects of Sanatana Dharma have become increasingly popular, today Sanatana Dharma finds itself standing at an important crossroads, certainly in America, but also in South Asia and globally. With profit-driven Americans increasingly exploiting Vedic elements for their own financial gain, we are beginning to see Sanatana Dharma as a unique and vital religious tradition being somewhat eclipsed. While elements of Sanatana Dharma become more popular in America, Sanatana Dharma itself is in danger of being assimilated into the greater cultural milieu, just another ingredient – albeit a nicely spicy one – of the great American melting-pot. We face the very real possibility of authentic Sanatana Dharma becoming co-opted into the greater American cultural matrix as nothing more than a menagerie of disparate elements used to market faddish New Age spirituality. We are in danger of losing the heart of Sanatana Dharma itself, as a unique and separate tradition of its own. And more, as these elements of Sanatana Dharma rise in popularity in America, they are tragically declining in South Asia.

For the sake of this present work, however, I will be focusing primarily on the American scene for now. The situation of Sanatana Dharma in South Asia will be saved for a future book.

8.4.6 The Challenges Sanatana Dharma Faces Today

For several decades now, I have observed that there are several concurrent factors that are responsible for the precarious situation that Sanatana Dharma currently finds itself in:

A) A Lack of Systematically Trained Dharma Leadership. The greatest challenge by far that Sanatana Dharma is facing in the world today is a distinct crisis of leadership. Every other major world religious tradition has systematic, comprehensive, and well-formulated means of training their religious and lay leaders. Such training usually includes (but is not limited to) training in the religion's theological tenants, critical thinking skills, debating/speaking/writing skills, comparative analyses of what other religions believe, principles of effective leadership, administrative training, etc.

The Catholic Church, for example, gives its priests years of such training in the seminary before they are seen as proper stewards for their congregations. Priests of the Catholic Jesuit Order, as one case in point, often rarely have anything less than a Masters degree, with many of these priests having Ph.D.s. Protestant/Evangelical Christian missionaries, Muslim Imams, Jewish Rabbis, and even Buddhist monks, undergo similarly rigorous training to lead their respective communities. When I was studying for my Ph.D. at the University of Wisconsin-Madison, for example, there were no less than 6 Buddhist monks and nuns working on their Ph.D.s in my department. Their plan, upon graduation, was to use their education to serve their respective Buddhist communities. I, as an American convert to Sanatana Dharma, was the only Sanatana Dharmi in the program. These other religious communities have understood that having a trained leadership is the greatest assurance of community survival.

The modern Vedic community, as it is currently situated, is severely lacking such effective leadership-creating institutions. Today, there are almost no traditional training facilities left that are designed to create a strong, knowledgeable, confident, and courageous Vedic leadership. Thus, modern Sanatana Dharma is lacking a well-trained leadership that can help defend Sanatana Dharma properly, and guide the Vedic community into the 21st century. The reasons for this current state are multiple: The primary reason has been due to the systematic eradication of our intellectual, spiritual, and *kshatriya* (warrior) leadership during the last thousand years of anti-Dharmic oppression. While leadership training institutions did exist for thousands of years in Sanatana Dharma in the form of *gurukulas* (children's schools run by qualified *gurus*), traditional *ashramas* (spiritual hermitages for adults) designed to train leaders in Vedic ritual, thought and philosophy, as well as diverse networks of Vedic educational facilities, these traditional institutions have been systematically destroyed over the last 1000 years during the aforementioned Hindu

Holocaust.

Another reason for the current crisis of leadership in Sanatana Dharma is the zealous overemphasis on economic development at the expense of religious development. Truthfully, encouraging our children to become courageous Dharma leaders has taken a back seat to forcing them to become engineers, doctors, IT professionals, and making as much money as possible. Unfortunately, more engineers and doctors and industrialists are not going to ensure the survival of our religious tradition – well trained and committed religious leaders will! Another factor has been a lack of economic, academic, technological, and strategically visionary resources. Most importantly, however, the reason why we are lacking the institutions necessary for creating a future wave of Vedic leaders is a complete lack of will. It must be understood that without a well-trained leadership, no community can survive.

B) Radical Universalism

Radical Universalism is the false teaching that "*all religions are the same*", that "*all religions are equal, with no important differences between them*". That Sanatana Dharma teaches such a preposterous notion is one of the greatest myths of the last century. Yet despite the fact that this dogma is not actually Vedic in origin, we hear it endlessly parroted by innocent, but unknowing, Dharmi parents; by Sanatana Dharma community leaders; and often even by badly trained and popularity-seeking "*gurus*" who come to the West with a greater yearning to gain a following, than to represent pure and authentic Sanatana Dharma. Without going too deeply into the social, philosophical, theological and historical problems posed by this false notion, suffice it to say that the dogma of Radical Universalism has philosophically weakened Sanatana Dharma to its core, has forced

Dharmi youth to question the maturity and rationality of Vedic teachings, has made Vedic "philosophy" look silly in the eyes of qualified intellectuals, and have left us open and defenseless to attack by Christian missionaries, Marxist terrorism, and Islamic aggression. I would ask that you please read my work on this topic "*Radical Universalism: Are All Religions the Same?*" for further clarification on this important topic.

On an important note, Radical Universalism is not to be mistakenly confused with Dharmic universalism, as some less knowledgeable commentators have erroneously stated. Dharmic universalism is the correct idea that Sanatana Dharma is a philosophy and religion that is open to all people regardless of their national or ethnic origin, and that Dharma is a universal Truth that applies to all people at all times. This is correct. The dogma of Radical Universalism, on the other hand, makes the fanatically sweeping claim that there are no fundamental differences between religions. Radical Universalism is a modern doctrine that is not found in classical Sanatana Dharma.

C) Anti-Dharmic Defamation

There is an academic/media/education/government matrix in America (and now duplicated to perfection in India) that fosters anti-Dharmic stereotypes, and has done so very successfully for decades. Rather than standing up and fighting against such anti-Dharmic portrayals of Sanatana Dharma (as every other stereotyped group in American has forcefully, loudly, and successfully done to defend their own communities), the Dharma community has been so slow to respond to these attacks in the past that many of the anti-Dharma bigots in academia feel they have a free reign to propagate any lies about Sanatana Dharma they wish. They also know that if the Vedic community ever even responds at all, it is usually too little, too late, and in a purely reactionary manner. We need to counter any and all attacks against Sanatana Dharma immediately, forcefully and professionally.

Some of us have, in fact, responded forcefully to anti-Dharma defamation in academia – including David Frawley, Koenraad Elst, Subhash Kak, Vishal Agarwal, Yvette Rosser, and myself, among others. However, the majority of instances in which Dharmis are engaged in the market place of ideas tends to be only when we need to respond to the attacks of others. Our interactions with academia, and other power-wielding institutions in America, have been almost purely defensive and reactionary in nature.

The time has now come to go on the intellectual offensive, and to engage in a conscious campaign of ideas. The world knows what the Christian perspective is; what the Islamic perspective, the Marxist perspective, the Feminist perspective are. Now is the time to vigorously educate the world on the precise nature of the Dharma perspective. Such positive pro-Vedic intellectual activity includes creating comparative analyses of Vedic philosophy vs. other thought systems (i.e., comparing Sanatana Dharma vs. Christianity, Sanatana Dharma vs. Marxism, Sanatana Dharma vs. Atheism, Sanatana Dharma vs. Post-modernism, etc., etc.). This category of positive Vedic intellectual activity also includes the creation of original critiques, commentaries, and position papers giving the Dharma perspective on the most important issues of the day: the Dharma perspective on the environment, on fiscal policy, on ethics, on terrorism, on women's rights, on race, on poverty, on euthanasia, etc. Unless we come to this crucial stage of positively and assertively projecting the Dharma perspective into the current realm of ideas, Sanatana

296

Dharma will not be taken seriously by either the non-Vedic world, or by our increasingly intelligent and cosmopolitan Dharmi youth themselves.

D) <u>Disaffected Dharmi Youth</u>

Too many young Dharmis today feel completely alienated from their religion and from their cultural roots. A large part of this problem is certainly due to the problems mentioned above. In addition, others have pointed to a) the lack of proper education for children about Sanatana Dharma, b) the inability of many Indian Vedic priests and leaders to answer their questions properly, and c) the overwhelming influence of popular American culture as additional reasons for why many Dharmi children question the value of their religion. These and many other causes have certainly contributed greatly to Dharmi youths' confusion about Sanatana Dharma. If we Dharmis can learn to stand courageously in the face of our many opponents, and serve as examples of strength to our children, I guarantee that our youth will follow our example – and far surpass it.

Having looked at a few of the major problems confronting Sanatana Dharma in American today, there are several solutions that the Dharma community must implement immediately if it is going to preserve Vedic culture and ensure a future for Dharmi children.

8.4.7 The Future of Sanatana Dharma in America

Sanatana Dharma, I feel, not only has a future in America, but America, more than any other nation on earth at present, is potentially the stage upon which a revitalized Sanatana Dharma as a global force can once again reemerge. America itself signals several potentially important attitudes and mindsets that Sanatana Dharma must adopt if it is to have a future at all. This is so for the following reasons:

A) Sanatana Dharma as a Multi-ethnic Community

Sanatana Dharma in America is very much a multi-racial, multi-ethnic phenomenon. In America, we are beginning to have a glimpse in microcosmic form of what the world would look like if Sanatana Dharma were to be the primary world religion, as I believe it will be in the not too distant future. Moreover, the example and fact of a multi-ethnic Vedic culture will display for the world the truly universal nature of Sanatana Dharma as the future religion of the world.

B) Ancient Dharma with a Modern Face

Sanatana Dharma in America will be instantiated as the most ancient religion on earth, but with a thoroughly modern face and attitude. American culture is a culture that fosters and celebrates success. It encourages a sense of practicality, excellence, a no-nonsense attitude, and high standards in every endeavor. These are all mindsets that Sanatana Dharma at one time also shared and taught when Vedic culture was historically at its greatest strength. It will now relearn these values from America.

C) Sanatana Dharma on the Cutting Edge

Here in America, more than anywhere else on earth, we will witness a revitalized Sanatana Dharma coupled with the most cutting-edge technology. The IT revolution will help to bring about a Dharma revolution globally as we begin to use the latest technology in the form of the Internet, DVDs, computer graphics, etc., to get our message out. Not only is Sanatana Dharma not opposed to the use of technology, but we must and will use such technology in Dharma *seva* (service).

298

D) Revitalized Dharmi Youth

Long have many bemoaned the Americanization of Dharmi youth. My prediction, however, is that in America, we will soon witness a veritable army of these very same Americanized, savvy, cool, energized and very practically-minded Vedic youth coming back to Sanatana Dharma. And when they do, they will be the vanguard of a new and truly American Sanatana Dharma that will instantiate the very best of both worlds – bringing together the very best of the most ancient with the very best of the most cutting-edge.

8.4.8 Sanatana Dharma is America's Future

Like two wings of the same powerful eagle, Sanatana Dharma and the best of American culture must be coupled together in partnership if either is going to have a meaningful future. If this can happen, not only will Sanatana Dharma have a future in America…but Sanatana Dharma will be America's future!

Futures, however, do not merely occur. Futures are made. If Sanatana Dharma is going to once again become the meaningful and influential global force that history shows us it once was, then it is incumbent upon each and every Dharmi to rededicate ourselves to our religion's future. We must learn not to merely be Nominal Hindus, but to be Conscious Dharmis – practicing our religion, studying the scriptures of our religion, and becoming living examples of God's grace (*prasada*) and compassion (*karuna*) alive in the world. It is up to each of us to be dedicated and loving stewards of this great religious heritage known as Sanatana Dharma. Sanatana Dharma's future is in the hands of every Conscious Dharmi.

8.5.1 The Sun of Dharma Arises in the West

Sanatana Dharma teaches us that nature, and the underlying metaphysical reality that directs nature's course, operates in cycles. What is prominent today will be anathema tomorrow. Nothing in nature is static. Poles shift, tendencies are altered, world-views are turned upside-down, failed civilizations perish and new ones take birth.

The Sun of Dharma once reigned over the entire earth, bathing all beings in the living light of Truth. Within the context of human history, we have seen that Sun then focus its living rays more pointedly upon the sacred geography of Aryavarta (roughly corresponding with today's Central and South Asian Himalayan region) for the last several thousand years. Today, that Sun of Dharma is quickly setting in the remnants of that sacred land of Aryavarta, as that land descends into the darkness of blind consumerism, secular materialism, Marxist tyranny, and the very worst of Bollywood culture. But that Sun, never to be truly ever set, is arising again in the West - of all places. The Sun of Dharma is slowly arising over American shores.

We are going to witness, and participate in, a Golden Dawn of Dharma in the Western world. Dharma, being Sanatana (eternal), never disappears entirely, but merely resituates itself where it can be best appreciated, understood, and practiced with fidelity, dignity and devotion. We see the very heart of Dharma in the form of Yoga, meditation, Vedantic philosophy, and Ayurveda, being practiced in the West today, though often without the proper understanding of what the actual religious context of these many ancient practices are.

A movement has taken birth in America designed to couple Americans' sincere interest in authentic spiritual practices with a proper understanding of authentic Sanatana Dharma philosophy. This movement can create in America nothing less than a Dharma Rashtra - a Dharma Nation - a new Vedic civilization dedicated to instantiating Dharmic ideals in the everyday lives of its people in such a manner as to ensure both material prosperity, combined with spiritual fulfillment.

More, it will only be by reconstructing authentic and Vedic-based Sanatana Dharma here in the West that the Sun of Dharma will again arise in the East. Once we've set the example here, the traditionally Dharmic nations of Asia will themselves eventually use the model they see here to reconstruct Dharma themselves. I see no other alternative right now to this scenario.

My personal goal and mission is, thus, to ensure the existence of a movement that will accomplish precisely this: A movement, based in America, and reaching out to both the traditional Indian Hindu community and to the non-Indian Yoga spirituality community, that is designed to teach pure, authentic Dharma in such a way as to communicate the most ancient wisdom in the most modern of ways. A movement that will spread Dharmic ideals into the deepest levels of the American psyche, and American institutions, and which will inform and transform the West on every level imaginable - philosophically, spiritually, politically, economically, culturally and religiously.

The creation of such a movement has now become manifest in the form of the International Sanatana Dharma Society.

America is potentially a new Dharma Rashtra - a Dharma Nation. America is the place where Dharma is most attractive to people - even if under different names, like "*yoga*", "meditation", "*ayurveda*", etc. It is here that we will re-instantiate a living, breathing Dharma Nation. America has the infrastructure, the interest, the intelligence, technology, wealth, media empires, sincere volunteers, etc. to effectively change the world for the better. It is up to us to create a new Dharmic civilization here in the most affluent, healthy, technologically advanced, communications-sophisticated, and politically savvy nation on earth. Once we have a Dharma Nation here, the rest of the world, including Bharata-mata, will follow.

Sanatana Dharma is the most ancient spiritual tradition known to humanity. Sanatana Dharma is the Eternal Natural Way. There was never a time when Dharma did not exist, nor shall it ever cease to be. Dharma itself, being an eternal manifestation of God's grace, can never come to an end.

Despite this fact, however, Dharma can periodically disappear from our own limited vision at certain times in history when the majority of humanity chooses to dedicate their lives to selfish material pursuit, rather than to the pursuit of Truth. Our current era is precisely one of those dark times in global history in which our society has turned its collective back on the life-giving principles of Dharma.

In order to end the widespread suffering, sense of meaninglessness, economic decline, social chaos, spiritual confusion, as well as ethical and moral degeneracy that we are witnessing today, we must revive Sanatana

Dharma. We must reestablish a Dharmic civilization - a Dharma Nation. And we must do so now.

As our direct response to the challenge of the negative energies of our dark era, known as the Kali Yuga, it is incumbent upon those of us who are still dedicated to upholding Dharmic principles to do everything in our power to revitalized Dharmic civilization today. Dharma forms the very basis of justice, peace, social harmony, positive culture, enlightenment, health, and all meaningful progress.

It is stated in the sacred *Mahabharata*: *dharmo rakshati rakshitaha*, "Those who preserve Dharma are likewise protected by Dharma." Does Dharma have a future? Yes it does. But that future is now dependent on those who are reading this book at this present moment.

Fourth Wave

- Grounding in Practice

Chapter 9: Taking Refuge in Dharma

9.1.1 Why Should I Be a Dharmi?

We live in an age in which people have found it increasingly challenging to express the life-giving principles of spirituality and religion with as much seriousness, enthusiasm and dedication as was once the case. All around us, we witness on a daily basis all the destructive ravages that materialism, consumerism, greed, anger, lust and self-centeredness have forced upon our once saner world. Much of the war, poverty, sense of depression and meaningless, and social ills that are rampant today are directly due to the clear failures of atheism and an unsatisfying lifestyle dedicated to the pursuit of material acquisitions to the detriment of our inner spiritual growth. We have substituted television for meditation, emailing for prayer, texting for real communication, the Internet for community, and sports for spirituality. Given all the daily challenges that we find ourselves facing today, it is understandable that some of us might find ourselves asking the question: "Why should I be Dharmi, a follower of Sanatana Dharma?"

What precisely does Sanatana Dharma have to offer us? How can this ancient, spiritual world-view and culture help us as individuals, help our family, and help to bring about a much better world?

The truth is there are many reasons why Sanatana Dharma (sometimes mistakenly referred to as "Hinduism") offers us the best way to find the happiness, peace and prosperity that we're all seeking. This small article will only offer a very small number of these many benefits of the Dharmic way of life. For more in-depth information, however, visit

Dharmacentral.com, the largest and most authoritative source of information on Sanatana Dharma available on the Internet today. In addition, take the time to read the other informative articles available on Dharmacentral.com.

Sanatana Dharma is the most ancient and respected religion in the world. Due to the spiritual peace, personal empowerment, overall health and satisfying lifestyle it offers its followers, Sanatana Dharma has survived intact for over 5000 years. It has survived – when many other religions didn't - because its teachings are time honored and true. Its lasting influence can be seen in the very name of our tradition, "Sanatana Dharma", or The Eternal Natural Way.

Dharmic ideas, philosophy, spirituality, and art have influenced more people in world history than any other religion on earth. Among those in the West who have been highly influenced by the teachings of Sanatana Dharma are: Schopenhauer, Herman Melville, Emerson, Thoreau, Whitman, Mark Twain, Romain Rolland, Einstein, Aldous Huxley, J. Robert Oppenheimer, Christopher Isherwood, J.D. Salinger, Arlo Guthrie, George Harrison, movie director David Lynch, and actresses Julia Roberts and Heather Graham, among the many thousands of other well-known writers, intellectuals, scientists, celebrities and artists who have incorporated aspects of Sanatana Dharma into their lives. Tom Brady, quarterback for the New England Patriots football team, keeps a four inch statue of Ganesha in his locker. Even today, tens of millions of Americans, Europeans, famous celebrities, scientists and scholars find spiritual solace and intellectual assurance in the amazing teachings of Dharma.

Sanatana Dharma is the most tolerant, peaceful, and non-fanatical religion in the world today. Unlike many other religions, Sanatana Dharma isn't based on blind belief, dogma, closed-mindedness or fanaticism. Rather, it is based upon your own intelligent discernment in searching for Truth, your personal experience with God, the guidance of the Vedic scriptures (the most ancient collection of writings in human history), the living example of hundreds of generations of liberated *yogis* and sages who traversed the path before us, and respect for you as a free person and an intelligent seeker.

In addition to having very rational and fulfilling religious principles, Sanatana Dharma is also a very practical path that offers us real tools for having more peace and joy in our lives. The Yoga, meditation, prayer and ritual practices of Sanatana Dharma have been scientifically proven in thousands of academic research studies to reduce stress, depression, anxiety, nightmares, and many other illnesses. These Dharmic practices have produced multiple millions of enlightened beings throughout world history, and have been proven to be just as relevant and effective in our own modern age. It is for this reason that hundreds of millions of the world's inhabitants practice meditational techniques today, almost all of which can be ultimately traced back directly to the tradition of Sanatana Dharma.

The Dharmic diet of lacto-vegetarianism (a diet free of meat, fish and eggs...but in which milk products are fine) has been shown by the entire medical community to be the healthiest and most nutritious diet in the world. The traditional Dharmic medical system of Ayurveda is now being studied in many of the top medical colleges in the world as a safe, natural and highly effective sister-modality to contemporary allopathic medicine.

And Yoga, the Dharmic path of self-realization, is now practiced by hundreds of millions of people outside of India for optimal health, stress-reduction, clarity of mind, as well as to experience the direct reality of their true spiritual selves. In American alone, about 20 million people practice Yoga on a regular basis. The reason why so many millions of intelligent, educated, health-conscious and spiritually-inclined people practice Yoga is very simple: They've seen that it works!

Of all the many reasons why you should be a Dharmi, however, the most important one is because it is through Sanatana Dharma that you can have a personal and vividly transformative experience of God. The ultimate goal of Sanatana Dharma is to experience God's presence in a radically personal and real way. When God is placed in the center of your personal life and your family life, there is no challenge, no problem, no illness, and no difficulty that you cannot face with courage and contentment. Sanatana Dharma is the most direct path there is for knowing God's love and grace in your life.

Sanatana Dharma is a religious path that is open to all human beings, regardless of your race, nationality, ethnicity, previous religious background or language. Sanatana Dharma is not "Eastern", "Indian", or "Asian". It transcends all nationalities and ethnicities. All that is required to achieve the maximum benefit that this dynamic path has to offer you is sincerity, humility, an openness to guidance and growth, and your own eagerness to know the Truth. Sanatana Dharma is open to all.

If you find the teachings, lifestyle and practice of Sanatana Dharma to be the answer to your spiritual search, the members of International Sanatana Dharma Society (ISDS) welcome you to embrace this spiritual heritage with joy and renewed vigor. Sanatana Dharma is God's gift to you and to our suffering world.

For much more information on how you can deepen your understanding of Dharma and begin your exciting journey on this spiritual path today, please visit: www.dharmacentral.com/dharmainfo.php

Sanatana Dharma is open to all sincere seekers and welcomes all who wish to adopt Dharma as their spiritual path. These are a few things you can do to get started in your practice of a Dharmic lifestyle. By protecting Dharma and supporting your spiritual community, you can become a great example for your family and your greater community.

Step A) **Beginning a Dharmic Lifestyle**

1. Consciously and openly identify with Sanatana Dharma as your spiritual path.

2. Begin to transition to a vegetarian diet.

3. Begin reading the *Bhagavad Gita*, the most important Dharma scripture.

4. Learn how to practice spiritual meditation.

5. Understand the philosophy of Dharma and accept the prin ciples of *karma*/reincarnation. Dharmacentral.com has a massive library of the very best information on Sanatana Dharma availa ble anywhere in the world today.

6. Study as deeply as possible the book *Sanatana Dharma: The Eternal Natural Way* and the companion book *The Sanatana Dharma Study Guide* (available at Dharmacentral.com).

7. Become a tithing member of the International Sanatana Dharma Society, the premier organization teaching Vedic spirit-

uality in the world today.

Step B) **Becoming a Dedicated Dharma Practitioner**

After declaring yourself a Dharmi, you may want to then deepen your understanding and practice of Dharma by incorporating a serious spiritual practice into your daily life. The best way to do this is under the guidance of a qualified and knowledgeable *guru*, or spiritual teacher. The following steps will help you with this deepening of your practice.

> 1. Study the philosophy and teachings of Dharma under the guidance of a qualified *guru* and take eventual initiation from that *guru*. Visit Dharmacentral.com for more information on how you can study with a qualified *guru*. Feel free to also get a copy of the book *Taking Refuge in Dharma: The Initiation Guidebook*.
>
> 2. Adopt a healthy spiritual lifestyle, including vegetarianism, avoidance of all intoxicants and narcotics, and following all the ethical principles of Dharma.
>
> 3. Practice regular spiritual meditation, reciting of sacred *mantras* and conducting *puja* on a daily basis.
>
> 4. Introduce others to Vedic spirituality by giving them copies of *Sanatana Dharma: The Eternal Natural Way*, and referring them to Dharmacentral.com

You are welcome to join the global Sanatana Dharma community. Join us in our active mission to share the beauty and peace of Sanatana Dharma with the world. Join the International Sanatana Dharma Society today!

For more information on the life-enhancing path of Sanatana Dharma, please visit Dharmacentral.com.

9.2.1 Choosing Sanatana Dharma as One's Spiritual Path

The members of the International Sanatana Dharma Society are dedicated to following a path that encourages them to look honestly within in a contemplative manner, to observing a spiritual discipline that leads to a gradual unfoldment of our true selves, and that results in self-realization and God-consciousness.

If you are interested in joining the International Sanatana Dharma Society, we ask that you possess deep sincerity, humility, openness, and a strong desire to know the Divine. If you are attracted to a Vedic-based path that focuses on thorough authenticity, a conscientious philosophical approach, and a clear and effective means of knowing God's presence in your everyday life, please consider becoming an official member today.

9.3.1 The Importance of the Guru in Sanatana Dharma

tad viddhi pranipatena pariprasnena sevaya
upadeksyanti te jnanam jnaninas tattva-darsinah

"Just try to learn the Truth by approaching a spiritual master. Inquire from him submissively and render service unto him. The self-realized soul can impart knowledge unto you because he has seen the Truth."
(*Bhagavad Gita*, 4:34)

The concept of practicing spiritual life under the guidance of an authentic and qualified *guru*, or spiritual teacher, has been central to the entire Dharmic world-view from the beginning of time, down to our present day. So important has the role of the *guru* always been in Vedic culture, that there is no Vedic tradition or *sampradaya* (school of thought) in all of

Sanatana Dharma that does not offer the greatest of respect to the importance of the *guru*. The great Vedantic text known at the *Vedanta-sara* paints the following dramatic picture in order to convey the importance of having a *guru* in one's spiritual pursuit:

janana-maranadi-samsaranala-santapto dipta-sira jala-rasim iva
upahara-panam sotriyam brahma-nistham gurum upasrtya tam anusarati

"Just as a person whose head is on fire runs to water, one who burns from the flames of birth, death, old age, and disease in the holocaust of material existence must run to a genuine *guru* for relief. Such a *guru* must be fixed in the Absolute Truth and well-versed in the scriptures. One should approach him with all that is needed for sacrifice and submit to him as a disciple, ready to carry out his every instruction." (*Vedanta-Sara,* 11)

In our present era, the term *"guru"* has become very well known even throughout the non-Vedic world, in addition to being known within Sanatana Dharma. Indeed, the very word *"guru"* has today become a part of the Standard English lexicon with such terms as "computer *guru*", "health *guru*", "economics *guru*", etc. being employed in daily usage. While the use of the word has become widespread, however, the sacrosanct importance of the station of *guru* is not as deeply understood in contemporary society as it once was. In the following section of this book, I will be briefly explaining the traditional Dharmic understanding of the importance of the *guru* in the life of the spiritual practitioner, as well as dispelling some of the more common myths often wrongly associated with the principle of *guru*.

Interestingly, the very word *"guru"* itself is actually a somewhat generalized term that simply means a competent teacher of any kind. Any skilled expert who is authorized to teach a specific subject can be considered a *guru* in the most general of senses. Thus, there can be a sitar *guru*, a martial arts *guru*, a medicinal arts *guru*, or a fine arts *guru*. When the word is used in the overtly spiritual sense, however, then we are talking about a *guru* of a categorically different nature. The spiritual *guru* is specifically designated as a "*sadguru*" or a teacher of Truth. It is the *sadguru*, the conveyer of Truth, who serves as the underlying model of any and all other types of *gurus*.

It has always been universally recognized that one can only learn a specialized field of important knowledge from a qualified and well-trained teacher, an expert on that particular subject who has both the theoretical knowledge, as well as the acquired experience, necessary to bring that knowledge to life. If one were to study to become a medical doctor, for example, it is understood that the only way to truly understand medicine is to go to a recognized school, and learn under the instruction of very experienced professors who themselves are recognized doctors trained and authorized to teach. If we attempt to learn to become a doctor by merely reading books on our own without the benefit of such expert guidance, we will be doing both our eventual patients and ourselves the greatest of disservices. Rather than curing our patients, in fact, we will most likely harm them due to our not having learned medicine from a living authority.

Similarly, it has been universally recognized in the Vedic tradition since the most ancient of times that if one wishes to understand and make progress in the realm of spirituality, one must also seek guidance under the most able spiritual professionals available. Such a spiritual professional is the *guru*.

According to the *Bhagavata Purana*:

> *tasmad gurum prapadyeta jijnasum sreyam uttamam*
> *sabde pare ca nisnatam brahmany upasamasrayam*

"One who is searching for the Ultimate Truth must surrender unto a spiritual master, a *guru*. A *guru* knows the inner meaning of the *Vedas*, is fixed in the Absolute Truth and is expert in the *shastra*, the revealed scriptures." (*Bhagavata Purana*, 11.3.21)

Of all types of *gurus*, the scriptures (*Shastras*) of Sanatana Dharma have recognized the Acharya as the most important form that the principle of *guru* can take. *Acharyavan puruso veda*, "Only one who has an Acharya can know the Truth." (*Chandogya Upanisad*, 6.18.2) It is only under the guidance of an Acharya who knows the Truth that a seeker can in turn know Truth.

The *sadguru* is a spiritual teacher. The Acharya, moreover, is considered to be a *sadguru* who has attained a much higher stage of personal spiritual development, and who thus has more responsibility in the realm of Dharmic leadership. An Acharya is a spiritual preceptor who represents a living lineage (*sampradaya*) of Sanatana Dharma, and who embodies the teachings of Dharma is his own life, thus teaching the world by his own personal living example. While every Acharya fulfills the function of a *guru*, not every *guru* can be considered an Acharya.

More than merely being a teacher in the formal academic sense, however, the Acharya *guru* is recognized as also being someone who possesses divine qualities due to his own years of practice and inner realization, and who thus perfectly personifies the fruit of spiritual teachings in his own life.

achinoti yam shastrartham achare sthapayaty api
svayam acharate yasma acharyas tena kirtitam

"An Acharya is one who fully understands the conclusions of the revealed scriptures. His own behavior reflects his deep realization, and thus he is a living example of divine precept. He is therefore known as an Acharya, or one who teaches the meaning of the scriptures both by word and deed." (*Vayu Purana*)

The qualified and authentic *guru* is not merely someone who teaches the Truth verbally, but who also lives that Truth perfectly, and who then reflects that Truth to his students in a living and dynamic way.

In the present, dark Age of Conflict (Kali Yuga), unfortunately, we more often than not encounter unqualified and self-anointed individuals who claim to be *gurus* while usually falling very far short of the true meaning of this term. A true *guru* is not merely a conning "miracle" worker pretending to pull sacred ash out of his sleeve like a third-rate magician; nor is he someone who merely gives comforting hugs but does not deliver philosophical truth that leads his disciples to liberation; nor is he simply an actor who is professionally photographed looking toward the skies above with a big toothy grin; nor is the *guru* someone who abuses his disciples sexually, financially, emotionally or spiritually with the consequent excuse that he was merely practicing some heretofore unknown form of "*tantra*". Rather, a true *guru* possesses an ability that no fake spiritual teacher can ever pretend to have. The true and authentic *guru* personifies the Truth in everything he thinks, says and does; and has the ability to help others achieve that very same Truth. Truth does not cheat.

Truth does not abuse. Truth does not need your money. Truth liberates you.

Often unqualified pretender *gurus* do not possess the prerequisite spiritual qualities, philosophical and *sadhana* (practice) training, and moral characteristics necessary to call themselves a *guru* in the authentic and scripturally based sense of this term. I have conservatively estimated that this is the case with a minimum of 95% of individuals who portray themselves as *gurus* today. The scriptures of Sanatana Dharma have given us very clear and unambiguous guidelines of many of the most important qualities necessary in order to recognize whether or not a person is in fact an authentic and qualified *guru*.[29] Some of these guidelines are outlined in the *Bhagavad Gita*:

> *duhkheshv anudvigna-manah sukheshu vigata-sprhah*
> *vita-raga-bhaya-krodhah sthita-dhir munir uchyate*

"One who is not disturbed in spite of the threefold miseries, who is not elated when experiencing pleasantness, and who is free from attachment, fear and anger, is called a sage of steady mind." (*Bhagavad Gita*, 2:56)

Thus, the *sadguru* (true *guru*) is inwardly detached and transcends the sufferings of this world, accepting material pleasure and pain, suffering and pleasantness with equal demeanor. It is as a result of the true *guru's* transcendent status - and the consequent detachment, peace, and gravitas (*dhira*) that the *guru* exudes at all times - that the true *guru* has the ability to help his student to similarly transcend the darkness of ignorance.

---

[29] For very clear guidelines on what constitutes a fraudulent *guru*, please read the chapter on this topic in my book *Taking Refuge in Dharma*.

More, the true *guru* exhibits certain necessary inherent qualities that are a reflection of the fact that he is presencing the Divine in his own life. Again, the *Bhagavad Gita* gives us several lists of these important transcendental qualities of the true *guru*, or the liberated sage, including the following important characteristics:

> The Blessed Lord said: Fearlessness, purification of one's existence, cultivation of spiritual knowledge, charity, self-control, performance of sacrifice, study of the Vedas, austerity and simplicity; nonviolence, truthfulness, freedom from anger; renunciation, tranquility, aversion to faultfinding, compassion and freedom from covetousness; gentleness, modesty and steady determination; vigor, forgiveness, fortitude, cleanliness, freedom from envy and the passion for honor--these transcendental qualities, O son of Bharata, belong to godly men endowed with divine nature. (*Bhagavad Gita*, 16:1-3)

In this way, the *guru* personifies the fruit of a sattvic (spiritually positive) lifestyle and of years of meditative practice.

A true *guru* is known, not merely by how much charisma he may possess, or by what cheap supposed miracles he seemingly performs, or by how popular he have become with the gullible masses due to well-formulated PR and marketing campaigns. Rather, the true *guru* is known by whether or not he personifies the qualities of a *guru* that are clearly outlined in the scriptures of Sanatana Dharma. Any person who claims to be a true *guru*, but who does not exhibit all the qualities of a true *guru* that are revealed in the scriptures of Sanatana Dharma, is a false *guru* and must be immediately rejected as a charlatan if the student is going to make any progress toward the goal of transcendental realization.

It is precisely because the true *guru* both personifies the very highest philosophical teachings (*siddhanta*), as well as the moral and yogic behavior described in the Vedic scriptures that the *guru* has the ability to deliver us from ignorance to wisdom, from darkness to the light, and from bondage to freedom.

According to the Vedic scriptures, when we find ourselves in the presence of such an authentic *guru*, it is almost as if we are in the very presence of God Himself; because like God, the *sadguru* has the ability to show us Truth, and to thus set us free. In the *Bhagavata Purana*, Sri Krishna confirms this in His instructions to His great devotee Uddhava:

> *acharyam mam vijaniyam navamanyeta karhicit*
> *na martya buddhyasuyeta sarva-deva mayo gurum*

[Krishna told Uddhava] "Know the Acharya as My very Self. I am the Acharya. Never envy the Acharya; never blaspheme him or consider him to be an ordinary man. Because the Acharya channels the infinite, He is greater than the sum total of all the finite. Thus, he is more important than all the gods." (*Srimad-Bhagavatam*, 11.17.27)

Further, Sri Krishna explains in the same sacred text that to even view the liberated Acharya as an ordinary man, and to not offer one's due respects to such an exalted *guru*, is considered by Him to be a great offence (*guru-maha-aparadha*):

> *yasya saksad bhagavati jnana-dipa prade gurau*
> *martyasad-dhim srutam tasya sarvam ku-jara-saucavat*

"The *guru* must be considered to be like the Supreme Lord Himself, because he bestows the light of transcendental knowledge upon his disciples. Consequently, for one who maintains the material conception that the *guru* is an ordinary human being, everything is frustrated. His attempts to make progress in spiritual life - his Vedic studies and scriptural knowledge, his penances and austerities, and his worship of the deity - are all as useless as the bathing of an elephant who rolls in the mud after his bath." (*Srimad-Bhagavatam*, 11.20.17)

Confirmation of these Vedic instructions on the nature of *sadguru* is found throughout the length and breadth of the Vedic scriptures. For example, in the *Padma Purana* it is explained that: *gurus nara-matir yasya va naraki sam*, "One who thinks that the *guru* is an ordinary man is said to live in ignorance." In this way, we see that the totality of the scriptures speak in one, unified and authoritative voice on the importance of the *guru* and the unique role of the *guru* in the life of one who claims the desire to know Truth.

Later in this same conversation, Uddhava replies to Sri Krishna's instruction in the same vein:

> *naivopayanty apachitim kavayas tavesha*
> *brahmayusapi krtam rddha mudam smarantam*
> *yo'ntar bahis tanu-bhrtam asubham vidhunvann*
> *acharya-chaittya vapusa sva-gatim vyanakti*

[Uddhava said to Sri Krishna] "O my Lord! Transcendental poets and experts in spiritual science could not fully express their indebtedness to You, even if they were endowed with the lifetime of Brahma, for You appear in two features - externally as the Acharya and internally as the Paramatman, the Supreme Self - to deliver the embodied living beings by revealing to them your devotional service and teaching them how to approach you on the path of divine love." (*Srimad-Bhagavatam*, 11.29.6)

In addition to explaining both the nature and the qualities of the *sadguru*, the scriptures also explain that it is likewise very important to understand the important qualities that must be present in a sincere and qualified student. In the *Katha Upanishad*, for example, we read the following:

shravanayapi bahubhir yo na labhyam
shrnvanto 'pi bahavo na vidyum
acharyo 'sya vakta kushalo 'sya labhda
acharyo jnata kushala nushishtam

"Many cannot even hear about the soul, and even after hearing about the soul, many cannot understand it; this is because it is hard to find an Acharya who is a genuine seer of the truth. Such a qualified Acharya is a great soul and is very rare. At the same time, realization of the truth can be had only by those disciples who carefully follow the qualified Acharya's teachings and become expert in the science of God. Such disciples are also very rare. Thus it is that only a few ever come to know the soul in truth." (*Katha Upanisad*, 1.2.7.)

To find a sincere and worthy student is thus explained as being just as difficult as finding a qualified and worthy *sadguru*. The highest attainment of transcendent Truth, and the personal spiritual liberation (*moksha*) that results from such a realization, is the most difficult goal to realize. Thus, Krishna states in the *Bhagavad Gita*:

Manushyam sahasreshu kashchid yatati siddhaye
Yatatam api siddhanam kashchin mam vetti tattvatah

"Of many thousands of men, one will attempt to reach perfection; and of the few who reach this goal, only a rare soul will perhaps know Me as I am." (*Bhagavad Gita*, 7:3)

When a sincere student and a qualified *sadguru* finally do find each other, and unite in the eternal process of spiritual exchange – the *guru* sharing his insight, instruction, and empowering presence with the student; and the student learning and growing spiritually with humility, sincerity, openness and eagerness – we then witness the perfect conditions necessary for the celebration and living of Truth. If you are seeking Truth, then seek the guidance of one who has seen the Truth. Seek the *sadguru*.

As for the necessity of a being with less intelligence/development/skills (a spiritual student, or *shishya*) deriving the necessary tools and sustenance for growth from a being (the teacher, or *guru*) who possesses what the former being is lacking, i.e., the *guru/shishya* relationship, such a relationship is not a matter of dogma, but of both logical and natural (Dharmic) necessity. In the same way that the relationship between mother and child is not a matter of man-made law that is somehow artificially imposed upon the mother and child, similarly, the relationship between *guru* and *shishya* is a natural and universally documented relationship that is as much a part of nature as an apple growing from an apple tree!

Knowledge of Transcendence derives from above, and not from below, in the same way that all spiritual realities, principles, etc. flow from their ontologically highest level, to then become increasingly concretized in relation to our ability to grasp them consequent to our own state of inner awareness/illusion. It is natural, then, that if we wish to know the Truth, then we can only access that Truth via someone who is "above" us in both knowledge and spiritual realization. That being who is above us, and who thus has the necessary tools, perspective and ability (*shakti*) to help us to grown spiritually, is the *guru*.

9.4.1 The Art of Questioning

The beginning of all spiritual life begins with asking the big questions: "Why am I here?" "Who am I?" "What is God's will for my life?" These and other such questions from the very basis of a self-reflective life. The process of sincere inquiry, and the reciprocal receiving of real and satisfying answers is a course of action that continues all throughout one's spiritual journey. This is one thing that, in fact, makes the path of Yoga and Sanatana Dharma very different from almost all other spiritual traditions. Unlike the Abrahamic religions, sincere questioning is actually actively encouraged in our spiritual tradition.

Sanatana Dharma is a spiritual world-view that is predicated upon the idea that we are all free and unique beings. We are respected as persons who have the ability to make our own choices in life, and who deserve to have our choices honored. As free beings, it is incumbent upon us to progress spiritually by the strength of our own sincerity, dedication, and free inquiry. The tradition of Dharma, from this perspective, can almost be called the religion of questioning and free inquiry.

Throughout the Dharmic scriptures (the Vedic literature), we see again and again thousands of examples of free and open dialogs that take place between students and teachers in an attempt to understand the truth of a particular question or philosophical problem. Whether in the *Upanishads*, *Puranas*, *Mahabharata*, *Bhagavad Gita*, or any of the other scriptures of Sanatana Dharma, we repeatedly read about various philosophical discussions that take place between either a *guru* and disciple, or a king and a *guru*, or a god and a human, etc. Indeed, only in Sanatana Dharma is there even a scripture known as the *Prashna Upanishad*, or the "*Upani-*

shad of Questioning". The most important of Dharmic scriptures, the *Bhagavad Gita*, is itself an open philosophical dialog between a princely warrior and God Himself serving in the role of the *guru*.

In the *Bhagavad Gita*, we have God Himself engaging in free and open dialog with His student Arjuna, in the attempt to bring Arjuna to a deeper understanding of the truth of his own self-identity, and his relationship with God. This vision of God as the Supreme Person who is compassionate, loving, and secure enough in His own being to have a down-to-earth conversation with His devotee is in stark contrast to how the Abrahamic (Judeo-Christian-Islamic) god is depicted in the Biblical and Koranic texts, as an unapproachable being who only engages in a one-way dialog with his followers. The encouraging of sincere and open questioning is found throughout our spiritual tradition like with no other religious tradition on earth.

It is understood in Santana Dharma that the process of questioning is in itself an art. The important thing to understand about the process of philosophical questioning is that the questioning itself has to follow the proper methodology if one is to receive real and truly authentic answers. Questioning is itself an art and a spiritual discipline. Above all, it is the motivational attitude, even more so than the cognitive abilities of the questioner, that is of operative importance. In other words, the important factor in questioning is not how smart the questioner thinks he is, but why the person is asking the questions in the first place.

A philosophical question to the *guru* needs to be presented in a way that is sincere, humble, open, and direct. Anything less than this attitude will not lead to real answers. Even a question as seemingly benign as "What is

324

God?", for example, can be asked in such a manner as to receive a real answer, or it can be asked in a manner that is arrogant and demanding. Only the former, asking with humility and openness, will lead the questioner to Truth. Asking with arrogance will only lead to further ignorance.

The *Bhagavad Gita* provides us with a very clear description of the science of asking questions of a *guru*:

"Attempt to learn that truth by approaching a spiritual teacher. Inquire submissively from him and render service to him. The self-realized sages will initiate you into true knowledge for they have themselves seen the truth." (*Bhagavad Gita*, 4:34)

It is only in approaching the search for truth with such an attitude of openness, humility, patience, and sincerity that the truth will be revealed to you.

In the same way that we can approach an embodied *guru* or sage with sincere inquiries, when we reach a very advanced stage, we can also engage in such a student/teacher relationship with God Himself as the *antaryamin*, or the inner witness within our hearts. While it is imperative that we have a living, embodied *guru* to whom we can approach and receive Divine knowledge, God is ultimately the source of all Truth, and the eternal Guru. Thus, through the process of meditation, we can both confirm the realizations that we receive from the embodied *guru*, as well as engage in a direct reciprocal relationship with God in which we can clarify inner doubts, receive answers to further queries, and deepen our understanding of both ourselves and the nature of reality.

There are always two people involved in spiritual inquiry: the student (*shishya*) and the teacher (*guru*). Likewise, the general process of inquiry consists of a two way process. It requires not only the asking of questions on the part of the student, but also the ability to receive and accept answers from the teacher. These two steps are necessary whether the teacher is an embodied *guru*, or God Himself. When we are inquiring directly from God, these two steps are found in the form of 1) prayer and 2) meditation.

Through prayer, we are communicating our concerns to God, and through meditation, we are allowing God to reveal Himself to us. Thus, the communication is a two way street, and not a one-way monologue. One of the problems that we often find with the Abrahamic religions of Judaism, Christianity, and Islam is that these religious constructs tend to lay a great emphasis on prayer alone, or speaking to their god and petitioning him, without any understanding of the reciprocal need of eventually stilling the mind in disciplined meditation and allowing their specific divinity to then reveal himself to them. Prayer, for the Abrahamic faiths is a one-way form of communication alone.

Too many of us want to speak to God, ask Him questions, ask for favors and gifts, but so few of us are ready to then sit in the silence of meditation and allow God to respond to our queries. Would it not at the very least be considered rude if someone were constantly speaking at you, asking you questions, petitioning you for favors, but never allowing you an opportunity to actually respond? This is what we are doing to God when we only pray, but never open ourselves in meditation for His response to us. In Sanatana Dharma, it is understood that "listening" to God in meditation is often of much greater importance than talking to

God, since it is in humbly and openly listening that we learn and grow. Both, speaking and listening to God, however, must be present if we are to fully experience what it means to commune with the Absolute.

It is in devotional meditation (*bhakti*) that we are in the most intimate communion with God. God, being purely spiritual in nature, the only way to truly communicate with, experience, and thus truly know God is in the pure realm of consciousness. In meditation, the pure *atman* that constitutes our true self is in closest proximity with God. And the deeper and more advanced the meditator is, in direct proportion is he able to experience and understand the eternal Truth free of egoic mediation. It is when there is no medium left separating the meditator from the object of meditation (God) that we can then experience pure and eternal knowledge being revealed to us directly from the mercy of God Himself. At this point of pure meditative absorption upon the Absolute, nothing remains unknown to us. This, of course, is the ultimate goal (*artha*) of meditation, and takes years of dedicated practice, sincerity, focused determination, and great devotion to attain.

As for the matter of getting immediate answers to ones questions through meditation, the answers that one gets will be in direct proportion to one's spiritual advancement, and the grace of both the *guru* and God. The path of Sanatana Dharma offers us the greatest, most systematic, and most effective vehicle for making spiritual advancement and for experiencing the infinite grace of the Divine.

9.5.1 The Process of Diksha

The formal process of entering the systematic spiritual path of Sanatana Dharma is known in the Sanskrit language as *"diksha"*, or spiritual initiation. The ancient process of *diksha* initiation is considered to be of crucial importance throughout the entire Vedic tradition as one enters a more serious and disciplined course of practice of Dharma spirituality. Through undergoing the ancient Vedic ceremony of *diksha*, one openly embarks on the path of Yoga, meditation, and spiritual practice under the skilled tutelage of a recognized *guru*, or spiritual teacher. In addition, the *diksha* process signifies one's acknowledged welcoming into the family of the great tradition of Sanatana Dharma, and the leaving behind of all previously held non-Dharmic beliefs and religious affiliations.

A follower of Sanatana Dharma is known as a Sanatana Dharmi, or, more simply, as a Dharmi.[30]

There are several important elements that occur as a result of the *diksha* process. First, *diksha* is a public acknowledgement that you are now dedicating yourself exclusively to the tradition and practice of Sanatana Dharma. It signals that Sanatana Dharma is your exclusive path to the Divine, and that you have left all other religious paths behind. More personally, it is designed to make you stronger in your own personal dedication to this path, as well as deepening your own realization and experience. Initiation is thus often a very moving and empowering experience since it signifies one's personal surrender to God, and the commencement of one's guided spiritual practice.

---

[30] Literally, "one who adheres to Dharma".

Second, the primary *mantra* that you will use in meditation is formally imparted to you. The primary *mantra* of meditation is **Aum Namo Narayanaya**. As a result of formally receiving the *mantra* in the *diksha* process, your meditative experience will now be deeper and more profound, since the *mantra* is now "charged" with the grace of God and Sri Guru. You will now be expected to meditate reciting a specific number of *mantras* per day, each and every day.

Third, during *diksha* initiation, there is a direct empowerment (*shakti-da*) that takes place from *guru* to *shishya* (student). This is a spiritual transmission of grace and power that helps the student in his continuing development of the student's practice and learning. The *guru* quite literally shares some of his own spiritual power with the student in order to strengthen the student for the practices that lie ahead.

The process of *diksha* signifies the commencement of a spiritual relationship between the *guru* and the student (*shishya*) that is both sacred and unique. With *diksha*, the *guru* pledges to faithfully serve the student as a guide and mentor. Similarly, the student pledges to follow the *guru's* instructions with trust, sincerity, humility, openness, and loyalty. A person typically only undergoes *tiru-mantra-diksha* (the first initiation, in which the Narayana *mantra* is conferred upon the student) once in their life. The bond between *guru* and *shishya* is a deep, loving and abiding relationship, and one's fellow initiates are seen as one's God-brothers and God-sisters.

9.5.2 Requirements for Initiation

A person is not eligible for initiation until they have already been studying and practicing Sanatana Dharma under the informal guidance of the *guru* (mainly via reading the *guru's* writings and listening to the *guru's* talks – either in person or via audio/video format) for some time. The precise duration of that time is completely at the discretion of the *guru*, but is **generally for a minimum of one year**. It is required that you be an official member of the International Sanatana Dharma Society for this period of time in order to have a formal connection with the *guru's* mission. Information about membership is available in the last section of this book, and at the main website of the ISDS: www.dharmacentral.com.

Once the *guru* accepts the student for formal initiation, the candidate for *diksha* initiation must be observing the following requirements both at the time of initiation, and thereafter:

- Acceptance of the philosophical principles of Sanatana Dharma as written in the Vedic literature and as taught directly by the *guru*.

- The strict observance of lacto-vegetarianism. This means the avoidance of meat, fish and eggs. Consuming dairy products, such as milk, cheese, butter and yoghurt, is completely acceptable.

- The strictest avoidance of all intoxicants and narcotics. This includes such substances as alcohol, marijuana, ayahuasca, hashish, cigarettes, etc. If a person uses these or any other psyche-altering substances, then he cannot claim to be a *yogi*.

- Strictly following all of the ethical precepts of Sanatana Dharma, including the Yamas & Niyamas of the Yoga system, in addition to the other ethical principles found throughout the Vedic scriptures. (*Please see the 'Yama & Niyamas' section in this book to read these ten ethical principles.)

• Acceptance of the Vedic scriptures as your scriptural guide.

• Belief in the principles of *karma*/reincarnation.

• Sincerity, humility, and a willingness to practice the path of Dharma under the guidance of a qualified *guru*.

9.5.3 Dakshina

Part of the traditional process of *diksha* includes what is called *dakshina*, or a gift to the *guru* in appreciation for his teachings and guidance. *Dakshina* is a symbolic gift that is given at the end of the *diksha* ceremony and represents the initiate's gratitude more so than the value of the gift itself. Thus, in accordance with the initiate's means and desire, *dakshina* can consist of a gift as simple as a flower, a fruit, or a stick of incense to a monetary gift of any amount. Again, it is ultimately the devotion (*bhakti*) and gratitude that is important, much more than the nature of the gift or donation. At the same time, the disciple must give to the maximal of their capability, and not use false devotion as an excuse to give to the minimal of their ability.

9.5.4 The Process of Initiation

Several ceremonial elements will take place on the day of initiation. First, there will be a *yagya*, or fire ceremony that will be conducted by a Vedic priest, and often by the *guru* himself. *Yagya* is one of the most ancient ceremonies on earth, with a known history of at least tens of thousands

of years. It is not only ancient, but is found in one form or another in all
pre-Abrahamic spiritual traditions.

During the 30–40 minute long
yagya ceremony, a small fire
will be ritually created in a
fireproof, ritual container in
the temple room. The fire itself represents the mouth of
God, into which various
sattvic (pure) items will be of-
fered. All the initiate candidates will sit around the fire, along with the
priest and the *guru*, during which the presence of God will be invoked.

Once the fire is established, the officiating priest will recite various sacred
mantras while offering assorted substances (herbs, incense, ghee, etc.) into
the fire. The purpose of this ritual is to invoke the presence of the gods
(*devas* and *devis*) and the grace of God, as well as to signal to the cosmos
and those present for the ceremony the solemnity of the vows about to
be undertaken by the initiates.

Second, after the *yagya* is over, everyone will move to the area in the temple in front of the seat of the Acharya (*acharya-asana*). During this
transition, everyone has a few minutes break to stretch his or her legs!
Then the Acharya will deliver a brief discourse on the significance of *diksha* and the nature of the oaths being undertaken.

Third, when the talk is over, the Acharya will call up each individual *diksha* candidate, one-by-one. As each person approaches the Acharya, he

332

will then whisper the *mantra* into the initiate's ear. The *mantra* given at the time of initiation is **Aum Namo Narayanaya**. It is specifically during this process that the *mantra* is now empowered within the heart of the disciple, and that the practice of *mantra* meditation will henceforth begin to have the most significant effect for the now-initiated practitioner.

In addition to giving the new disciple the empowered *mantra*, the *guru* will also give him a set of meditation beads (*japa-mala*) upon which to meditate. These beads were previously empowered by the Acharya by himself meditating upon them, thus infusing them with power. He will then place a set of sacred *tulasi* beads around the new disciple's neck signaling that he is now a devotee of Bhagavan Sri Krishna. Finally, the *guru* will utter the disciple's new Sanskrit spiritual name, by which he will now be known in the company of fellow disciples, along with an explanation of the significance of the new spiritual name.

Fourth, the newly initiated person will offer their respects to the *guru* by offering prostrated obeisances, followed by placing the symbolic *dakshina* gift in the *guru's* hands. The newly initiated disciple will then retake his seat.

Finally, the newly initiated students and congregational members will all together, as one group, a) shout out "Sanatana Dharma Jayate" (Victory to Sanatana Dharma), b) recite the Guru Pranama Mantra in unison (see below), and c) offer prostrated obeisances. This will conclude the initiation ceremony.

9.5.5 Guru Pranama Mantra

The following *mantra* is to be recited during the last step of the process
mentioned above, as well as when offering food, coming into the *guru's*
presence for the first time in the day, and for other ceremonial occasions.

> *nama aum vishnu padaya*
> *krishna preshthaya bhutale*
> *srimate dharma pravartaka*
> *acharya iti namine*

"I offer my respectful obeisances unto he who has taken shelter at the
feet of Sri Vishnu, Sri Dharma Pravartaka Acharya, who is very dear to
Lord Krishna."

9.5.6 Vows Undertaken by the Shishya

During the *diksha* ceremony, the student makes several vows that he is
expected to uphold to the absolute best of his ability. These are oaths
(*vrata*) that cannot be broken and that are to be followed for the rest of
the student's life, until either amended or changed by the *guru's* clear instructions. These vows include the following:

To meditate daily on the **Aum Namo Narayanaya** *mantra*, using a *mala*
(chain of beads) made of sacred *tulasi* wood, as instructed by the Acharya.

To follow all the ethical principles of Sanatana Dharma found in the primary Vedic scriptures,[31] with a special emphasis upon the ten principles known as Yamas & Niyamas.

> To be a strict vegetarian for life.

> To live a thorough Dharma lifestyle, as instructed by the Acharya, to the best of his ability.

> To offer compassion to all sentient beings by sharing the teachings of Dharma with them in accordance with their individual ability to understand.

> To assist the Acharya's mission by being a member of the International Sanatana Dharma Society, by volunteering your time and donations to the ISDS, and by taking part in the programs of the ISDS.

> To serve Dharma, God, and Guru with all of your thoughts, words, and deeds.

> To always maintain loyalty, fidelity and deep devotion (*guru bhakti*) to the person, the teachings and the mission of the *guru*.

The Yamas and Niyamas: The Ten Codes of Dharma

All initiated followers of Sanatana Dharma are expected to uphold the following ten Codes of Dharma as the minimal ethical requirements for spiritual advancement.

---

[31] The primary scriptures include: *Bhagavad Gita, Srimad Bhagavatam, Vishnu Purana*, the fourteen major *Upanishads, Yoga Sutras, Brahma Sutras* and *Narada Bhakti Sutras*.

Yamas (proscriptions)

a) Non-violence   (*ahimsa*)

b) Truthfulness   (*satya*)

c) Non-stealing   (*asteya*)

d) Godly conduct   (*brahmacharya*)

e) Non-attachment   (*aparigraha*)

Niyamas (prescriptions)

a) Contentment   (*santosha*)

b) Discipline/austerity (*tapasya*)

c) Study of scriptures   (*svadhyaya*)

d) Devotion to God   (*Ishvara-pranidhana*)

e) Cleanliness   (*shaucha*)

Chapter 10 Dharma in Practice

10.1.1 The Inner Dimensions of Sadhana Practice

Sanatana Dharma is expressed both philosophically and practically. As human persons who are naturally multi-dimensional beings, we interact with reality in a variety of ways. We both receive input from our external environment, as well as convey output. The ways in which we experience input from our surroundings include the physical, emotional, mental, intellectual, and spiritual ways of perceiving. Conversely, we act within the world in three expressed ways: via the volitional output of our thoughts, our words, and our actions. Through these three means, we affect the world around us, communicating our inner being to our outer reality. It is in all three of these ways of expression that we are meant to practice spiritual life.

While spirituality is certainly meant to be experienced in an intellectual way, it must ultimately be understood through direct practical experience if it is going to be a living spirituality that has the power to change us within and to deepen our understanding of the Divine. Philosophy is necessary, but not sufficient, for serious spiritual growth. Even a good spiritual idea, if not also experienced in the most immediate of ways, is only a reflection of the surface level of Truth without grasping the substance of Truth. Thus, in Dharma practice, ideally the pursuit of philosophical wisdom must be actively coupled with daily practice. In Sanskrit, such daily spiritual practice is called "*sadhana*". *Sadhana* consists of two integral aspects: a) the inner dimension and b) the outer dimension.

The inner elements of our practice serve as the internal volitional foundation for any fruitful practice. It is the inner approach that we take to our personal practice that makes the external disciplines of Yoga, meditation, *puja*, and study effective. These internal elements include: sincerity, humility, openness, and yearning for God.

Sincerity is reflected in the honesty, trust, and patience with which we approach the spiritual path. If we are not honest with ourselves about what it is we claim we are actually searching for, then we cannot be fully honest with our *guru* (spiritual teacher), with others, or with God. Having trust is not to be equated with having blind faith, but rather having confidence in the path we are on due to our previous positive experiences with our *sadhana*, coupled with the knowledge we have gained from the study of scripture (*shastra*). We trust in what we know works, and in what we know is true. Patience is one of the hardest virtues to practice. But with the power of patience, and a willingness to detach ourselves from the idea that we need to achieve immediate results within our own subjective timeframe, we can achieve success in our journey toward self-discovery.

The crucial virtue of humility is too rarely spoken of today by many of our contemporary era's supposedly authentic *gurus* and spiritual guides. We know, however, that historically every true saint, sage, *yogi*, and *guru* has highly praised the incomparable importance of this virtue in the spiritual seeker. Indeed, we can measure the legitimacy of a spiritual teacher in direct proportion to that teacher's depth of humility, and corresponding lack of egotism and false aloofness.

Humility is one of the most important qualities that a spiritual seeker can have. Humility is the direct abandonment of the false ego that keeps us blocked from receiving God's grace and the instructions of the authentic *guru* (spiritual teacher). Humility is the very opposite of the delusional power of false ego (*ahamkara*) that keeps us bound to the negative and self-defeating thought patterns and actions responsible for our suffering. Humility allows us to view ourselves and our situation from the perspective of the Infinite, rather than from the perspective of the limited ego and our unlimited desire.

With an attitude of healthy openness, we allow ourselves to be receptive to the ever-new realizations and experiences that will deepen our personal understanding of Truth. Progress means elimination and new acceptance. We must be open to the fact that our perceived realities, our attachments, and our pet ideas will be constantly challenged and transcended on the spiritual path, and that God often has enormous surprises in store for our limited ego and intellect! It is only when we open ourselves to God's grace, consciously and willingly, that we begin to experience God's presence in our lives in a vivid and meaningful way. To experience God's grace, however, requires that we yearn for that grace.

Every accomplishment begins with a desire to achieve a goal. If we want to accomplish any large task, such as earn a Ph.D., or an M.D., or to lose weight, become healthy, or accomplish any other significant undertaking, having a nonchalant attitude toward our goal will guarantee that we won't succeed. We all know that in our everyday lives, we cannot achieve anything of importance unless we have a yearning and a deep desire to achieve our goal. The more of ourselves we invest in the task, the more we will strive with focus and dedication to be successful. In the same manner in which we need to yearn to achieve even a material goal in this world, we also need to have a strong yearning to know Truth if we are going to have the necessary inspiration to practice our *sadhana*. We must yearn to know God with as much longing as a lost child has when she craves to be reunited with her mother. Only with such an intense spiritual desire will we have the determination we need if we wish to know God.

Our outer reality is a reflection of our inner state. The outer processes of spiritual practice, such as meditation, Yoga, *puja* (ritual worship), and study, can only be effective when coupled with those inner qualities capable of bringing our *sadhana* to life. Allow sincerity, humility, openness, and yearning for God to be your vehicle toward Truth. Then, our effort along the spiritual path, coupled with God's loving grace in our lives, will ensure that we will achieve the goal: spiritual freedom.

10.1.2 General Principles of Daily Sadhana

Sanatana Dharma is certainly a world-view and a philosophical system. More than merely an intellectual exercise, however, Sanatana Dharma is also a lifestyle, a spiritual discipline, and a daily practice. It is in the active practice of Vedic spirituality that we encounter the very heart of the Vedic path. Philosophy without practical application is akin to licking the outside of a bottle of honey in an attempt to know what the honey inside the bottle tastes like. Spiritual practice is opening up the bottle and tasting deeply the sweetness of the honey. The term "*sadhana*" means a path of spiritual practice under the protective guidance of a qualified Acharya (spiritual teacher). By following a daily spiritual practice under the guidance of Sri Guru, we can continuously deepen our experience and realization of the Divine. When a person feels called to devote himself more fully to a systematic spiritual discipline to achieve self-realization and God-realization, they then begin to follow a *sadhana* practice.

The following is a collection of practical, scripturally based guidelines from the teachings of the *sadhana*-specific portions of the Vedic scriptures that will help us to more fully develop our innate spiritual potential. These many practice teachings are derived from such scriptures as the *Upanishads, Bhagavad Gita, Yoga Sutras, Narada Bhakti Sutras, Shandilya Bhakti Sutras,* and a wide array of other Vedic works. These guidelines are not meant to be exhaustive or fully detailed, but to provide a helpful introduction to the spirit of *sadhana.*

Sadhana, or spiritual practice, must be performed regularly with sincerity, humility, openness, and determination. Just as we all perform our daily routines of eating, sleeping, and bathing without fail, similarly we should practice our daily spiritual *sadhana* without fail in order to refine our inner selves and to advance in spiritual life. It is a discipline. As is true of any disciplined endeavor, you will experience the fruits of *sadhana* in direct proportion to the dedication that you bring to your practice.

As my own *guru,* Bhakti Rakshaka Sridhara Swami, would often say, progress is a process of new acceptance of the positive coupled with elimination of the negative. Through our *sadhana* practice, we undergo a simultaneous process of accepting deeper and richer states of devotional consciousness (*bhakti*), along with the elimination of unwanted faults (*anarthas*), unfounded fears (*bhaya*) and negative psychological patterns (*samskaras*).

As we engage in the process of spiritual *sadhana,* we should monitor our progress every day by asking ourselves if today we have improved ourselves in some way. This improvement can be achieved incrementally by either positively gaining a more profound insight or experience of devotional consciousness, or else by progressing in the negation of a negative fault that we have in ourselves. Through this daily process of cultivation of the spiritually positive and elimination of the negative traits that have hampered our realization of Truth, we gradually and deliberately come closer to the goals of self-realization and God-consciousness.

The two keys to a successful *sadhana* practice are *abhyasa* (practice) and *vairagya* (non-attachment). Patanjali confirms this in his *Yoga Sutras* (1:12), where he states "Yoga is achieved through both practice and non-attachment." I will explain the importance of these dual principles separately.

Abhyasa: Sri Krishna explains that *sadhana* may seem difficult at first, but eventually it becomes natural to us. "That which in the beginning may be just like poison but at the end is just like nectar and which awakens one to self-realization is said to be happiness in the mode of goodness." (*Bhagavad Gita*, 18:37) Attaining spiritual progress requires just as much work, concentration, discipline and repeated practice as does any other challenging art that we wish to learn. If one wants to be a violin virtuoso, or a martial arts master, or a great visual artist, there is no substitute for constant practice in order to hone one's craft. This same principle applies to making spiritual progress as well. Merely claiming sincerity is not enough if one is not also ready to make that sincerity come to vivid life in one's actions.

<u>Vairagya</u>: At the same time, however, even if we are practicing *sadhana* rigorously, if we have too much of an impatient attachment to achieving the goal immediately, then we are focusing on the distraction of our impatient mental state more so that what we should be focusing on, which is devotion toward God. We are meant to perform our duty of meditation upon the Divine in a peaceful and patient manner, without allowing constant worry to be a source of anxiety. *Sadhana* must relieve anxiety, not cause it! If we can perform all our spiritual practices with consistency and free of ego, we will know the very highest of spiritual attainments.

Spiritual activity occurs on three levels of human activity: in our thoughts, in our words and in our actions. The *Srimad Bhagavatam* states: "Oh Lord Narayana, I offer to you whatever I do according to my nature, using my body, words, mind, senses, intelligence and purified consciousness. I give all this to you - thinking it is for your pleasure." (*Srimad Bhagavatam*, 11.2.36) We must always strive to spiritualize our activities in everything that we think, say and do.

Sadhana in Thought

1. Above all else, always think of Lord Krishna, as continuous awareness of God is the essence of all scriptural injunctions. When you wake up in the morning, remember Lord Krishna before rising from bed. At night, offer your obeisances to Him before sleeping. Throughout the day always meditate upon His name and keep you consciousness situated in His divine person. By remembering the Supreme we can be like the lotus leaf, which always remains dry above the water level despite being situated within the water.

2. We must associate with like-minded devotees, learning from their example and insights, and developing their godly qualities in ourselves. We must allow their good counsel to enter our intellects and refine us from within. This process is known as *sat-sangha*. *Sat* means that which is good, eternal and true. *Sangha* means association. Thus *sat-sangha* is good association. *Sat-sangha* is coming directly in contact with the Lord through reciprocal association with His devotees. By always keeping spiritually positive association and avoiding negative and dark association, we will quickly begin to reflect the divine qualities of the Lord, and to presence His grace in our lives. The International Sanatana Dharma Society is predicated upon the fellowship dynamic of *sat-sangha*. Thus, for those who cannot find such association where they are, it is advised that they become members of the International Sanatana Dharma Society to receive such positive spiritual association.

3. The initiated disciple must study the sacred Vedic literatures very systematically and reverently, especially the *Bhagavad Gita*, *Bhagavata Purana*, *Patanjali Yoga Sutras*, *Upanishads*, and *Narada Bhakti Sutras*. Try to spend time bathing your intellect each day in these sacred texts, and discuss them with other devotees whenever possible. There is no difference between Lord Krishna and Lord Krishna's instructions. By reading the *Bhagavad Gita* and hearing Sri Krishna's *upadesha* (teachings), we are directly associating with the Supreme.

4. Contentment (*santosha*) is an internal treasure that brings about peace of mind. Contentment is not attained merely by acquiring external objects. Do not let the senses force you to chase unnecessary material possessions. Learn to control your material yearnings and to be content with the blessings that God has given you. One cannot extinguish a fire

by pouring fuel on top of it. Trying to satisfy all of your material desires, however outrageous they might be, will only increase the fire of material suffering. Learn to extinguish this fire by removing the fuel of material attachment. Only through simple living and high thinking can we attain contentment and detachment in spiritual life. Because no two people are the same, detachment will mean different things for different people. Ultimately, detachment is an internal state, more than a matter of how much you possess.

Sadhana in Words

5. Learn to spiritualize your speech by making your utterances reflect the perfection of spiritual reality. Speak truth (*satya*) at all times. This means both refraining from lying, as well as positively sharing the truth of Sanatana Dharma with everyone who expresses a sincere interest and has the ability to understand. Never unduly criticize people or engage in gossip. Mature spiritual practitioners do not speak behind others' backs, do not spread rumors, and do not revel in scandal. Try not to discourage people in the pursuit of their positive dreams, or raise your voice at others out of pride or anger. Instead, see your speech as a gift from God meant to inspire others to be the very best they can be. Always offer kind encouraging words to others.

6. Each day, all initiated disciples should meditate upon the names of Sriman Narayana (God) on *japa malas* (meditation beads) made of *tulasi* wood. In the present Age of Conflict (*kali yuga*), there is no method quite as effective for attaining spiritual realization as meditating upon the sacred names of the Absolute. This is confirmed in the *Brihad Naradiya Purana* (38:126), where it states:

harer nama harer nama harer namaiva kevalam
kalau nasty eva nasty eva nasty eva gatir anyatha

"In this age of Kali, there is no alternative, there is no alternative, there is no alternative for spiritual progress other than the chanting of the holy name, the chanting of the holy name, the chanting of the holy name of Lord Hari (Narayana)."

It is very rare throughout the Vedic scriptures that a statement is repeated three times. It is only when the scripture in question wishes to emphasize the great importance of a statement that it will repeat a phrase three times, as is the case in the above verse. Thus, according to this *Purana*, the most effective process for making spiritual progress in our day and age is to meditate upon a *mantra* that consists of the name of Hari (one of the many names of Narayana).

The most effective of all such *hari-nama*, or divine name, *mantras* is the *mantra*:

Aum Namo Narayanaya

A *shishya* (student) is expected to recite a minimum of one round of this *mantra* on his *japa mala* in daily meditation. One round consists of 108 *mantra* recitations. While one round is the absolute minimum number of *mantras* to be said in each 24 hour period, however, there is no maximal number of times that the *mantra* can be recited in meditation. The quality of our practice must always take precedence over the quantity. However, to have a maximal of both quality and quantity together is always the most effective course of practice if our goal is to deepen our spiritual realization.

Sadhana in Action

7. Each day the *shishya* must strive to increasingly deepen his understanding of his *gurudeva's* teachings, to practically assist his *gurudeva's* teaching mission with enthusiasm, and to offer his respects to him.

8. Always try to offer practical service (*seva*) to God in accordance with your own specific capacity, means, skills, and understanding. No two human beings in existence are the same. No two humans are perfectly "equal" in every way. We are all different and unique, with individualized skills, temperaments, desires and abilities. To offer service to God that is actually in accordance with your own nature (*svadharma*) is to offer Him service that is an honest expression of your deepest and sincerest nature. As Krishna explains, He prefers that our service be reflective of our own unique nature rather than the nature of another:

"It is far better to discharge one's prescribed duties, even though faultily, than another's duties perfectly. Destruction in the course of performing one's own duty is better than engaging in another's duties, for to follow another's path is dangerous." (*Bhagavad Gita*, 3:35)

If you are an intellectual, then write about Krishna and teach others His philosophy. If you are a good manager or warrior, then lead in a Dharmic manner. If you are a good businessperson, then create prosperity and donate a portion of your wealth to God's devotees. If you are great at construction or labor, then work for God; build His temple! Whoever we are, whatever skills we have, wherever we find ourselves in our lives, we all have something that we can offer in service to the Divine.

9. Have an altar in your home where you keep a sacred image (*murti*) of

Lord Krishna, or other forms of the Lord. Offer daily worship to the *murti* with incense, flowers, water, a ghee wick lamp, and with what ever else is within your capacity. Only in the eyes of those lacking metaphysical depth would this process be misconstrued as "idol" worship. It is not. The science of *murti* worship is an active process of meditation in which we symbolically offer pure and pleasing items to God while meditating upon our own sense of increasing surrender (*prapatti*) to God. In this way, we systematically deepen our consciousness of surrender.

10. Give up unhealthy habits such as smoking, the use of narcotics and drinking alcohol. The best way to give up such destructive habits is to not surrender to them or think that you are helpless to their power, but to instead transcend them. You can transcend such negative tastes by replacing them with a positive taste. Replace these destructive habits with the spiritually beneficial activity of service (*seva*). Service to God in the company of devotees is one of the sweetest and most enjoyable methods to advance in spiritual life.

11. Practice non-violence (*ahimsa*) by avoiding harming other living beings unnecessarily. The principle of non-violence is not to be mistaken with the idea of pacifism. Sanatana Dharma does not believe in pacifism in any form. On the contrary, Sanatana Dharma is a warrior tradition. Sanatana Dharma is not a religion that encourages us to become victims; rather it teaches us to not victimize others. Sanatana Dharma encourages us to show active and rational compassion toward others. Compassion, forgiveness, kindness, and love can conquer our internal enemies of anger, greed and lust.

12. A *yogi* must observe a proper spiritual diet by eating vegetarian and sattvic (pure, healthy and organic) foods. He should eat a healthy diet and avoid meat, fish, and eggs, as these foods increase the lower tendencies and will result in negative *karma*. When possible, he must offer all food to Lord Krishna before eating and partake of the remnants as *prasadam*, or God's grace.

13. As followers of Dharma, we are called upon to strive toward ethical excellence, and to not seek excuses for unethical behavior. Sanatana Dharma upholds the very opposite of ethical relativism. Rather, Sanatana Dharma calls upon all honest spiritual practitioners to exhibit the very highest virtuous behavior in their lives at all times. The details of such spiritually beneficial behavior are found throughout the totality of the Vedic scriptures. In the *Bhagavad Gita*, for example, Bhagavan Sri Krishna provides the following list of ethical behavioral traits that the sincere *yogi* should cultivate:

> Humility, pridelessness, nonviolence, tolerance, simplicity, approaching a true spiritual master, cleanliness, steadiness and self-control; renunciation of the objects of sense gratification, absence of false ego, the perception of the evil of birth, death, old age and disease; nonattachment to children, wife, home and the rest, and even-mindedness amid pleasant and unpleasant events; constant and unalloyed devotion to Me, resorting to solitary places, detachment from the general mass of people; accepting the importance of self-realization, and philosophical search for the Absolute Truth--all these I thus declare to be knowledge, and what is contrary to these is ignorance. (13: 8-12)

There are similar values found throughout the length and breadth of the Vedic scriptures that we are expected to uphold. To cultivate such virtues makes us *arya* - noble.

14. Every day, we must offer compassion to others by helping them in their spiritual understanding and development. Actively sharing spiritual knowledge with others is the highest form of kindness, so engage in teaching Lord Krishna's instructions in the *Bhagavad Gita* to those who have expressed a sincere interest. It is important, however, in our outreach efforts to others that we learn how to teach, and that we do not merely preach. The goal is simply to inform others about the truth of Sanatana Dharma in such a manner that, if they have an open heart and an engaging intellect, they will naturally be attracted to learn more, and possibly begin to practice the Vedic path.

Thus, in the above ways, and more, strive always to follow the teachings of Sanatana Dharma in your everyday life, and to thus reflect God's goodness in all your thoughts, words, and deeds. If we can perform all our spiritual practices with consistency and free of ego, we will know the very highest of spiritual attainments.

10.2.1 Yoga: The Heart of Sanatana Dharma

Despite its very ancient origins, Yoga has experienced an explosion of popularity in America in the last few decades. Tens of millions of people have tried Yoga to different degrees. Famous celebrities are known to be avid Yoga practitioners. Mothers and fathers, lawyers and college students are all doing Yoga. Yoga's recent surge in popularity is due to the fact that it offers a very easy, rational and enjoyable way to achieve deep levels of relaxation and physical reinvigoration.

Despite its amazing growth in popularity, though, even many serious practitioners of this ancient art see Yoga as nothing more than a series of powerful physical exercises designed to give one a perfect body. While Yoga will certainly give us the physical health, energy, stamina and strength that we are all seeking, this is not the primary goal of Yoga. Yoga is infinitely more than just the "aerobics of India."

First and foremost, Yoga is a systematic process of spiritual unfoldment. Yoga forms the very heart of the Sanatana Dharma tradition. Yoga is a 5000-year-old system of self-knowledge and God-realization, the aim of which is to unleash our full human potential--including our physical, ethical, emotional, mental, intellectual and spiritual dimensions. Yoga is an active philosophy and practical discipline that brings about a harmonization of all these various aspects of the human experience.

The Sanskrit word "*yoga*" means "to unite." Accordingly, the path of Yoga teaches us how to integrate and heal our personal existence, as well as harmonize our individual consciousness with God. The practice of Yoga spirituality brings about a greater sense of harmony between self, God and the world around us. As a direct result of this harmony, we then experience the peace, fulfillment and joy that we have always craved. Moreover, Yoga is a system that has the state of meditative awareness as both its means and its goal.

Above all else, the aim of yoga is active, focused and conscious meditation on the Absolute. Devotional meditation upon God is at the very heart of any good Yoga practice. For this reason, Yoga has often been called "meditation in motion." All the other aspects of Yoga exist in order to ensure that the *yogi* can achieve a deep state of meditative communion with both his true self, as well as with the Absolute. Indeed, even if we were to do all the various physical poses of Yoga perfectly, unless we are also doing these poses in a meditative frame of mind, then we are not really doing Yoga at all. Meditation on God, with love and devotion, is the foundation and goal of all Yoga practice.

While the physical component of Yoga is certainly of importance, it is only one of the eight traditional limbs of Yoga practice, all of which have meditation on God as their purpose. These are the eight limbs of the complete Yoga system as they are found in the famous Yoga scripture known as the *Yoga Sutras*, written by the sage Patanjali. Briefly, the eight limbs are:

Yama: These are five positive ethical guidelines (restraints, or abstinences) that include non-violence, fidelity to the Absolute, non-stealing, truthfulness and non-attachment.

Niyama: These are five positive behaviors, including cleanliness, contentment, self-discipline, self-study and devotion to God.

Asana: These are the actual physical exercises that people usually associate with Yoga. These powerful poses are designed to give our bodies strength, flexibility and energy in order to engage in meditation. They also contribute to the deep sense of relaxation that is necessary in order to lovingly meditate on the Absolute.

Pranayama: These are the energizing breathing exercises that produce vitality, overall health, inner calm, and greater integration between the physical and subtle bodies.

Pratyahara: This is detachment from the ever-present fluctuations of life. Through this practice, we can transcend all the trials and sufferings that life often seems to throw our way and begin to see such challenges in a positive and healing light.

Dharana: This is the practice of powerful and focused concentration.

Dhyana: This is devotional meditation on God, designed to still the agitations of the mind and open the heart to God's healing love.

Samadhi: This is blissful absorption of one's individual consciousness in the essence of God. In this state, the *yogi* experiences the direct presence of God in his life at all times. The *yogi* does not "become" God, which is logically and existentially impossible, but rather comes to the point of having nothing but God as the very center of his consciousness. The result of *samadhi* is peace, bliss and happiness without end.

These eight limbs together constitute the complete system known as classical *ashtanga* (eight-limbed) Yoga. When Yoga is diligently practiced under the guidance of a well-trained spiritual teacher (*guru*), it can lead to liberation from all illusion and suffering. By sincerely and patiently following the path of Yoga, you can achieve peace of mind, health of body, and the bliss of soul.

10.3.1 Meditation – The Heart of Yoga

The basic process of meditation is found, in one form or another, in many of the world's pre-Abrahamic religious traditions. All authentic Vedic paths agree that the way to attain true and lasting happiness is to come to a deep and substantial knowledge of oneself and of one's place in the cosmos. The only way to know one's inner self is by means of the science of meditation. As the most ancient and systematic spiritual tradition known to humanity, the process of meditation is found in its fullest form in the Yoga system of the Sanatana Dharma tradition.

For as long as there have been human beings, there have been people doing what only human beings do best: Asking philosophical questions. A few examples of such questions include:

> Who and what am I, really?
>
> What is life's ultimate meaning?
>
> Is this world that I see around me, and which I take to be so real, the only reality there is?
>
> Or is there something infinitely greater?

Inevitably, in order to help find the answers to these and similar questions, men and women throughout the ages have turned to the process of meditation. Meditation, however, is not just for a few special seekers dedicated to unraveling life's deepest mysteries. Meditation is a natural process that is accessible to all sincere spiritual seekers.

The only way to know one's inner self is by means of the science of meditation. As the most ancient and systematic spiritual tradition known to humanity, the process of meditation is found in its fullest form in the Sanatana Dharma tradition.

There are many wonderful benefits that you can experience by taking up the practice of regular meditation. These include inner calm and peace of mind; reduction of stress and anxiety; greater control over your own mind and its activities; keener intelligence and sharper concentration; becoming more centered and balanced; discovering who we truly are within; a deepening sense of communion with God; and personal joy and happiness.

10.3.2 Beginning Meditation with Breath Concentration

The following is a simple, yet very effective, guide to beginning the practice of meditation.

In order to practice meditation, you first have to find a quiet and uncluttered spot to sit. Such an environment contributes to the creation of a quiet and uncluttered mind. Once there, sit in a comfortable, yet alert, position. Have your back and spine straight, but not strained. Do not slouch or recline, or else you might fall asleep – and the goal of meditation is not to sleep, but to be very much awake. Having a very firm meditation cushion to sit on is very helpful in this regard. Also, it is fine if you need to initially have your back against a wall for added support.

As you sit in your comfortable position, try to put aside all negative thoughts and anxieties that may be bothering you at the moment. Allow your thoughts to be on hold for just a little while. Tell yourself that you can always come back to them later. But for right now, you wish to surrender to peace.

Listen with relaxed, yet keen and alert, attentiveness to the rhythm of your own breathing. Feel, and even hear, the life-giving air as it enters and leaves your lungs. Concentrate all of your attention on nothing other than the sound and the feeling of your own breath. With every out-going

breath, allow the stress and anxiety hidden in your body and mind to just
be released. Allow fears and doubts to simply leave. With every in-
coming breath, imagine the calm and peace of a love-filled universe entering your lungs, and into the deepest levels of your very being. If your
mind temporarily wanders away - and it will! - then just gently and patiently bring the mind's awareness back to its task of focusing only on the
breath.

Try this for about 10 minutes as a preparation for *mantra*-meditation,
slowly increasing the time over the next few weeks. After you have
calmed the mind with breath concentration, you can now move on to the
more spiritual aspect of meditation by using a sacred *mantra*.

10.3.3 Mantra – Meditation Upon God's Name

There are many different techniques of meditation. Of all the various
forms, however, the most ancient, effective and easiest is known as
"Mantra Meditation." This type of meditation uses a *mantra*, or a transcendental sound vibration, to achieve its goal. The word "*mantra*" comes
to us from the ancient Sanskrit language and is actually composed of two
words. "*Man*" means "the mind," and the word "*tra*" means "to liberate."
A *mantra* is thus a sacred sound frequency that frees the mind from anxiety and illusion.

While there are a wide variety of *mantras*, the Vedic scriptures teach us
that not all *mantras* are equal. In order for a sound vibration to be considered a real *mantra*, it cannot merely be a made-up string of sounds, but
rather must have been directly revealed in the Vedic scriptures. The most
effective *mantras* for achieving the specifically spiritual goals of self-

realization and God-consciousness are those Sanskrit *mantras* that have the names of God included within them, and which are directly designed to bring about a state of *bhakti* - or devotional consciousness.

AUM

The most ancient and important of all *mantras* is the foundational *mantra* Aum (sometimes misspelled as "om"). First revealed as far back as the *Rig Veda* (circa 3,800 BCE), the *mantra* Aum is found in almost every known scripture of the Sanatana Dharma tradition. Aum is the sound representation of God in God's omni-present form as the very sustainer of all existence.

Everything that exists in empirical reality has its very being grounded in the presence of the Absolute. It is only as a result of God being present in every piece of matter – from the tiny atom, to the planets, to our very own bodies – that all these things can even have their existence. There is nothing and nowhere in which God is not present. Indeed, if we could point to anything in which God were not present, we would be pointing to nothing at all! More, it is God's presence that gives our cosmos its very form and integrity as a well-ordered system.

Aum is both a name of God, as well as the sound representation of God's omni-presence in reality. Aum is the very sound underlying God's sustaining presence in the universe.

10.3.4 How to Meditate

In order to practice meditation, you first have to find a quiet and unclut-

tered spot to sit. Such an environment contributes to a quiet and uncluttered mind. Once there, sit in a comfortable, yet alert, position. Have
your back and spine straight, but not strained. Don't slouch or recline, or
else you might fall asleep – and the goal of meditation is not to sleep, but
to be very much awake!

As you sit in your comfortable position, try to put aside all negative
thoughts and anxieties that may be bothering you at the moment. Allow
your thoughts to be on hold for just a little while. Tell yourself that you
can always come back to them later. Listen with relaxed, yet keen and
alert, attentiveness to the rhythm of your own breathing. Feel, and even
hear, the life-giving air as it enters and leaves your lungs. Concentrate all
of your attention on nothing other than the sound and the feeling of
your breath. With every out-going breath, allow the stress and anxiety
hidden in your body and mind to just be released. Allow fears and doubts
to simply leave. With every in-coming breath, imagine the calm and peace
of a love-filled universe entering your lungs, and into your very being. If
your mind temporarily wanders away - and it will! - then just gently and
patiently bring it back to its task of focusing only on the breath.

Try this for about five minutes as a preparation for *mantra*-meditation,
slowly increasing the time over the next few weeks. After you have
calmed the mind with breath concentration, you can now move on to the
more spiritual aspect of meditation by using a *mantra*.

10.3.5 Mantra Meditation

There are many different techniques of meditation. Of all the various
forms, however, the most popular, effective and easiest is known as

"Mantra Meditation." This type of meditation uses a *mantra*, or a transcendental sound vibration, to achieve its goal. The word "*mantra*" comes to us from the ancient Sanskrit language and is actually composed of two words. "*Man*" means "the mind," and the word "*tra*" means "to liberate." A *mantra* is thus a sacred sound frequency that frees the mind from anxiety and illusion.

The Mantra

The most powerful of *mantras* that one could use is known as the Tirumantra (the "Auspicious Mantra"):

$$ॐ\ नमो\ नारायणाय$$

Aum Namo Narayanaya

The English translation of this *mantra* literally means: "I offer my respects to the Absolute, the Sustainer of all beings." It is said in the Vedic literature (*Narayana-Upanishad*) that if one recites this *mantra* sincerely and with devotion, one will achieve peace, fulfillment and self-realization. More, one will also achieve God-consciousness, an immediate awareness of the grace of God in one's life.

Immediately after doing the breath concentration exercise described above, sitting in the same position, with your eyes closed, begin to repeat the *mantra*, **Aum Namo Narayanaya**, out loud and with devotion.[32] Focus all of your attentive energy on the sound and the vibration of the *mantra*, hearing the *mantra*, and even feeling the soothing vibrations of the *mantra* in your chest near the heart region. After chanting the *mantra* for 10-15 minutes, end your meditation by again focusing on your breath for about five minutes. We sums up the process of *mantra* meditation below.

Mantra Meditation Session

A full *mantra* meditation session consists of three steps:

1) Breath
2) *Mantra*
3) Breath

A) Sit in a comfortable place with your eyes closed and your body alert and erect. Begin with focusing on your breath in silence, doing the breath concentration exercise described above, for about 5 minutes. This process will still the mind.

B) Immediately after breath concentration, sitting in the same position with your eyes closed, begin to repeat the *mantra* **Aum Namo Narayanaya**, out-loud and with devotion. Focus all of your attentive energy on the sound and the vibration of the *mantra*, hearing the *mantra*, and even feeling the soothing vibrations of the *mantra* in your chest near the heart region. Recite and meditate upon the *mantra* for about 10-15 minutes.

---

[32] To hear the exact pronunciation of this *mantra*, and many of the *mantras* discussed in this book, please purchase the CD "Mantra Meditations", available at Dharmacentral.com.

Adjust the volume and speed at which you are saying the *mantra* in such a way that it sounds most natural and effortless to you. This process will awaken the self.

C) Then end the meditation session with another 5 minutes of silent breath concentration in a similar manner as you did in step (A). Allow the purifying effects of the *mantra* to silently reverberate throughout your inner being.

A good meditation session lasts for about 20 - 30 minutes per day. There is, however, no maximal time limit for how long you can meditate. It is explained in the Yoga literature of ancient Vedic culture, and by great Yoga masters throughout history, that if you can cultivate a daily meditation practice, and perform meditation with sincerity, humility, patience and with devotion, then you will achieve peace, fulfillment, wisdom and direct realization of God's presence in your life.

With a daily practice of meditation, you will slowly begin to see your stress and anxiety levels start to reduce. You will also begin to experience a deep inner peace that will seem very familiar and comforting. This is because you will be accessing the deepest well of inner peace that is natural to your true self. The only way to experience this joy of meditation is to try it. So dive deeply into the reality of your own inner peace.

10.4.1 Bhakti: The Heart of Meditation

The most important path of Yoga that is described in the *Bhagavad Gita* is called *bhakti*, or devotional consciousness. This Yoga consists of developing a loving, devotional attitude towards the Supreme. It is a path that is meditative, contemplative and worshipful in nature. Often modern commentators on Yoga mistakenly attempt describe *bhakti* as the "*yoga* of the emotions." This Yoga is not, however, to be confused with mere emotionalism or sentimental piety. As we will see in this section, Bhakti-yoga is just as much a rigorous philosophical system as are any of the other branches of Yoga.

The very essence of the teachings of the *Bhagavad Gita* are that Yoga and *bhakti* are ultimately synonymous and inseparable aspects of one another, Yoga being the means to achieve the highest goal of human life, with *bhakti*, or devotional consciousness, being the very goal of Yoga itself.

In the sixth chapter specifically, Lord Krishna and His student, Arjuna, delve very in-depth into a practical philosophical discussion of the practice of *ashtanga-yoga* (not to be confused with the very modern "Ashtanga" of Prattabhi Jois, but the original eight-fold system), also known by the name *raja-yoga*, or the "King of Yoga". In this verse, Krishna explains to His disciple Arjuna what He personally considers to be the highest *yogi* of all.

> *yoginam api sarvesham mad-gatenantar-atmana*
> *shraddhavan bhajate yo mam sa me yuktatamo matah*

"Of all Yogis, he who always abides in Me with great faith, worshiping Me in transcendental devotional service, is most intimately united with Me in Yoga and is the highest of all." (*Bhagavad Gita*, 6:47)

The Sanskrit word for "abides in Me with great faith..." is *shraddhavan* (*shraddhaavaan*). In the tradition of Yoga and Sanatana Dharma, the word "faith" has a very different meaning than it does for the much more recent Abrahamic religions (Judaism, Christianity and Islam). Rather than designating an unhealthy system of blind belief that flies in the face of objective experience, the Dharmic sense of faith (*shraddha*) means something more akin with the term "assurance". As an example, when we board an airplane to travel to a distant city, we do so with the assurance that we will reach our destination. That assurance is not based upon blind faith, but upon the fact that we have taken many planes before and always made it to our destination. Such assurance is based upon previous experience, and is therefore the very opposite of baseless or blind. Thus, *shraddha* is not referring to blind faith.

Abiding in God means cultivating God-realization (*brahma-vidya*) with an attitude of complete surrender to Him, which is the ultimate goal of the path of Yoga and of Sanatana Dharma. To abide in God means to increasingly meditate upon God with devotional consciousness (not to ever be confused with "emotion"), experiencing the presence of God within, and eventually having a direct experiential realization of God as the very foundation of our being, the loving center of all reality, and our ultimate spiritual refuge. The result of such God-realization is unlimited freedom (*moksha*), unending bliss (*ananda*), and perfect transcendental knowledge (*jnana*).

The basis of all positive and healthy relationships is love. This is where the cultivation of *bhakti* comes into the picture. "Worshiping Me in transcendental devotional service" is rendered in this verse as "*bhajate yo mam*" in the Sanskrit. What this means is quite literally experiencing love of God and reconnecting with God as the source of our being, the foundation of our existence, and as our very best friend.

Having a direct realization of our intimate connection with the Absolute is the entire goal of the Yoga system in its complete, pure, and authentic form. The Yoga and *bhakti* manual known as the *Bhagavad Gita* offers us a systematic and intellectually satisfying path through which, under the expert guidance of an authentic and self-realized *guru* (spiritual teacher), we can both philosophically grasp and practice this path, and thus achieve spiritual joy.

Practitioners of *bhakti* (known as *bhaktas*) generally view the Absolute in very personal terms, as opposed to the sometimes more amorphous concept of the impersonal aspect of Brahman. Krishna, who is speaking as an incarnation (*avatara*) of the Divine, recommends this path throughout the entire course of the *Bhagavad Gita*. For example, in the eighth chapter He says:

> *purushah sa parah partha bhaktya labhyas tv ananyaya*
> *yasyantahsthani bhutani yena sarvam idam tatam*

"The Supreme, who is greater than all, is attainable by devotional consciousness. Although He is present in His abode, He is all-pervading, and everything is situated within Him." (8:22)

It is possible to have an immediate and intimate experiential knowledge of the omnipresent Absolute, then, by the process of *bhakti*. The efficacy of the *bhakti* system is attested to throughout the entire text of the *Bhagavad Gita*. In the eleventh chapter Krishna tells Arjuna:

> *mat-karma-krn mat-paramo mad-bhaktah sanga-varjitah*
> *nirvairah sarva-bhuteshu yah sa mam eti pandava*

"One who is engaged in devotion to Me, free from the contaminations of previous activities, who is friendly to every living entity, certainly comes to Me, O son of Pandu." (11:55)

For the *bhakta*, the goal of life is nothing less than achieving a state of pure and transcendent loving absorption of the mind's contemplative faculties in the Absolute. This is done by transcending our false sense of self that is caused by ego, and embracing our true spiritual self. The goal of Bhakti-yoga is to replace our unhealthy sense of self-centeredness with a liberating affirmation of God-centeredness. Interestingly, *bhakti* is viewed in the *Bhagavad Gita* as being both a means for attaining the goal, as well as being the very goal itself. Unlike the other forms of Yoga discussed in the *Bhagavad Gita*, only *bhakti* is seen as being both the means, as well as the goal. Consequently, the state of *bhakti* is presented in the *Gita* as being the foundation of the entire philosophy of Yoga itself.

10.4.2 Bhakti Yoga

As we have seen, it is in *bhakti*, specifically, that the four paths of Yoga presented in the *Bhagavad Gita* (Jnana-yoga, Karma-yoga, Raja-yoga and Bhakti-yoga) achieve their integral unity and ultimate purpose. Unlike any other salvific Yoga concept, *bhakti* most thoroughly interpenetrates all strata of possible human concern and activity. With *bhakti*, we acquire unadulterated wisdom directly from our unmediated experience of God, who is the source of all wisdom. Thus the goal of Jñana-yoga, the Yoga of wisdom, is achieved. Likewise, in *bhakti*, we are dedicating all our activities in the loving service of God. So the detached activity that is the goal of Karma-yoga is achieved. And with *bhakti*, the personal self-realization and liberation that is the aim of Ashtanga-yoga is also achieved. As a direct result of the pervasiveness of *bhakti*, Jnana-yoga, Karma-yoga and Ashtanga-yoga find their perfect fulfillment in *bhakti*. It is only in the devotional element that intellect, action, mystic attainment

366

and loving relationship with the Absolute all meet in a systematic manner.

Devotional contemplation is practiced in a very comprehensive way. This necessarily includes the acquisition of wisdom. According to Swami Vishvesha Tirtha, "Two elements constitute devotion - knowledge and love. The harmonious fusion of knowledge with love is devotion" (Tirtha, 1983). The term "devotion" is not to be mistakenly interpreted as referring to some sentimental form of irrational religious emotionalism. The practice of *bhakti* is not contrary to acting in accordance with reason; on the contrary, *bhakti* is seen as the necessary prerequisite for attaining true, transcendental knowledge. Indeed, Krishna clearly states in the tenth chapter that spiritual intelligence, itself, has its origin in devotional contemplation:

tesham satata-yuktanam bhajatam priti-purvakam
dadami buddhi-yogam tam yena mam upayanti te

"To those who are constantly devoted and worship Me with love, I give the intelligence by which they come to Me." (*Bhagavad Gita*, 10:10)

Bhakti-yoga is a spiritual discipline that is grounded in a highly developed philosophical system. Most of Sanatana Dharma's greatest philosophers, including Narada, Ramanuja, Madhva, Jayatirtha, Nimbarka, Vallabha and Chaitanya, have upheld the view that *bhakti* is the preeminent path to self-realization. The path of *bhakti* has been, historically, one of the most important philosophical schools of Sanatana Dharma. Unlike some schools of philosophy, though, *bhakti* does not limit its field of concern merely to the intellectual realm. *Bhakti* is a dynamic way of life and practice, in addition to being a school of philosophy.

The reality of *bhakti* as being synonymous with Karma-yoga is described in many parts of the *Bhagavad Gita*. Devotional meditation involves not only the engagement of one's mind and heart, but of every aspect of the *yogi's* inner constitution, including the impetus for activity. In describing the practical aspects of *bhakti*, Krishna explains, "engage your mind always in thinking of Me, offer your obeisances and worship to Me. Being completely absorbed in Me, surely you will come to Me" (9:34). The discipline of *bhakti* requires that the *yogi* do everything as a conscious devotional offering to the Supreme. All that one does, thinks and desires must be engaged in with a consciousness of detached devotional contemplation of the Absolute. All of the daily activities of life must be performed in a serene mood of dedication to the Absolute. This includes even such everyday activities as eating and drinking. Krishna confirms this in chapter nine of His *Bhagavad Gita*:

> *patram pushpam phalam toyam yo me bhaktya prayacchati*
> *tad aham bhakty-upahrtam asnami prayatatmanah*
> *yat karoshi yad asnashi yaj juhoshi dadasi yat*
> *yat tapasyasi kaunteya tat kurusva mad arpanam*

"If one offers Me with love and devotion a leaf, a flower, fruit or water, I will accept it. O son of Kunti, all that you do, all that you eat, all that you offer and give away, as well as all austerities that you may perform, should be done as an offering unto Me." (9:26-27)

In this way, the *yogi* lives his life in such a manner that, whatever seemingly mundane activity he may be engaged in, he is performing it in a state of devoted focused concentration on the Absolute.

Consequently, the *yogi* consciously makes the effort to spiritualize all of

368

his activities, thoughts and communications with others. Due to the self-less and devoted nature of his consciousness, the *yogi's* actions, thoughts and words are all transcendentally situated. They are spiritually trans-formed. B.R. Sridhara Swami, a prominent 20th century Bhakti-yoga teacher, describes this shift in consciousness that takes place within the heart of the *yogi* in the following way:

> Everyone is thinking of themselves as many masters of many things, but this is all heart disease (*hrid-rogam*). This is all con-ceived in a diseased state of consciousness. In a healthy state, when the heart is quite wholesome, we can see the Supreme Whole, and we can see that everything is meant only for His sat-isfaction. (Sridhara, 1985)

The goal of Bhakti-yoga is nothing less than the development of a totally theocentric lifestyle and consciousness, a life in which one's entire being is infused with the bliss and peace of loving devotional contemplation of the Absolute.

10.4.3 The Descent of the Infinite

The *Bhagavad Gita* considers Bhakti-yoga, or loving devotion to Krishna, to be the highest form of Yoga, and the unifying essence of *jnana*, *karma* and *ashtanga*. It is significant that the *Bhagavad Gita* specifically points to Krishna as the focal object of *bhakti*. The speaker of the *Gita*, Sri Krish-na, is not portrayed in the work as being an ordinary individual. Indeed, He is seen as a divine incarnation (*avatara*) of God. According to Howard Resnick: "In the *Bhagavad Gita*, Lord Krsna declares Himself to be the Supreme Godhead, and He specifically asserts His supremacy over the well-known gods or demigods of the Vedic and Hindu pantheon. Indeed,

Krsna is the source of all the other gods that inhabit the cosmos, for He is the source of all that exists." (Resnick, 1995)

Krishna, Himself, confirms the categorically distinct ontological status of His nature, in comparison to ours, when He states to Arjuna,

Sri bhagavan uvacha
bahuni me vyatitani janmani tava charjuna
tany aham veda sarvani na tvam vettha parantapa

"Many, many births both you and I have passed. I can remember all of them, but you cannot..." (4:5). Sri Krishna presents Himself as being the infinite Absolute, Brahman, voluntarily manifest in a finite form. An *avatara* represents the Infinite revealing Itself in the world of the finite, the Eternal making Itself known in the realm of time.

According to the *Bhagavad Gita*, and Vedic philosophy in general, God periodically descends to Earth during times of extreme crisis and tribulation in order to alleviate humanity of its misery. Krishna explains to Arjuna:

yada yada hi dharmasya glanir bhavati bharata
abhyutthanam adharmasya tadatmanam shrjamyaham
paritranaya sadhunam vinashaya cha dushkrtam
dharma-samsthapanarthaya sambhavami yuge yuge

"Whenever and wherever there is a decline in religious practice, O descendent of Bharata, and a predominant rise of irreligion - at that time I descend Myself. In order to deliver the pious and to annihilate the evil, as well as to reestablish the principles of religion, I advent Myself millennium after millennium." (4:7-8)

There are several different types of *avataras*, of which we will briefly discuss two of the most prevalent categories: a) *purna-avatara* ("full incarna-incarnation"), and b) *avesha-avatara* ("empowered incarnation").

Purna-avatara: When God descends upon the Earth in His full and direct form, this is known as a *purna-avatara*. The have been 10 major full incarnations throughout history. Examples of such *purna-avataras* include Kurma, Rama and Krishna. Sri Krishna was the very last *purna-avatara* to have appeared on our planet. The next *purna-avatara* to appear is Kalki, who will manifest upon the Earth 432,000 years after the beginning of the Kali Yuga, which commenced at midnight on February 18, 3102 BCE. Thus, any individual who either claims, or allows his disciples to claim, that he is a full *avatara* of God previous to the clear arrival of Kalki is a false *avatara* and must be publically rejected by all sincere devotees of Sanatana Dharma. There will not be another full *avatara* until the arrival of Kalki approximately 427,000 years from now.

Avesha-avatara: When, on the other hand, God directly empowers a human being to serve on His behalf to restore Dharma to the world, such a divinely empowered human is known as an *avesha-avatara*. An *avesha-avatara* is still a human being. Ontologically, he is an *atman*. But he has so emptied himself of any sense of artificial I-ness (*asmita*), and so filled himself with love for God and a deep sense of mission to save the world, that when we look upon such a human *avesha-avatara*, it is as if we are looking upon God Himself. There have been numerous avesha-avataras in the world. Historically, such *avesha-avataras* have included Gautama Buddha and Chaitanya Mahaprabhu, among many others. In the 20th century, specifically, the great Acharya, Srila Prabhupada, was one such instance of an *avesha-avatara*.

It is only with this concept of *avatara* in mind that we can properly comprehend the many statements of Krishna in the *Bhagavad Gita* regarding devotion to Himself as the incarnation of the Absolute.

Understanding the principle of *avatara*, and thus the unique position of Sri Krishna as the last full incarnation of God on Earth, present over 5200 years ago, it is by cultivating devotional consciousness toward Krishna as the *avatara* for our current age that the fulfillment of all Yoga can be realized.

10.4.4 The Difference Between Devotion and Emotion

The central message of the *Bhagavad Gita*, the most important scripture in all of Sanatana Dharma, is that *bhakti*, or devotion to the Absolute, constitutes the most effective and highly recommended path in all of the Yoga and Sanatana Dharma tradition. It is truly unfortunate, however, that despite the almost universally held importance of *bhakti* in the history of Yoga, there seems to have always been a good deal of misunderstanding on the part of many about what the terms "*bhakti*" and "Bhakti Yoga" actually mean. I've read even many supposedly knowledgeable authors write that *bhakti* is the Yoga of "emotion", or that it somehow precludes any involvement with *jnana* (knowledge, or intellectualism), philosophy, or serious Yogic *sadhana* (practice). Nothing could be further from the truth.

The word "*bhakti*" is derived from the Sanskrit verb root "*bhaj*", meaning "to share in, resort to, experience, partake of, cultivate, worship, go to", etc. The object of this "experiencing" or "partaking in" is, of course, God. In this definition, we can begin to recognize in seed form what the foundational basis of Bhakti Yoga consists of.

Bhakti is a trans-emotional state of consciousness that we are meant to cultivate and uncover as the natural essence of our soul, and Bhakti Yoga is a complex and rigorous system of Yoga designed to bring its adherent to a progressively deeper state of meditative absorption (*samadhi*) in the Divine. Thus, the term "*bhakti*" denotes both a state of trans-empirical perceptual awareness and phenomenological experience, as well as a philosophical system and praxis designed to bring about such a higher state of awareness of the Divine.

Bhakti is meditation in its fullest and deepest manifestation. *Bhakti* actually denotes devotional meditative absorption. Unlike any other system of Yoga, *bhakti* stands apart from all other systems in that it actually constitutes both a means (*upaya*) toward the goal of God-realization (and thus it is a Yoga), as well as the end (*artha*) of Yoga itself in the form of a spiritual state of pure egolessness and God-consciousness. *Bhakti* is not only the most effective and most highly recommended means of enlightenment, but *bhakti* **is** enlightenment.

"Devotion" in this correctly understood *bhakti* sense is radically different from "emotion" (*abhitapa*). *Bhakti* is a state of consciousness that is transcendent in essence and which reflects the innermost, latent nature of the *atman* (true self) as being functionally contingent and ontologically sustained by the Absolute. *Bhakti*, or devotion in this more phenomenological sense, represents the true functional nature of our soul. There is nothing material, or emotional, or sentimental about *bhakti* at all.

Emotion (*abhitapa*), on the other hand, is held universally by all the schools of Yoga and Dharmic spirituality to be a purely material-originated phenomenon that arises from *manas* (mind), *chitta* (psyche), desire (*kama*) and anger (*krodha*). Thus, materially inspired emotions are unreal, temporary and negative in the truest, spiritual sense. Emotions that stem from materialistic likes and dislikes are akin to phantasms that – while certainly experienced in a very real way when we have them – are nonetheless not of lasting importance. This is especially true of negative emotions that arise from our illusion of being separate from God.

Material emotions, for the *yogi*, are to be transcended. Devotional consciousness, for the *yogi*, is to be cultivated.

This being said, Sanatana Dharma does not teach that emotions are inherently an evil or unwanted instrument. Emotions are in and of themselves actually neutral tools. They are tools that can be used for either good or for self-bondage. The emotive mechanism is just as much a neutral tool as is our mind, body, intellect, etc. Just as is true of our mind, body, and intellect, it is not that any of these tools are inherently either good or bad. Rather, they are good if they are under our control, and bad if they are not under our control.

When a person has an uncontrolled mind, they are considered to be mentally disturbed. When a person has an uncontrollable body, then they are experiencing some sort of physical illness. In the same way, when a person has emotions that are uncontrolled, they tend to be emotionally unstable and thus unpeaceful. And peace is a direct manifest symptom of

374

spiritual transcendence.

To have normal, reactive emotions toward things that happen in our lives is natural. Emotions arise as a result of external occurrences that affect us, which we then perceive as either good or bad. Just like if someone hits us, we feel physical pain, in the same way if someone hurts us emotionally, we then feel emotional pain. Emotions are a natural effect to external stimuli – or at least to our perceptions of such stimuli.

But if we were to cry for the next six weeks because we gently stubbed our toe, then we would be overreacting to a very miniscule amount of physical pain, and we would not really be in control of our physical reactions. In the same way, if we overreact and give in to a sea of uncontrollable emotion with every incident that happens to us, big and small, then we are not serving ourselves, but rather being slaves of our uncontrolled emotions.

So the idea that is espoused in Dharma spirituality is not to artificially repress, ignore, or stifle our emotions, mind, intellect, ego, body, etc., but to see them in their proper place in relation to spirit, our true self, and to then control and thus transcend their power over us. It is a simple matter of having control over our emotions, rather than allowing our emotions to have control over us.[33]

A prevalent misconception that many have is that God-realized, or enlightened, people are necessarily emotionless people because they have

---

[33] The great sage Bharata Muni mentions eight powerful emotions in his work known as the *Natya Shastra*. These eight emotions are: love, mirth, fury, compassion, disgust, horror, heroic mood, and amazement.

learned to transcend emotion. Nothing could be further from the truth. God-realized people are certainly not emotionless. On the contrary! They can be the most fun people to be with. God-realized sages can laugh, can cry, and can even exhibit anger when appropriate - and especially in the defense of Dharma. God-realized people can be emotional; but such emotions tend to be positive emotions that are used in God's service, as well as spiritual *bhava*, or transcendent states of consciousness that the unwise might mistakenly confuse with material emotions. God-realized persons: 1) try not to be ruled by their emotions; 2) tend to focus on more positive emotions (love, compassion, pity, joy, etc.); 3) and ultimately the emotive states that they experience most deeply are the transcendental mellows of love between themselves and God, and not the lower, reactive emotions that arise from sense perception.

In the highest state of self-realization and God-realization, our material emotions are keenly surpassed and are subsequently replaced by devotional ecstasy and states of rapturous spiritual elations (*rasa*) the likes of which nothing in our present perceptual state can comprehend. To experience such bliss, we must practice Bhakti Yoga, the Yoga of devotional consciousness. The greatest textbook on Bhakti Yoga is the *Bhagavad Gita*. Beginning with devoted study of the *Bhagavad Gita*, coupled with daily meditation upon the Absolute under the expert guidance of an authentic spiritual teacher (*guru*), we can know the bliss of love of God.

10.4.4 Papatti: The Path of Self Surrender

Bhakti Yoga finds its culmination and its perfection in the process of *prapatti*, or self-surrender to God. It is for this reason that the 66th verse of the 18th chapter of the *Bhagavad Gita* has been considered by all the great Acharyas of the past to be the culmination of this entire scripture. In this culmination verse, Sri Krishna says to Arjuna:

sarva-dharman parityajya mam ekam sharanam vraja
aham tvam sarva-papebhyo mokshayishyami ma suchah

"Abandon all varieties of false religiousity and simply surrender unto Me. I will deliver you from all negative reactions. Do not fear."

It is in such complete surrender of the totality of our very selves as a humble offering of love at the feet of God that we most directly transcend the false ego that has entrapped us in illusion, and take the most courageous leap of healthy faith toward the Divine. This is the case because self-surrender to God is in every way the very opposite volitional trajectory of self-involvement in false ego. It is our false ego that has convinced us that we are the center of all things, and that only our self-centered interests matter. When we cultivate an attitude of self-surrender, we are taking our selfish concerns out of the center of our awareness and placing God, instead, in that center of awareness. It is the most radical rejection of illusion that can be performed on the spiritual path. It is also the most radical embrace of the Divine that can be conceived. Self-surrender to God is the final culmination of all religious and spiritual pursuit.

The act of self-surrender to God (*prapatti*) is not merely one dramatic instance in time in which we throw our hands up into the air out of desperation and simply make the emotional declaration that "God, I am yours!" It is not a one-time act, but rather, *prapatti* is a process and an attitude that is continuously cultivated in one's life to increasing depths.

It is in prapatti that we begin to vividly experience a reciprocal loving relationship with the Divine in a consciousness of pure devotion (*shuddha-bhakti*).

We are always surrendering 24 hours a day to something or someone. The vast majority of the time, however, we are surrendering to the wrong something or someone due to our own illusion. Thus, we are often surrendering to our own ego, fears, anger, and confusion rather than relinquishing these destructive tendencies. We surrender to what we are told by the media, by teachers and professors, by our friends, by government representatives, and by our own chattering and ever-changing minds. It is only when we make the conscious and spiritually-motivated decision to surrender specifically to the Divine, however, that the surrendering process is now being properly utilized in our deepest and most meaningful self interest. Whether we use generic names like "Source", "Divine", "Higher Power" or "God", or use the very personal and transcendental names that are revealed in the Vedic scriptures is up to us. The important thing is to understand to whom we are surrendering. As we have now seen from the above examples, not all surrender is the same. This is why we need the *sadguru*, the true spiritual master, to guide us.

10.5.1 The Science of Prayer and Meditation

> May God lead us from the unreal and to the Real.
> May God lead us from darkness to Light.
> May God lead us from death to immortality.
> Unto all, may peace prevail.

> (*Brhadaranyaka Upanishad*, 1:3:28)

There are a few important concepts, practices and features of spirituality
that we find common to each and every religious tradition. Prayer is certainly one of these demonstrably common elements of spirituality.
Whether we are speaking of the larger world religions of Sanatana
Dharma, Buddhism, Christianity or Islam, or any of the numerous indigenous religions of the world, prayer is one of the most prevalent
foundations upon which the practice of all religions is based. Regardless
of our language, religion, ethnicity or philosophy of life, every human
being has resorted to prayer at one time or another – even if only in
times of great need. The importance of prayer in the Western religions
might be more familiar to many reading this. However, the nature and
central place of prayer, coupled with the practice of meditation, as it is
expressed in the Vedic tradition might be less understood my some who
were raised in the Abrahamic faiths. In the following section, we will examine the very important role that prayer plays in Vedic spiritual practice,
the intimate and mutually dependent relationship between prayer and
meditation, as well as what the Vedic concept of prayer and meditation
has to teach all spiritual seekers today.

10.5.2 Prayer in the Sanatana Dharma Tradition

Sanatana Dharma itself is known to be the most ancient continuously
practiced religious tradition on earth. The earliest work in the Vedic
scriptural canon is the *Rig Veda*, which was first composed approximately
3800 BCE. It is only one of a vast collection of revealed texts that com-
prise the Vedic canon of sacred texts. Sanatana Dharma is a religion that
is predicated upon the importance of direct personal experience of the
Divine. All people, regardless of their ethnicity, educational level or sta-

tion in life, can experience God's love and grace in their lives if they will merely approach God with humility, love, and pure intention. Upholding a panentheist monotheistic theological outlook, Sanatana Dharma teaches that God is both the transcendent source of all reality, as well as being omnipresent in all things, sentient and non-sentient alike. There is no place in existence that is devoid of God's grace and presence.

One of the most effective and direct tools that human beings have at their disposal for communicating with God is the process of prayer. The profound importance of prayer is stressed throughout all the scriptures of Sanatana Dharma. The *Rig Veda* itself, for example, consists of many hundreds of prayers directed both to God, and to the many elemental divinities (*devas* and *devis*) who populate the natural and celestial realms as God's servants. In the later scriptural text, the famous *Bhagavad Gita* (first recited around 3100 BCE), Arjuna offers fervent and sincere prayers to Krishna, the incarnation (*avatara*) of God and speaker of the teachings of the *Bhagavad Gita*. Likewise, a vast number of beautifully composed devotional prayers are offered in almost every other important Sanatana Dharma scripture, including the *Mahabharata*, *Ramayana*, *Upanishads*, *Puranas*, etc. The central importance of prayer in the Sanatana Dharma tradition is evidenced throughout the entire sacred literature of Sanatana Dharma.

10.5.3 Diverse Objects of Prayer

There is one Supreme Absolute (Para-Brahman) who is recognized as such by the scriptures (*Shastras*) of Sanatana Dharma. The primary name of that Supreme Absolute is Sriman Narayana. In addition to this primary name, the Absolute is also known by an infinite number of secondary and tertiary names, all of which point to Sriman Narayana. All other gods and goddesses (*devas* and *devis*) in existence are recognized by the Vedic scriptures to be mere servants of Sriman Narayana. Being a monotheistic religion, Sanatana Dharma teaches that the most important forms of prayer are those that are offered directly to the Absolute – God. God being the source and origin of all things perceivable and conceivable, it is when we go directly to this Divine Source that our hopes, our requests, our praise, and our prayers are unimpededly communicated to God. Thus, it makes most sense to offer our prayers directly to God, and not to lesser divinities.[34] Despite this recommendation, however, it is recognized by the Vedic system that people are very diverse in their many interests and aspirations, and so will offer prayers to a multitude of different beings, and for a variety of different reasons.

Being motivated by varying desires, people pray for many different reasons, and to many different objects of prayer. Not every spiritual seeker is necessarily seeking God after all. In our day-to-day lives, we will find people, including ourselves, often offering prayers to many different sorts of beings. Some pray to demigods and demigoddesses, some to ancestors, spirits, "channeled" entities, or other lesser divinities. Many of us who otherwise would not consider ourselves especially religious even offer forms of "prayer" to politicians or to our boss if there is something that we want them to do for us. Arguably, marriage proposals are even forms of prayer, the suitor supplicating his object of romantic devotion to bestow her grace and undying love upon him. Thus we find that the

---

[34] "Men of small intelligence worship the gods, and their fruits are limited and temporary. Those who worship the gods go to the realm of the gods, but My devotees ultimately reach My supreme abode." - Sri Krishna, *Bhagavad Gita*, 7:23

phenomenon of prayer is universal, regardless of whether or not we even know that we are praying.

10.5.4 The Two Forms of Prayer

Regardless of what we chose to pray to God for, either material gain or spiritual enlightenment, all prayer that is directed toward God is considered to be positive and good. Since God is the ultimate source of all gifts, who else would be more appropriate to turn to in times of need? Prayer itself, however, can really be distinguished into two distinct types. The first of these is prayer in the form of an appeal. With this sort of prayer, we are praying for a specific result. Whether we are praying for a new car, the healing of a health concern, or even world peace, with prayers of appeal we are asking that the object of our desire be bestowed upon either us or upon those we care for. While all prayer to God is good, still Sanatana Dharma considers prayers of appeal to be not the most advanced or self-beneficial form of prayer. The second form of prayer is in the form of pure devotional praise. With this form of prayer, we are not asking for any particular object, or the bestowal of a specific desire or need. Rather, we are simply praising God out of a sense of pure devotion and appreciation for all that God is. This kind of purely devotional outpouring of prayer is a way of simply saying "I love you" to God, without the desire for any result or remuneration. When we offer a prayer of praise, it is God, and not merely our own needs, that is exclusively at center stage. Because of its thoroughly desireless and pure nature, prayers of praise are considered to be the highest form of prayer. With prayers of praise, self-surrender to the will of God becomes possible, and the bondage of illusory ego is completely transcended.

Again, in Sanatana Dharma, the highest form of prayer is prayer that is directed exclusively toward God, and that is done so selflessly and for the sake of praise. Accordingly, we find such prayers offered throughout the Vedic scriptures. One of the most important of these prayers is found in the *Rig Veda*, and is known as the Gayatri *mantra*. The Gayatri prayer is possibly the oldest prayer found in Sanatana Dharma, and is recited by millions of Dharmis each day. Traditionally, Vedic priests recite this prayer three times per day, at sunrise, in the afternoon and at sunset. Below is the full Gayatri *mantra* in both its original Sanskrit, along with my English translation.

Gayatri Mantra

Aum bhur bhuvah svah
Tat savitur varenyam
Bhargo devasya dhimahi
Dhiyo yo naha prachodayat aum

I invoke the Earth Plane, the Astral Plane, the Plane of Intellect, and the Plane of Absolute Truth. The resplendent effulgence and divine brilliance of God is pure and venerable. We pray and meditate on God to inspire our minds and illuminate our intellect with His divine light.

Whether recited in Sanskrit or English, the beauty and grace of this prayer is clearly evident. As a prayer of praise the Gayatri *mantra* is said to have the ability to purify our minds and hearts with the divine light of God's love.

10.5.5 Two-way Communication with God

Many of the prayerful *mantras* of the Sanatana Dharma tradition are designed as both prayers, as well as focal points for meditation, the Gayatri *mantra* among them. Prayer and meditation, both, are crucial forms of communication with God. Communication is always bi-directional. We speak, but then we must also listen with proper attentiveness. If we are having a conversation with someone, we know that it would be rude to simply do all the talking without giving our conversation partner a chance to respond. In the same way, it is important that we not only speak our thoughts and desires to God in the form of prayer, but that we also listen for God's response in the form of meditation. It is in meditation that we commune most directly with God, and thus have the opportunity to truly listen to His sweet voice within our hearts.

10.6.1 Performing Puja Meditation

The ultimate goal of Sanatana Dharma (the Eternal Natural Way) is to re-establish our innate relationship with God. We do this by cultivating devotion consciousness (*bhakti*) in meditational awareness. One of the most effective means of devotional meditation is known as *puja*. *Puja* involves the direct meditative worship of God by making various symbolic offerings to God with devotion at your home altar or at a temple altar.

Puja is not merely a ritual or ceremony. It is not "ritualism". Rather, it is an active meditation in which we are systematically transforming our consciousness into a mode of natural surrender of our selves to the Supreme Self that is God. In the process of *puja* meditation, we offer various pure substances to the *murti*, or divine image, of God. With each item that we offer, we are meditating on the fact that we are, in actuality, offering our inner being at the lotus-feet of the Divine. This section of the book will provide an introduction to *puja* meditation.

In order to perform the *puja* ceremony, you first have to have a home altar. An altar can be as simple as a small table or shelf in your home, or as elaborate as putting aside an entire room or a section of a room just for the purpose of doing spiritual practice (*sadhana*). How elaborate you would like your altar to be is up to you.

The most important thing to keep in mind is that, more important than how large your altar might be, is how much awareness and sincerity you bring to your *puja* practice. In the *Bhagavad Gita* (9:26), Sri Krishna Himself explains: "If one offers Me with love and devotion a leaf, a flower, fruit or water, I will accept it." The quality of devotion with which we offer anything to God is much more important than the quantitative value of what we offer.

10.6.2 Establishing a Home Altar

The altar must be raised off the ground; should be in a quiet, clean, well-lit, and accessible area of your home; and must be large enough to hold all the necessary *puja* items comfortably. An altar should never be placed in a bathroom, or any other unclean area of the home.

Once you have picked your altar, you then need to pick out your image of God for worship. The image of God is termed a *murti* in Sanskrit. It is important to understand that an authorized *murti* is not an "idol", a "graven image" or merely the blind worship of some imaginary statue concocted in the mind of some flawed human being. Rather, the *murti* represents a trans-substantive portal (a transparent via medium) through which the very presence of God is made accessible in the material world. It is a yogic focal point of meditation, concentration and veneration through which the unseen, Transcendent Being becomes approachable by His devotees where they find themselves currently situated within the material realm. Thus, the *murti* is a direct manifestation of God's limitless grace upon His devotees.

For an image to conform to the precise yogic mechanism of *murti puja* (devotional meditation on the image of God), the *murti* must correspond to the exact specifications outlined in the revealed Vedic scriptures that impart the nature of these precision-tuned instruments of meditative awareness. Such scriptures include the *Agamas*, *Pancharatras* and *Tantras*. Thus, the authorized *murti* forms of God are not to ever be confused to be man-made or concocted whims of an imperfect imagination, but rather represent the crystal clear glimpses of spiritual reality that were experienced by the greatest of our sages (*rishis*), and subsequently passed down to us via the scriptures that they revealed.

It is strongly recommended that your main deity (*murti*) be either of Krishna, or Radha-Krishna; Narayana, or Lakshmi-Narayana; Rama, or Sita-Rama; or of another avatara (incarnation) of Narayana. If you have a choice, it is always better to have both the masculine and feminine aspects of the Divine together on your altar.[35] Thus, *murtis* of either Radha-Krishna, Lakshmi-Narayana, or Sita-Rama are best to have. The image can be either a statue or a printed image. If it is a printed image, please

---

[35] For more information on the masculine and feminine aspects of God, please read the book entitled *The Shakti Principle*.

place it in a respectfully decorative frame. This main image of God should always have the center and most prominent place on your altar. It is this specific *murti* that will be your primary focus of meditation during *puja*.

In addition to the main image of God, it is important to also have a framed photo of your *guru* on the altar. This photo should be smaller than the main image of God, and placed to the side, directly by God's feet. If you also feel inspired to have one or more images of *devas* or *devis* (lessor gods or goddesses, respectively) on your altar, you may do so. These can include, for example, images of Ganapati, Sarasvati, Parvati, Durga, or Shiva. These also should be smaller than the main *murti*, and off to the sides of the altar.

From the very earliest dawn of religious consciousness in human beings, people have attempted to approach and know the Divine by the use of various intermediary devices. Such vehicles of worship and meditation have included divine images, sacred relics of saints, and hallowed objects of many descriptions. The use of *murti*s, or divine images, as a meditational vehicle for approaching God is nothing new, and is not limited to only the Sanatana Dharma tradition. It is a revealed spiritual science.

10.6.3 Conducting Puja

There are several items that you will need to perform *puja*. At a minimum, you will need: a) incense and an incense holder; b) a lighter or matches; c) a bell to ring; d) a ghee-wick lamp, ghee-wicks and ghee.

You must be bathed and clean before performing *puja*.

Sitting before your altar, you want to first center yourself by closing your eyes and taking a few normal breaths with awareness, allowing yourself to be at peace and open to God's grace.

Opening your eyes, place your hands together in 'namaste' gesture and offer your obeisances to the *murti*, reciting "Jaya Sriman Narayana" (Victory to Sri Sri Lakshmi and Narayana).

Light a stick of incense. The begin ringing the bell rhythmically with your left hand. Gently wave the incense stick in your right hand in a clockwise circular motion – three times to the face of the image, three times to the belly, three times to the feet, and finally four times around the entire image. Then place the incense stick in a safe holder. The offered incense is now *prasada*, or the sanctified grace of God. Smelling its aroma is spiritually beneficial because its scent was first accepted by God.

Next, light the ghee wick lamp. Offer the ghee wick lamp with your right hand, ringing the bell in your left hand in the same manner and with the same numbers as the incense was previously offered (three times to the face, belly and feet, then four times around the entire image). When you are done, quickly pass your hands over the flame of the ghee wick lamp and place your hands to your forehead for a blessing. The flame of the ghee-wick, too, is now sanctified *prasada*. Thus, seeing the flame and smelling its aroma will be spiritually beneficial.

You may then offer other items in a similar manner to how you offered the incense and ghee-wick lamp. Other items that you can offer include: a flower, water, or some simple food such as almonds or raisins (which are afterwards eaten as a sacrament, or *"prasada"*).

After the *puja* is over, you may again place your hands in the 'namaste' gesture and offer your obeisances to the altar. Offering obeisances is performed by placing your forehead to the ground while having the top of your head facing the deity. Please then recite the following *mantras*.

10.6.4 Puja Mantras

> *aum ajnana timirandhasya*
> *jnananjana shalakaya*
> *chakshur unmilitam yena*
> *tasmai sri guruve namaha*

"I offer my respectful obeisances to my spiritual teacher, who has opened my eyes, which were blinded by the darkness of ignorance, with the torchlight of knowledge."

> *he krishna karuna sindho*
> *dina bandho jagat pate*
> *gopesha gopika kanta*
> *radha kanta namo'stu te*

"Oh Krishna, ocean of mercy, You are the friend of the distressed and the source of creation. You are the master of the cowherdmen and the lover of the gopis, especially Radha. I offer my respectful obeisances unto You."

> *tapta kanchana gaurangi*
> *radhe vrindavaneshvari*
> *vrishabhanu sute devi*
> *pranamami hari priye*

"I offer my respects to Radha, whose bodily complexion is fair and who is the Queen of Vrindavana. You are the daughter of King Vrishabhanu, and are very dear to Lord Krishna."

Sriman Narayana Charanau Sharanam Prapadye
Srimate Narayanaaya Namah

"I seek refuge at the feet of Sriman Narayana. My salutations to Sriman Narayana."

Having completed the *puja*, this would now be an ideal time to now perform your daily meditation practice in front of your altar, smelling the sweet aroma of the incense and ghee-wick.

10.6.5 Where Do I Get Puja Supplies?

The best resource for *puja* supplies, including sacred images, is the online store called Krishna Culture: www.krishnaculture.com. Ghee and Incense are available in a wide variety of places, including any Indian grocery store, Whole Foods or natural health store.

10.6.6 The Validity of Murti Meditation

The use of images as a path through which finite humanity can approach the Infinite has been found in every traditional culture, religion, and nation on earth. The use of images as a way to know the Divine has been the overwhelming norm – and not the exception – in the history of the world's many religions.

The almost sole exception to this means of approaching God has occurred in the relatively recent religions of the Western world. For the majority of adherents of the Abrahamic sects (Judaism, Christianity, and Islam), the use of images as tools for meditation and prayer has been looked upon as a taboo religious activity. Many Western religions consequently oppose the practice of what they superstitiously term "idol" worship. The leaders of these Abrahamic sects have repeatedly condemned worshipers who employ images of divine figures as "Devil worshipers", "idolaters", "heathens" and "infidels", among other uncharitable descriptions. Those who use icons as a means of worship have faced persecution, denunciation, and even death at the hands of such "idol" smashers.

But is the conscious use of sacred imagery in worship and meditation really to be considered "idol worship" and consequently condemned? Followers of Sanatana Dharma are known to use sacred images as focal points for meditation and worship, and have suffered significant persecution as a result.

The concept of an "idol" in Abrahamic dogma does not refer merely to any iconographic image that is used in worship. Rather the term "idol" refers specifically to an image that is made up, concocted in the mind of its maker, and then claimed to be a divinity. An idol in the proper sense of the term refers to something that one worships as a result of his own whim, and not as a result of the teachings of sacred scriptures. This, however, is not what Dharmis are doing when we venerate sacred images. Dharmis are not idol worshipers because the images that we employ in worship are not contrived by humans.

Rather than "idols", Dharmis worship what are properly called "*murtis*". *Murti* worship is a divine science revealed to humanity in order to facilitate our closeness to God. Sacred Vedic images are not the fanciful creations of the human imagination. Rather, such sacred images were revealed to Vedic worshipers by perfected sages (*rishis*) who have directly experienced the nature of the Divine. To use objects as a focus for devotional prayer and contemplation is perfectly authorized, as long as these images are God-revealed.

The science of employing divine imagery is found in sacred revealed texts known as the *Agamas* and *Pancaratras*. In these texts, the entire science of image veneration is laid out in a logical and reasonable manner. For example there are very exacting specifications for precisely how such images must be created, including the exact dimensions of the images, the rituals necessary to create them, and what sacred *mantras* must be recited during the process. Indeed, even the exact size of every toenail has to be in accordance with certain strict specifications. Only when these images are in accord with these exact specifications do they then become vehicles of the Divine, and proper objects of veneration and meditation.

In following these exact requirements of the sacred texts of Sanatana Dharma the worshiper is performing a very special sacred process known as *murti* meditation, which is categorically distinct from "idol" worship.

The term "idol" is a clearly derogatory term used by unthinking followers of anti-Dharma ideologies to persecute and revile the profound spiritual tradition of Sanatana Dharma. In the same way that other derogatory terms have been removed from civilized human discourse, the term "idol" must never be used again by either Dharmis or non-Dharmis to refer to the sublime science of *murti* worship.

Indeed, even Dharmis themselves have often been guilty of using the term "idol" in ignorance of the nature of their own religion. Whether the term is used by either Dharmis or non-Dharmis, the use of the term "idol" to refer to our sacred imagery must be immediately stopped. Rather we must begin to use such proper Sanskrit terms as *murti, archa*, etc. when referring to our sacred imagery.

Our own ignorance of our own religion is just as inexcusable as is a non-Dharmi's ignorance of our religion. Let us take pride in the divine gift that the *rishis* have bestowed upon us in the form of *murti* worship.

10.6.7 Pitri Puja: Honoring Our Ancestors

No living being exists in complete isolation. No one is an island. We share the cosmos with a multitude of other beings with whom we live in interdependence. This interdependent myriad of beings exists in a vertical, hierarchical relationship with one another, from the lowest amoeba to the highest demigod. Living beings also exist in temporal, historical and genetic relationship with one another. While the past may be gone from our immediate vision, those who affected past historical events, both great and small, are the creators of our present day reality. We are because they were. Each of us, and our families, owe the blessings that we enjoy today at least as much to our direct ancestors as we do to our own hard work and initiative. Knowing this, we must always be thankful to our ancestors. Our ancestors are as much a living presence in our world now as they were when they inhabited physical forms in the past. Their lives have a very real influence upon us today.

All pre-Abrahamic cultures understood the tremendous importance of remaining closely connected to the past if the present was to be invested with any spiritually significant meaning. They also understood that the most personally relevant and accessible portal to the empowering wisdom and goodness of the past was through their own direct, familial ancestors - those who shared their particular bloodline and DNA. Indeed, to honor and respect our specific family's ancestors was considered to be as sacred a duty, and as much a part of being a spiritual person, as worshiping the gods, the *guru*, or the Supreme Absolute.

It was for this reason that all traditional cultures engaged in what is often called ancestor worship (*pitri-puja*). There is no pre-Abrahamic culture on Earth that did not take great care to honor its ancestors in one form or another, often with each household maintaining a family altar in the home specifically meant to honor the family's ancestors, and even the nation as a whole maintaining public altars to honor the greatness of the nation's progenitors, the volksgeist of the entire people of the nation. This is a very important spiritual responsibility and tradition that used to be practiced universally by individuals, families and nations in the ancient past. The process of ancestor worship now needs to be revived in the modern world if we are to retain our sacred connection with our own cultural-spiritual heritage.

All followers of Sanatana Dharma should regularly engage in *pitri-puja*. Ancestor worship must again become a regular, household practice in modern times if we are to maintain a healthy connection with the hereditary current of power and blessings that our ancestors wish to deliver unto us. If you have not yet instituted the practice of ancestor worship in your own home, please consider doing so. The following brief section describes how to begin performing ancestor worship (*pitri-puja*) right away.

PERFORMING ANCESTOR PUJA

The easiest way to begin performing *pitri-puja* is to first establish an ancestor altar in your home. This sacred space does not need to be large in size, and can be as simple as a bookshelf, the top of a short piece of furniture, or a mantelpiece. It can be the natural place in which you keep photos of your departed relatives. The altar should be no higher than eye level, and ideally around waist level in height. Place a clean and pleasant cloth on the surface area, along with either photos and/or mementos on top of the cloth of any deceased relatives who you feel especially close to. You can have anywhere from one to dozens of such photos and items on your ancestor altar, depending on the room you have on the altar and the guidance of your own inspiration.

Each day, perform a simple *puja* ceremony in which you offer a stick of incense and a small cup of water for your ancestors to drink. Then recite the following *mantras*:

Aum Namo Vah Pitrah Saumyah Svaha

("Oh Dear Ancestors, I offer you my obeisances. Please accept this offerring.")

Aum Sarva Pitrah Svaha

("I make this offering to all my ancestors")

In addition, you may recite the Pitri Gayatri *mantra*:[36]

---

[36] You should especially recite the Pitri Gayatri *mantra* if you have had *brahmana* initiation. Otherwise, even if you have not had *brahmana* initiation, it is acceptable to recite the Pitri Gayatri *mantra* if you are living a sattvic lifestyle. You must

Aum Pitr Ganaya Vidmahe
Jagat Dharine Dhimahi
Tanno Pitro Prachodayat (Aum)

After reciting the above *mantras* with devotion, sit and commune with the spirits of your ancestors, asking them to share their wisdom with you, to keep you strong and faithful to Dharma, and to empower and bless you and your family in every way.

10.7.1 Eating as Meditation: How to Prepare Prasada

The very essence of all forms of Sanatana Dharma is Yoga. And the heart of Yoga is meditation. With any activity that is done in Yoga, whether doing any of the *asanas*, *pranayama*, study of scriptures, etc., these activities are only considered to be Yoga in the true sense of the word when we are in a simultaneous meditative state while performing them. Thus, if you are performing an *asana* (Yoga pose) to technical perfection, but without awareness, then you are not doing Yoga in any real sense. If on the other hand, your attempt to do an *asana* is far from perfect, but you are in complete concentration, struggling with sincerity and devotion to God as you are struggling to perform the *asana*, then, and only then, are you truly doing Yoga. For Yoga is meditation. Yoga is about what the mind and consciousness do...not just what the body does.

The ancient classical Yoga tradition had God-realization as its highest goal. Authentic Yoga is also sometimes known as the Prapatti Marga, or

---

be living a sattvic lifestyle in order to recite any *gayatri mantra*. See *The Sanatana Dharma Study Guide* for more information on living a sattvic life.

the path of complete self-surrender to the grace of God. One of the unique features of this form of authentic Yoga spirituality is the concept of Prasada-Meditation. The Sanskrit word "*prasada*" is literally translated as "mercy," or "grace." Specifically, *prasada* refers to the divine grace of God. Everything we do, are and think should be done in a consciousness of dedication to the Absolute, with love and devotion (*bhakti*). Such a state of active devotional meditation will ensure that we make continued progress on the spiritual path and in our own individual Yoga practice and Dharma *sadhana*.

For the *yogi* (practitioner of Yoga), this meditative lifestyle of devotional surrender is all encompassing, and is extended even to the preparing and eating of food. With Prasada-Meditation, we make the preparing of food, the offering of food to God with devotion, and the eating of the food offered, into a powerful devotional meditation. If, as a meditative discipline, we can offer our food to God with devotion before eating it, not only are we not implicated in the potential *karma* involved in acquiring the food, but we can actually make spiritual progress by eating the offered food. Our devotion, and God's grace, subtly transforms the food offered from material nutrition to spiritual mercy (*prasada*).

10.7.2 Guidelines

Before we can offer any food to God, however, we must first follow some important guidelines while preparing the food. First, God only accepts purely vegetarian offerings - offerings that are acquired without pain and suffering on the part of any creature. So, we have to strictly avoid cooking any meat (including chicken; a bird is not a vegetable!), fish and eggs. Second, we cannot offer any onions, garlic or mushrooms.

This may seem like an odd proscription; but the Vedic scriptures, as well as the ancient natural medicinal system of Ayurveda, explain that these foods excite the more passionate elements (*rajas*) of the human psycho-physical constitution. Third (and this can sometimes be tough), we must not taste the food before it is offered to God. The preparing of *prasada* is done as an active devotional meditation. So the goal is to prepare delicious foods, not with our own satisfaction in mind, but thinking only of the satisfaction of God. Therefore, He should be the first to "taste" the fruits of our labors.

Keeping this meditative goal in mind, it is important to have an atmosphere in our kitchen that is conducive to creating a meditative and devotional state. We should be in a calm, peaceful and contemplative frame of mind while preparing food for God, thinking to ourselves as we prepare the food that we are acting for God's satisfaction, and not just our own.

Finally, as in any spiritual endeavor, it is important to maintain a high standard of cleanliness while preparing, cooking, and offering the food. The kitchen, utensils and foods that are used should be clean. We ourselves also should be clean and bathed before beginning Prasada-Meditation, or any other meditation for that matter.

If we can follow all of the above guidelines and, most importantly, maintain a meditative consciousness of love and devotion for God as we are performing these activities, then God will gladly accept our offering.

10.7.3 How To Offer Food to God

It is helpful if you have an altar already set up somewhere in your home, apartment or dorm. At the very center of this altar should be either a sacred image or a picture of God in any of His sacred forms. For example, an image of any of His incarnations - Rama, Krishna, Narasingha - or any other form, such as Srinathaji or Venkateshvara, is fine. In addition, you can include images to the side of your altar of your *guru*, saints, or other *devas* or *devis* on your altar - Durga, Ganesha, Sarasvati, etc. Images of God, however, should be the central focal point of any altar used for meditation. If you do not have an altar, then placing a simple image of God somewhere special will do.

When the food is ready, take a small sampling of each preparation, along with a glass or cup of water, and place them all on a special plate that is used only for offering food to God. This plate must never be used for any other purpose than offering food to God in Prasada-Meditation. Place the plate of food and the water before the sacred image. Offer a little incense to God. Then, in a meditative and devotional state of mind, sit with eyes closed in meditation and recite several sacred *mantras*. First recite the following *mantra* once:

> *namo brahmanya devaya go brahmanaya hitaya cha*
> *jagad dhitaya Krishnaya govindaya namo namah*

"I offer my respectful obeisances to the Supreme Absolute Truth, Krsna, who is the well-wisher of the cows and the *brahmanas*, as well as all sentient beings in general. I offer my obeisances to Govinda, Krishna, who is the pleasure reservoir for all the senses, and especially the senses of His devotees."

This is to be followed by reciting the *tiru-mantra* three times:

Aum Namo Narayanaya

After chanting this *mantra*, then remain in silent prayer for about 3 minutes and request the Lord to accept your offering.[37] After you have offered the food in this way, the food that you have cooked is now sanctified and considered to be *prasada*, food transformed into the grace of God. The individual food items on the offering plate should be re-merged into the food in the pots. Having thanked the Lord for accepting your offering, the *prasada* can now be eaten. By partaking in such food, we show our devotion to God, and thus make spiritual advancement.

The food should also be eaten with meditative awareness, peacefully and respectfully. While eating the *prasada*, please always be conscious and aware that you are partaking in the special grace of God. Eat with reverence, and enjoy!

10.7.4 Mantras Recited Before Eating

The eating of food is a sacred act. This is the case because God is the source of all foodstuffs and the vitality that they contain. It is for this reason that every civilized culture has one form or another of prayer or ritual that is to be performed before eating one's meal. In order to become more aware of God's grace during the eating process, the following *mantras* can be chanted before having food.

---

[37] If you have *brahmana* initiation, recite the *gayatri mantra* three times silently as God partakes of the offering.

1) Take some water in your right hand, and sprinkle it around the plate, encircling the food in a counterclockwise direction while chanting the *gayatri mantra.*

Aum Bhur Bhuva Svaha
Tat Savitur Varenyam
Bhargo Devasya Dhimahi
Dhiyo Yo Nah Prachodayat

2) Then take a small bit of the food and put it in your mouth. Recite the below *prana-mantras* (offering respects to the five *pranas*).

Aum Pranaaya Svaaha
Aum Apanaaya Svaaha
Aum Vyanaaya Svaaha
Aum Udanaaya Svaaha
Aum Samanaaya Svaaha

The process of offering a bit of food to the five *pranas* serves the triple purpose of activating the *pranas*, activating the *agni* force that leads to proper digestion, as well as making us aware of the energizing power of the food that God's gift us all with. Then, recite:

Aum Brahmane Svaaha
Brahmana Atma Amrita Tvaaya

3) Start eating. While eating food, it is desirable that you keep God in mind.

4) At the end of eating, sip a bit of water, enough to wet your throat, and recite the below *mantra.*

Amrita api dhaanam asi. ("Let this food confer longevity to me.")

10.7.5 Important Vedic Holy Days

Vedic culture is a rich, diverse and immeasurable tapestry of beautiful celebrations of the Transcendent. There are many dozens of holy days that are observed in the Vedic tradition. Some of these, however, are of much more importance than others. These are not just secular holidays, such as Labor Day or President's Day, in which we are just happy to have a day off. Rather, we use these days to deepen our spiritual understanding and experience as we contemplate the meaning of the day.

The following is a list of the most important holy days that all followers of Sanatana Dharma should observe each year. Please note that the Vedic calendar (known as the Yugabda calendar) is based upon a lunar calculation, and not the solar calculation of the West. As a result, it is not possible to give exact days of each holy day, since these will vary from year to year. Consequently, the exact dates are only approximations. Check with your local Vedic calendar (this information is easily available Online) for the exact dates within any specific year.

Rama Navami (early April)

This is the appearance day of the *avatara* (incarnation) Sri Rama. Rama appeared upon the Earth to rule as a perfect Chaktravartin, or Dharma Ruler, thus showing the world what it means to personify Dharma both in one's self and in governance. *Puja* to Sri Sri Sita Rama is performed on this day, along with a daylong fast that is ended with a feast of *prasada*.

Ramanuja Jayanti (late April)

This day celebrates the appearance in this world of the greatest Vedic philosopher in history, Sri Ramanuja Acharya (1017–1137 CE). He is responsible for reviving pure Vedic philosophy in the Kali Yuga, for reintroducing Bhakti Yoga to the world, and for writing the *Sri Bhashya*, the most important commentary ever written on the *Brahma Sutras*, the scriptural foundation of Vedanta. A half-day fast is observed on this day in Sri Ramanuja Acharya's honor, as well as a special *puja* to him.

Guru Purnima (early July)

On this day, the principle of Sri Guru is celebrated throughout the Vedic community. We offer our obeisances to our own *guru*, and to all legitimate *gurus*, on this day. In addition to offering respects to our spiritual masters, we offer our respects to all the teachers who have positively impacted our lives. *Puja* is offered to the *guru*, and donations are given to the *guru*.

Sri Krishna Janmashtami (late August or early September)

This is the appearance day of the *avatara* (incarnation) Sri Krishna. Devotees of Sri Krishna will fast on this day until midnight, finally breaking the fast at midnight with a feast of *prasada*. We will also engage in *kirtana* (devotional songs) and reading the sacred story (*divya-katha*) of Krishna's appearance and activities all throughout the day. *Puja* to Sri Sri Radha Krishna is performed throughout this day as well. This is the most important and joyous of all the Vedic holy days.

Navaratri (late September/early October)

Navaratri means "Nine Nights" and is dedicated to the goddess principle. Over the course of nine nights, the sacred feminine power (Shakti) in the form of the goddess Durga is worshipped with elaborate *pujas* and festivities. Each of the nine nights is dedicated to a different aspect of the goddess.

Dipavali (mid-October or mid-November)

This day is also known as the "Festival of Lights". It celebrates the return of Sri Sri Sita Rama to their capital city of Ayodhya after 14 years in exile. The *Ramayana* explains that when Sita and Rama were flying back to the city in Their *vimana* (flying vehicle), the residents of Ayodhya were so overjoyed that they lovingly lit up millions of small lamps throughout the city so that Sita and Rama could easily find Their way back to them. This holy day celebrates the victory of good over evil, and the triumph of the light of Truth over the darkness of ignorance. On this day, we light *dipas* (ghee-wick lamps) and place them both inside and outside the house in commemoration of the return of Sita and Rama to Ayodhya.

Chapter 11   Living Dharma Today

11.1.1 Balancing Spiritual and Material Life

It seems that there are an infinite number of demands on our schedules today compared to even just a generation ago. People today are riddled with jobs, classes, active Internet lives, family, and an ever-increasing barrage of information coming at us at lightning speed. While adding Yoga, meditation and a satisfying spiritual life on top of all this material activity is crucial to balance out the stress and anxiety that is inexorably linked with modern life, combining our spiritual and material lives often seems to be a pretty daunting goal. By focusing on the quality of our spiritual practice over the quantity, as well as learning how to lead a balanced lifestyle, we can eventually learn how to be successful in both our spiritual and material lives.

Sanatana Dharma is a path that believes in avoiding obsessive extremes in lifestyle. The idea of spiritual life is ultimately one of healthy balance, with a deep focus on the quality of our practices. The path of spiritual *sadhana* (practice) teaches us that balance in all things is necessary to making spiritual progress. In the *Bhagavad Gita*, for example, Sri Krishna shares the following wisdom with us:

> *naty-asnatas 'tu yogo 'sti na chaikantam anasnatah*
> *na chati-svapna-silasya jagrato naiva charjuna*

"One can have no success in Yoga if one eats too much or eats too little. Nor can one be successful if one sleeps too much or does not sleep enough." (*Bhagavad Gita*, 6:16)

We are meant to engage in spiritual practice in a way that is healthy, realistic, and conducive to our advancement. Thus, we have to avoid extremes in our life, and live our life in such a way that we can come to a happy compromise with A) our *sadhana* (practice) and B) our material duties in life.

As far as knowing where the line lies between balance and obsession, that will vary in accordance with the individual. A good indicator that you may be over-extending yourself in *sadhana* at the expense of the other important aspects of your life is precisely when *sadhana* begins to be seen as a dreadful burden rather than a joy, and to produce anxiety rather than peace in your life.

When we are performing *yoga-asanas*, for example, we know that we have pushed our bodies too far when an *asana* has gone from being merely challenging to then being painful. At that point, we are being given a hint by our body that it is time to pull back a little, and if we go further into an *asana*, in complete disregard to our body's natural cautioning signals, we may end up injuring ourselves.

In the same way that we need to hear and respect what our body is communicating to us in *asana*, we also need to hear what our inner self is telling us with our *sadhana* practice. It is important to always challenge ourselves in a healthy and progressive manner. But if we go beyond that fine line, from wholesome challenge to unhealthy extremes, from devotion to fanaticism, then we need to adjust ourselves accordingly and reassess just how much we can do in accordance with our capabilities, the time we have, our other demands in life, and our goal in spiritual practice. Again, the crucial principle in Yoga, meditation and any spiritual *sadhana* is always quality over quantity.

If, on the other hand, our problem is not that we feel that we are pushing ourselves too much spiritually, but that we actually want to perform more *sadhana* than we are at present, but simply do not have the time, then this is a different concern. This is still a matter of balance, but it is now a matter of a balance of priorities. In this case, there are several options that one can follow. These include: A) reassessing just how important other specific, non-spiritual activities are to one's life. Are there some activities – even just one or two – that can be put on hold or scaled down to give you more time? Can you take one less class, work a few less hours a week, spend less time surfing the Internet, watch a few less movies per week, or make some other minor adjustments? B) Another course of action is maximizing the time that you do have, performing tasks more efficiently as much as is feasible, and thus freeing up more time for spiritual life than you even knew you had.

What spiritual practitioners often find is that, interestingly, when we take somewhat of a leap of faith and put our spiritual life first in a healthy and realistic way, what then happens is that the rest of our life quite naturally becomes more balanced and efficient. Our material life conforms to our spiritual life. When we make room in our lives for meditation, Yoga, and spirituality in general, we consequently find the energy, inspiration, focus, and determination to maximize what we're doing in the rest of our lives. A healthy and balanced spiritual life is the key to ensure a happy and prosperous material life.

11.1.2 Being a Dharma Activist

It sometimes seems that the dual worlds of spirituality and social-political involvement are mutually exclusive concerns. Dharma offers us a profound vision of harmony, truthfulness and spiritual unity. Social activism, on the other hand, often seems to be predicated upon seeing natural divisions among people, and maneuvering among such social divisions in order to achieve a practical strategic end. How can we reconcile being engaged in the world as social-political activists, along with the inevitable subsequent recognition of the inherent and natural differences between individual persons and diverse peoples, while also being on a spiritual path the goal of which is to transcend the egotistical mistake of mere social-identification? There are several thoughts that we need to reflect on in this regard.

First, it is important to understand what exactly is meant by the word "ego" (*ahamkara* in Sanskrit). Ego is a false, or illusory, sense of self that arises from identifying with things/persona/situations that are actually alien to the true, spiritual self (*atman*). To act out of illusory ego is to act out of a mistaken identification with an artificial self. Thus, the two word term "*aham-kara*" means literally "I maker", or the artificially constructed self. When we act out of a sense of illusion (*maya*), or a false identification with what we are not, we are then acting egotistically. Of course, there is a natural and necessary causal correspondence between living egotistically and subsequently acting out of selfishness, self-centeredness, envy, unjustified anger, lust, hedonism, etc. One's inner identity dictates one's outer behavior. If we identify with our natural, spiritual self, then we are acting in a spiritually whole and healthy way. When we identify with the artificial construct of illusory ego, then we are acting in a manner that is fragmented, unreal and unhealthy. So, in summary, to act out of any sense of false identity, coupled with the attendant emotions and motivations of selfishness, etc., is to act out of ego (*ahamkara*).

Second, while it is true that ultimately we are not merely these bodies, and that we ultimately transcend materiality in our spiritual essence as pure *atman* (soul), we are nonetheless spiritual beings having a material experience. While the spiritual realm is possessed of infinitely more substantial reality than is the empirical realm, the empirical does have its own legitimate reality, and attendant natural laws, structural integrity and rules, that need to be taken into account. Dharma philosophy asks us to realize our ultimate spiritual identity, while also simultaneously acknowledging the fact that we are currently situated in a material world with its own inherent laws that need to be respected. So, while it is egotistical to identify solely with the body at the expense of spiritual self-realization, it is not egotistical to acknowledge the concrete material facts of characteristic differences in human beings, natural social hierarchies, unavoidable inequalities among all people, and genetic inheritances...just as long as we also recognize the fact that, ultimately, it is the spiritual *atman* that informs, and is superior to, the material body. This is how a person can very easily be both a Dharmi and an activist at the same time. In fact, I would argue that the only way to fully understand the metaphysical meaning behind the many natural differences between people that we encounter in the world around us is precisely through a proper understanding of Dharma - or Natural Law.

Third, both the metaphysical and physical principles of this world are a manifestation of Dharma, and are thus a reflection of the Eternal Truth.

It is exactly the laws of nature that are responsible for the social alterations that have resulted in the existence of many different political
stances, and in the inherent superiority and inferiority of these different
stances. We must have the philosophical discernment and moral vision to
acknowledge, for example, that:

> A) Evil, tyranny, radical materialism, greed and psychopathocra
> cy are very real factors currently inhabiting many of the institu
> tions of power and must be opposed.

> B) The vast majority of people in any given society are innocent
> in nature and are only lacking compassionate leadership and
> guidance.

> c) Dharma offers the most compassionate, logical and workable
> solutions to combating tyranny, giving the common people a
> true voice, and forming a society that is based upon justice, natu
> ral law, healthfulness and spiritual culture.

To acknowledge these concrete social-political realities is not an expression of ego. Rather, it is an inherent expression of the yogic wisdom
(*buddhi*) and innate powers of discernment (*viveka*) that are the very fruit
of spiritual practice, which is in turn an expression of Dharma. Being a
seeker of truth means having the ability to accept that truth in each and
every sphere of experience - including the social and political.

Again, to identify ourselves with the reality our given situation, either
spiritual or material, is to live in accordance with Dharma. To misidentify
ourselves with a mistaken assumption of any given situation is ignorance,
and thus is a state that arises from illusory ego, and is to live in opposi-
tion to Dharma. To merely acknowledge the fact that Dharma reflects
the highest form of truth, human organizational principles, and world-
view accessible by human life on this Earth is not a reflection of ego, but

is a reflection of compassion toward all beings. We have a duty to Dharma to actively preserve reality and to honor truth in all spheres of human endeavor. To honor what is true is not egotistical. It is Dharmic.

11.1.3 Twenty Things You can do to Support Dharma

1. Consider becoming a monthly tithing member of the International Sanatana Dharma Society. Your donations go toward the creation of books, videos, documentaries, CDs and other media created to share the teachings of Dharma with a suffering world. In addition, your donations help support the necessary infrastructure to ensure that our worldwide Dharma movement continues to expand. Please visit Dharmacentral.com to become a donating member today.

2. Join a local Sanatana Dharma Temple or Satsangha group organized by the International Sanatana Dharma Society.

3. Distribute copies of *"Sanatana Dharma: The Eternal Natural Way"* and other ISDS publications to your friends, family and all sincere spiritual seekers you know. Let others know about our books via social media and by writing positive reviews of our books.

4. Join the Sanatana Dharma Forum online discussion group found on Dharmacentral.com to feel more connected to our global online Vedic community. (To be established in 2016)

5. Contact the managers of your local Yoga centers and request them to offer copies of *"Sanatana Dharma: The Eternal Natural Way"* for sale at their Yoga shop.

6. Print out and put up flyers about Sanatana Dharma on local bulletin boards in your city or neighborhood. Dharma flyers can be obtained at Dharmacentral.com.

7. Be an Internet guerilla! Use e-mail, blogs, tweets, and newsletters to broadcast the message of Dharma Online. Spread empowering information available at Dharmacentral.com throughout the Internet.

8. Contact the International Sanatana Dharma Society to host a Dharma event in your community, your Yoga center, your university, or at your workplace.

9. Dharma begins at home. Nurture, support, and involve your children and family in practicing Dharma.

10. Use music, art, stories, drama, film, and other creative media to explore themes of Dharma and spirituality. Art and culture is a powerful and positive way to teach Dharma.

11. Broadcast a positive Dharma message by using a Dharma flag, poster, badge, t-shirt, or bumper sticker. These can be obtained at www.dharmacentral.com.

12. Join a Dharma study circle centered on "*Sanatana Dharma: The Eternal Natural Way*", "*The Sanatana Dharma Study Guide*", and other publications of the International Sanatana Dharma Society. Self-education is a fast track toward spiritual understanding and empowerment.

13. Become an active volunteer for your local branch of the International Sanatana Dharma Society, or on any of the many ISDS projects currently available. Information on such projects is available at either Dharmacentral.com or Sanatanadharmaforum.com.

14. Forward any of the many hundreds of Dharma memes that we have available in many different languages. These are available at Dharmacentral.com

15. Organize a fundraiser for the International Sanatana Dharma Society in your community.

16. Share links to all of our inspiring and educational videos available at Youtube.com/dharmanation.

17. Vote. Voting is your hard-earned right and your official voice. Run for elective office, especially on the local level. Be a voice for Dharma, reasoned sanity, and balance. Read the book *"The Dharma Manifesto"* for more information.

18. Attend the annual Sanatana Dharma Conference, sponsored by the ISDS.

19. Donate a house, building or land to the ISDS for use as a local temple and/or *ashrama*.

20. Donate your time, volunteer assistance and funding to the International Sanatana Dharma Society.

Chapter 12 Resources

12.1.1 International Sanatana Dharma Society

If your goal is to be considered as a candidate for possible initiation, then it is required that you be actively involved as a formal member of the International Sanatana Dharma Society both prior to and after initiation.

The International Sanatana Dharma Society (ISDS) is a global spiritual movement dedicated to practicing and teaching the ancient Vedic religious tradition in its fully authentic and unaltered form. Our goal in spiritual practice is to accept no watering-down or compromises to the time-honored integrity of the Vedic philosophy and lifestyle. The only way to practice and truly benefit from Dharma spirituality is to practice Dharma on its own sacred terms, and not merely as a further extension of our illusory ego (*ahamkara*).

Our religion is known in the Sanskrit language as Sanatana Dharma, or the Eternal Natural Way. We thus call ourselves "Dharmis", or followers of Dharma. Members of the ISDS follow Sanatana Dharma exclusively as their chosen religious path. We do not mix and match pure Vedic spirituality with any other religious traditions, modern "new age" innovations, or pop spirituality. We exclusively identify with, and practice, Sanatana Dharma as our path to Self-realization and God-consciousness.

We know truth by means of a) the instructing words and guidance of the enlightened *guru* (*guru-vani*), b) the guidance of the revealed Vedic scriptures (*shastra-pramana*), and c) the use of our own reasoning faculties

416

(*vichara*), philosophical discernment (*viveka*) and personal experience (*anubhava*). Sanatana Dharma is not a religion of blind faith, fanaticism, or wishful thinking. It is a religion of acquired spiritual/philosophical wisdom, coupled with direct personal experience of the transformative presence of God.

The teachings and practices of the ISDS are based directly upon the Vedic scriptures. Our scriptures consist of the entire *shruti* and *smriti* cannons of the Vedic literature, but with special emphasis on the teachings of the *Bhagavad Gita, Upanishads, Bhagavata Purana, Vishnu Purana, Brahma Sutras, Yoga Sutras* and *Narada Bhakti Sutras.*

Who We Are

Aum Tad Vishnu Paramam Padam
"The abode of Vishnu is the highest state of existence."

- *Rig Veda*, 1:22:20

Members of the ISDS recognize the Vedic scriptures' clear declaration that Sriman Narayana (also known as Vishnu) represents the supreme form of Godhead (Brahman), and we express special devotion to the *avatara* of Sriman Narayana for this age: Bhagavan Sri Krishna and His divine consort (*divya-shakti*) Srimati Radharani. Sri Krishna was on the earth over 5100 years ago, and is the speaker of the famous *Bhagavad Gita*, the most important scripture for our current age. The meaning of life is to revive our innate devotional consciousness (*bhakti*) toward the Supreme Godhead, and to reunite ourselves with Sriman Narayana in eternal loving union.

Our spiritual practice (*sadhana*) consists of the full classical Yoga system (*ashtanga*) permeated throughout with a consciousness of *bhakti* (devotion). *Bhakti*, or devotional consciousness, is understood to be both the highest means of liberation, as well as the ultimate goal of spiritual life and culture. Thus, *bhakti* is not merely the most effective means (*upaya*) for spiritual liberation; it is also the ultimate goal (*paramartha*) of life. Members of the ISDS all strive to achieve self-realization (*atma-jnana*), leading finally to God-consciousness (*brahma-vidya*). Our primary form of meditation is *mantra* meditation upon the divine sound vibration **Aum Namo Narayanaya**.

Members of the ISDS only acknowledge the leadership of as a truly enlightened sage, a Sadguru (true *guru*), who is capable of guiding his disciples to the deepest realization of wisdom and spiritual liberation, and all members strive to follow our *guru's* spiritual teachings in our daily lives with sincerity, loyalty and fidelity.

12.1.2 Distinctly Authentic Approach to Vedic Spirituality

There are several features that make the International Sanatana Dharma Society (ISDS) fundamentally distinctive when compared to any other Hindu / Dharma / Yoga movement on earth today.

1) **Guru Principle**: We recognize that it is only under the expert guidance and grace of an authentic *guru* that we can traverse the path to liberation safely and effectively. We are guided, both as individual disciples and as a movement, by a living and extremely qualified

representative of the Vedic ideal.

2) **Scripturally-Based**: We scrupulously base everything the ISDS does and teaches upon a clear understanding of the Vedic scriptures. Our approach to philosophy, spiritual practice, meditation and lifestyle are all rooted directly in the teachings of the scriptures. Indeed, in-depth and guided study of the Vedic scriptures is one of the most important ongoing practices that our members engage in.

3) **Academic Excellence**: Our members strongly strive to couple their meditative spiritual practice with a very scholarly and philosophical grasp of the philosophy, theology, culture, history and application of Sanatana Dharma. Mystical attainment can never be used as an excuse for intellectual lethargy on the part of the spiritual practitioner. Success on the spiritual path is only possible with the integrative partnership of both subjective spiritual experience (*anubhava*) coupled with wisdom and understanding (*buddhi*).

4) **Quality over Quantity**: In our philosophy and practices (both personal and as an organizational structure), the ISDS always emphasize the spiritual quality of our activities over mere quantity. Thus, rather than artificially focusing on merely having a large mass following, we instead strive to have a smaller membership of truly exceptional and sincere spiritual practitioners. Consequently, we have sometimes been called somewhat elitist or exclusive in whom we accept as members and formal students. We are fine with that! Our goal is to serve those who are sincerely ready for the real thing: an authentic path the goal of which is having a direct experience of truth. We also seek to create the Dharma leaders and teachers of the future who will carry on the traditions of the

most ancient spiritual path on Earth. The ISDS represents nothing less than the cutting-edge Vedic vanguard. The ISDS is thus not for everyone. But if you are willing to learn and practice authentic Vedic spirituality in a mood of humility and sincerity, and to experience growth in your spiritual life in a manner that is truly meaningful, then you are very welcome to join.

5) **Vedic Authenticity**: We are radical traditionalists in our approach to the Vedic way. We seek to practice Dharma in as traditional, authentic, orthodox and uncompromisingly real a manner as is possible in the modern era. There is nothing new, "New Age", or concocted in how we teach or practice the Vedic way. Moreover, we do not "mix and blend" our practice or understanding of Sanatana Dharma with those of other, non-Vedic paths. If you are interested in the ISDS, the teachings of Sanatana Dharma, or being involved in our movement, please do so knowing that what you will be taught and will be following nothing less than the authentic and ancient religion of Sanatana Dharma - the Eternal Natural Way.

6) **Comprehensiveness**: As students of the Vedic way, we understand that Sanatana Dharma is so much more than merely a religious tradition. Rather, the world-view, arts and sciences of Vedic culture are meant to very naturally extend into every field of human concern. This includes not only the spiritual, but also the social, political, economic, scientific, medical, artistic, musical, culinary, martial, cultural, civilizational and philosophical realms of human endeavor. The ISDS seeks to not only help our members in their own individual spiritual progress, but to also extend the truths of Dharma over the entire sphere of human endeavor. Our goal is to positively change all of society on the most fundamental of

levels, and to thus affect the respiritualization of global civilization.

7) **Effective Sadhana**: The essential foundation of following Sanatana Dharma is *sadhana*, practicing the meditational and yogic techniques in a disciplined and daily manner. The powerful spiritual disciplines that the ISDS teaches its members are highly effective, authorized and scripturally based, with an emphasis on Yoga, *mantra*, *puja*, and meditation as revealed in the *Upanishads*. The *sadhana* techniques of the ISDS work because they are authentic and taught expertly.

8) **Highest Ethical Standards**: Many in the West have all too often found themselves exploited by unethical "spiritual teachers" who falsely claimed to be representing the pure Yoga and Dharma tradition, but who only turned out to be amoral abusers of their innocent followers. The ISDS is unyielding in its commitment to upholding and educating all its members in the very highest ethical standards that form the core behavioral expectations of Vedic culture. Our strict code of ethics includes adherence to the Yamas and Niyamas of Yoga philosophy. Both the initiated students and the leaders of the ISDS are expected, without exception, to strictly observe the following ethical standards: a) no intoxicants (including alcohol, cigarettes, marijuana, hashish, ayahuasca, etc.), b) strict lacto-vegetarianism (no meat, fish or eggs), c) no illicit or exploitative sexual behavior (sexuality should be confined exclusively to the institution of marriage).

12.1.3 Becoming a Member of the ISDS

We recognize that membership in the ISDS is not for everyone. It is only for a small number of individuals who possess the deep sincerity, the philosophical discernment, and the inner strength necessary to truly embrace the path to total liberation in a vividly meaningful manner. Our students are dedicated to following a path that encourages them to look honestly within in a contemplative manner, to observing a spiritual discipline that leads to a gradual unfoldment of their true selves, and that results in Self-realization and God-consciousness.

If you are interested in joining the International Sanatana Dharma Society, we ask that you possess deep sincerity, humility, openness, and a strong desire to know the Divine. If you are attracted to a Vedic-based path that focuses on thorough authenticity, a conscientious philosophical approach, and a clear and effective means of knowing God's presence in your everyday life, please consider becoming an official member today.

The following are requirements for membership:

1. You must consider Sanatana Dharma to be your exclusive and chosen spiritual tradition.
2. You must do your utmost to learn and to put into daily practice the teachings of the *guru* of the ISDS.
3. All members are expected to tithe monthly in accordance with their means.

Please choose a generous amount below, and start giving your tax-deductible monthly membership donation today!

Membership Tiers

1. **Basic Membership**: $120 min. annual donation. ($10 per month)

2. **Family Membership**: $240 min. annual donation. ($20 per month)
3. **Supporting Member (Dharma Warrior)**: $600 min. annual donation. ($50 per month)

4. **Patron Member (Dharma Knight)**: $1200 min. annual donation. ($100 per month)

5. **Life Member (Dharma King/Queen)**: $5000 min. one time donation.

For more information on how to become a member, please visit: Dharmacentral.com/members

12.1.4 Books and Periodicals

Books by Sri Dharma Pravartaka Acharya

The Dharma Manifesto
The Vedic Way of Knowing God
Living Dharma: The Teachings of Sri Dharma Pravartaka Acharya
Radical Universalism: Are All Religions the Same?
Vedanta: The Culmination of Wisdom
The Dharma Dialogues
Taking Refuge in Dharma: The Initiation Guidebook
The Shakti Principle: Encountering the Feminine Power of God
The Art of Wisdom

Sanatana Dharma: The Eternal Natural Way

The Sanatana Dharma Study Guide

The Vedic Encyclopedia

The Dharma of Wellbeing

Books by A.C. Bhaktivedanta Swami Prabhupada

Bhagavad-Gita as It Is

Krsna: The Supreme Personality of Godhead

The Nectar of Devotion: The Complete Science of Bhakti Yoga

The Perfection of Yoga

Sri Isopanisad

Easy Journey to Other Planets

The Science of Self-Realization

Raja-vidya: The King of Knowledge

Books by Dr. David Frawley

Universal Hinduism: Towards a New Vision of Sanatana Dharma (Introduction by Sri Dharma Pravartaka Acharya)

From the River of Heaven: Vedic Knowledge for the Modern Age

Awaken Bharata: A Call for India's Rebirth

How I Became a Hindu: My Discovery of Vedic Dharma

Yoga, the Greater Tradition

Vedantic Meditation: Lighting the Flame of Awareness

Beyond the Mind

Yoga and the Sacred Fire: Self-realization and Planetary Transformation

Ayurveda and the Mind: The Healing of Consciousness

Gods, Sages and Kings: Vedic Secrets of Ancient Civilization

Books by Stephen Knapp

Proof of Vedic Culture's Global Existence
The Power of the Dharma: An Introduction to Hinduism and Vedic Culture
Yoga and Meditation: Their Real Purpose and How to Get Started
Avatars, Gods and Goddesses of Vedic Culture
The Soul: Understanding Our Real Identity
How the Universe was Created and Our Purpose In It

Periodicals

ISDS Well-Wishers Newsletter
Hinduism Today Magazine

Dharma Websites

Dharmacentral.com

Dharmacivilization.com

Dharmanation.org

Youtube.com/DharmaNation (Our official Youtube video channel)

Facebook.com/pages/International-Sanatana-Dharma-Society/111383025561439

Appendix

Sanatana Dharma by the Numbers

Three Gunas: *sattva / rajas / tamas*

Three Kandas: *karma-kanda / jnana-kanda / upasana-kanda*

Three Margas: Vaishnava / Shaiva / Shakta

Three Material Challenges (Tapa-traya): (1) Challenges arising from the mind and body, (2) challenges inflicted by other living beings, and (3) challenges arising from natural catastrophes over which one has no control.

Three Planetary Systems: Svarga (upper) / Bhu (middle) / Patala (lower)

Three Pramanas: *pratyaksha / anumana / shabda*

Three Tattvas: Brahman / Jiva / Jagat

Three Truth Verifiers: Shastra / Acharya / Vichara

Four Sampradayas: Sri / Brahma / Rudra / Kumara

Four Vedas: *Rig / Sama / Atharva / Yajur*

Seven Mothers: the real mother, the wife of a *guru*, the wife of a king, the wife of a *brahmana*, the cow, the nurse and mother earth.

Seven Physical Layers: skin, flesh, blood, marrow, bone, fat and semen.

About the Author

Sri Dharma Pravartaka Acharya is universally acclaimed as one of the world's most respected and qualified Dharma teachers and Vedic spiritual leaders. Dr. Deepak Chopra has exclaimed in 2002: *"You've done truly phenomenal work teaching the pure essence of Yoga"*. In a similar manner, Dr. David Frawley has said about Sri Acharyaji, *"Sri Acharyaji represents the Sankalpa [the will] of the Hindu people and the cause of Sanatana Dharma. I urge all Hindus everywhere to give him your full support, assistance, and encouragement in his crucial work. He needs and deserves our help."* Indeed, *Hinduism Today Magazine* has proclaimed him one of the top five scholars of Hinduism on earth.

Sri Acharyaji began his personal spiritual journey over 40 years ago at the tender age of ten when he read the *Bhagavad Gita* for the very first time. It was at the age of ten that he began his rigorous practice of Yoga, meditation, *pranayama* and many other ancient Vedic techniques of spiritual awakening. At approximately twelve years old, he took Yoga lessons from Sri Dharma Mittra and Sri Swami Bua in New York City. Only a few short years later, he took on the lifestyle of a fulltime Vedic monk, living a life of celibacy and great austerity for close to eight years. This monastic training culminated in Sri Acharyaji being awarded the status of *brahmana* (Vedic priest) by his *guru*, B.R. Sridhara Swami, in 1986 at his *guru's ashrama* in India.

He coupled his decades of intense spiritual practice and study with advanced academic achievements, earning a B.A. in philosophy/theology from Loyola University Chicago, as well as an M.A. and Ph.D. in religious studies from the University of Wisconsin-Madison. His entire

428

university career was funded by academic fellowships awarded to him as a result of his scholastic excellence and brilliance.

Explaining to his doctoral advisor in 1995 that *"I don't want to just study the history of religion...I want to make religious history"*, Sri Acharyaji eventually left academia to devote himself exclusively to spiritual teaching and to the preservation of the great tradition of Sanatana Dharma.

Sri Acharyaji occupies his full time teaching Dharma spirituality to diverse audiences. In addition to leading classes, *satsanghas*, seminars and lecturing on Sanatana Dharma widely, Sri Acharyaji is a renowned author of over ten authoritative books, as well as a personal spiritual guide (*guru*) to a rapidly increasing following of many thousands of enthusiastic students from both the Indian and the non-Indian communities. Sri Acharyaji was the Resident Acharya (Spiritual Preceptor) of the Hindu Temple of Nebraska from 2007-2009, which represents the first time in American history that a Hindu temple has ever made such an esteemed appointment. Sri Acharyaji is considered by many contemporary *gurus* and leaders of the Vedic community to be the most cutting-edge, authentic and highly qualified Vedic *guru* in the world today.

For more information about the life and teachings of Sri Dharma Pravartaka Acharya, please visit his website: www.dharmacentral.com

Glossary

Abhaya:	Fearlessness.
Abhyasa:	Practice.
Acharya:	Spiritual Preceptor. *Guru.* Representative of a spiritual lineage.
Acharya-asana:	Seat of the Acharya.
Agni:	The Vedic god of the altar fire who mediates between the gods and humans. He is first mentioned in the *Rig Veda.*
Ahamkara:	The artificial and illusory sense of self, lit. "I-maker."
Aham Pratyaya:	I-Cognition. The healthy sense of "I" as distinct from others.
Ahimsa:	Non-violence, including vegetarianism.
Ajna Chakra:	Spiritual centre at the eyebrows.
Ajñana:	Ignorance, non-knowledge.
Akasha:	Ether.
Anahata Chakra:	Energy center located at the heart region.
Ananda:	Bliss, happiness, enjoyment.
Anitya:	Non-eternal, temporal, fleeting, transient. The ever-changing nature of experience.
Anga:	Body, limb, member.
Antahkarana:	The fourfold internal organs: Manas, Chitta, Buddhi and Ahamkara.
Anubhava:	Experience.

Aparigraha:	Non-possession, one of the five *yamas* (abstinences) of *ashtanga-yoga.*
Apavarga:	Liberation, emancipation. Synonymous with *moksha.*
Apunya:	absence of merit, evil, non-virtuous. The opposite of *punya.*
Artha:	Aim, purpose, goal, meaning.
Asana:	The physical poses of the Yoga* system.
Ashrama:	A retreat, hermitage, or secluded place where the principles of yoga and meditation are practiced.
Ashuddhi:	Impure, sullied.
Asteya:	Non-stealing, non-theft, one of the five *yamas* (abstinences) of *ashtanga-yoga.*
Atman:	The true, eternal, essential self.
AUM:	Divine sound representing the omni-presence of God. The primordial sound out of which all other sounds are born.
Avatara:	A Divine descent of God into the earthly manifestation. *Avataras* of God come to earth to uphold Dharma and to battle *adharma.*
Avidya:	Ignorance.
Bhagavad Gita:	The Song of God. The primary scripture of Sanatana Dharma*.
Bhakti:	Devotional consciousness.
Brahmachari:	Celibate student.

Brahmacharya:	Sexual restraint, one of the five *yamas* (absti nences) of *ashtanga-yoga*.
Buddha:	Awakened. The *avatara* of God seen as the founder of Buddhism.
Buddhi:	Wisdom Faculty, intellect, understanding.
Chaitanya:	Consciousness.
Chakra:	Wheel, circle. Symbol of Dharma. One of sev en psychic energy centers in the subtle body.
Chit:	Knowledge.
Chitta:	Mind-substance, reason, intelligence.
Chitta-vritti:	Activity of mind, thought, fluctuations of the mind.
Chitta-vritti-nirodha:	Restraint or restriction of fluctuations of the mind. The first definition of Yoga given by Pa tañjali in his *Yoga Sutras* (1:2).
Chetana:	Mind, understanding, sense.
Dana:	Charity.
Darshana:	View, perspective, observation, seeing. The phi losophical systems of Sanatana Dharma are known as Darshanas. They all recognize the insights of the *Vedas* as their foundation. Dar shana also means to view a sacred image or to have the audience of a sage.
Dakshina:	Gift in gratitude to the spiritual teacher.
Deha:	Physical body.
Desha:	Place, locus, nation.
Deva/Devi:	Lesser gods/goddesses of Vedic spirituality. Similar to angels.

432

Dharana:	Concentration, the sixth of the eight limbs of Yoga.
Dharma:	Natural Law/Way. Intrinsic principles of cos mic operation.
Dharmi:	A follower of Sanatana Dharma.
Dhyana:	Meditation, the seventh of the eight limbs of Yoga
Diksha:	Spiritual initiation by a qualified *guru*.
Duhkha:	Dissatisfaction, pain, sorrow, frustration.
Drashtr:	The seer, experiencer, consciousness, *atman*.
Drashtuh-svarupa:	The true, spiritual form of the experiencer, or consciousness. That which is known when thought is stilled.
Drishti:	Drishti is the focus of the eyes in meditation in which one attempts to attain concentration alignment, and inner and outer balance. One actually does this to prevent distractions, but should be looking inwardly and not concentrate on the physical object. The object of focus could be the tip of your nose, in between your eyebrows, or a sacred image (*murti*) of the Divine.
Grihasta:	Householder.
Guna:	The three constituents of prime matter, which are: *sattva* (lightness, radiance or illumination), *rajas* (activity or passion), *tamas*: (darkness, hea viness or inertia).
Guru:	Teacher. Spiritual mentor and guide.
Hare Rama Mantra:	Hare Rama Hare Rama Rama Rama Hare Hare /

Hare Krishna Hare Krishna
Krishna Krishna Hare Hare.

Hiranyagarbha:	The founder of Yoga; the first cosmological principle to emerge out of the infinite Reality; also called Brahma.
Indriya:	The sense organs.
Ishvara:	Literally master, lord, or king. Another term for God. Narayana.
Ishvara-pranidhana:	Devotion to Ishvara, selfless action, one of the five *niyamas* (observances) of Yoga.
Jada:	Insentient, lifeless.
Japa:	Repetition of a mantra.
Japa-mala:	A sting of 108 beads used for *mantra* meditation.
Jaya:	Mastery, conquering, victory.
Jivatma:	The individual self, a living individual.
Jñana:	Wisdom, knowledge, understanding.
Kali-yuga:	The present historical cyclic era. The Age of Conflict.
Kama:	Passion, desire, lust.
Karma:	"Action". The principle that for every action, there is a reaction.
Karuna:	Compassion toward all sentient beings.
Kala:	Time.
Kaivalya:	Isolation, aloneness, single, unitary, uncompounded. Synonymous with *moksha*, or spiritual liberation.

Kapila:	The sage who originated Samkhya philosophy.
Klesha:	Affliction, pain, distress. According to Patañjali there are five *kleshas*: *avidya* (ignorance), *asmita* (I-am-ness, the artificial sense of self), *raga* (attraction), *dvesha* (aversion), and *abhinivesha* (clinging to life). He also outlines four states the *kleshas* exist in: *prasupta* (dormant), *tanu* (weakened or attenuated), *vichinna* (intercepted), and *udara* (fully active or aroused).
Klishta:	Afflicted, hindered.
Kosha:	*Koshas* are the five sheaths that cover the overall human system. These are the *Annamaya kosha* (Food Sheath), *Pranamaya kosha* (Pranic Sheath), *Manomaya kosha* (Mental Sheath), *Vijnanamaya kosha* (Intellectual Sheath) and *Anandamaya ko sha* (Blissful Sheath).
Krishna:	The last incarnation of God who appeared on earth over 5100 years ago. The speaker of the *Bhagavad Gita*. The primary form of God to be worshipped in this age.
Kriya:	*Kriyas* are classical Yoga techniques aimed at inner purification. This provides a cleansing process of one's inner body that results to high er knowledge and state of consciousness.
Krodha:	Anger, wrath, passion.
Kurukshetra:	(Lit. "the field of the Kurus") the setting of the *Bhagavad Gita*.
Maha Jagad Guru:	Great World Teacher.
Manas:	Mind, the storehouse of data, impressions, and memories.
Mandala:	Region.

Mantra:	A Divine, liberating sound vibration.
Mantra-dhyana:	*Mantra* meditation.
Maya:	Illusion.
Moksha:	Liberation, spiritual freedom.
Murti:	Sacred image placed on altars and used in wor shipful meditation.
Namaste:	"I bow to the Divinity within you". A respect ful greeting.
Narayana:	A name of God. The "Sustainer of All Beings".
Narayana-mantra:	Aum Namo Narayanaya. "I offer my respects to that Absolute Who is the sustainer of all be ings".
Niyama:	Observances. One of the eight limbs of Yoga. The *niyamas* are *shauca* (purity), *santosha* (con tentment), *tapas* (austerity), *svadhyaya* (self-study) and *Ishvara-pranidhana* (devotion to Ishvara or God).
Paramatman:	The supreme Self; the transcendental Self of our self; God.
Patañjali:	The author of the *Yoga Sutras* believed to have l ived around 300 B.C.E.
Prakriti:	Material nature. Prime matter. The power of creativity.
Prana:	Life energy, life force, or life current. These finer-than-atomic energies have inherent intelli- gence, as opposed to atoms and electrons, which are considered to be blind forces. The Chinese call this life force *chi*.
Pranayama:	Yoga breathing exercises. *Pranayama* is one of the eight limbs of Yoga.

Pratyahara:	Withdrawing the senses in order to still the mind in meditation. One of the eight limbs of Yoga.
Prasada:	"Grace". Food or other objects offered to God and thus sanctified.
Prema:	Divine love.
Puja:	Worship ceremony.
Purusha:	Pure consciousness, the seer or witness.
Rishi:	Seer, sage, perfected yogi, revealer of sacred texts.
Sadhana:	Spiritual practice or discipline.
Sadhaka:	One who performs *sadhana.*
Samadhi:	Absorption of our consciousness in God, unitive awareness, eighth limb of Yoga.
Samsara:	The wheel of material existence. The cycle of birth and death.
Samskara:	Stored impression or tendency of past action. An embodied memory.
Sanatana Dharma:	The Eternal Natural Way. The true name of the spiritual tradition commonly mislabeled "Hinduism".
Sankalpa:	Formative will; determination.
Santosha:	Contentment. One of the *niyamas**.
Sat-sangha:	True/Good association.
Sattva:	Illumination, lightness, one of the three *gunas.*

Satya:	Truthfulness, one of the five *yamas* (abstinences) of Yoga.
Seva:	Service/voluntary action performed in devotion to God.
Shakti-da:	Spiritual empowerment transmitted by God or by the *guru*.
Shanti:	Peace.
Shastra:	Scripture.
Shauca:	Purity, one of the five *niyamas* (observances) of Yoga.
Shishya:	Initiated student.
Shriman-Narayana:	The highest name of God in Sanatana Dharma. It denotes both the male and female aspects of God together, Mother-Father God in the form of Sri Lakshmi and Narayana.
Siddhi:	A perfection, or mystic power.
Sukha:	Happiness, pleasure.
Sukshma:	Astral, subtle.
Sundaram:	Beautiful, noble.
Sutra:	(Lit. "thread") brief statement or aphorism often used to convey Dharma philosophy in brevity of form.
Svadhyaya:	Self-study, one of the five *niyamas* (observances) of Yoga.
Svarupa:	(Lit. "own form") The *atman's* eternal, spiritual form.
Tamas:	Heaviness, darkness, inertia. One of the three *gunas*.

Tapas:	Austerity, asceticism, challenging oneself. One of the five *niyamas* of Yoga.
Tattva:	Literally "that-ness", essence, a metaphysical Real in the Aristotelian sense.
Trataka:	Meditation consisting of gazing at a particular spot or flame.
Trikala-jnana:	Knowledge of the past, present, and future.
Trishna:	Craving, thirst.
Tri-Tattva:	The "Three Reals": the Absolute (Brahman), Materiality (Jagat), and the finite self (Atman).
Tulasi:	A plant that is very dear to Lord Krishna, and thus sacred.
Upadesha:	Sacred teachings.
Upanishads:	Ancient Vedic philosophical scriptures. There are 108 *Upanishads* in total.
Vasana:	Stored trait or tendency of past action.
Veda(s):	"Knowledge". The sacred scriptures (*sha stras*) of Sanatana Dharma.
Vidya:	Wisdom, science, knowledge.
Virodha-vardhana-vada:	Marxism. The "Theory of Growth through Conflict".
Viveka:	Discrimination, discernment.
Vritti:	Fluctuation(s) of the *chitta* (mind-substance).
Vairagya:	Detachment.
Vedanta:	Philosophical school propounded by Bada rayana Vyasa. It contains the teachings of the

Upanishads and investigates the nature and rela
tionship of the three Reals (Tri-tattva): the Ab
solute (Brahman), Materiality (Jagat), and the
finite self (Atman).

Yagna: Fire ceremony.

Yama: Restraint. One of the eight limbs of Yoga

Yamas & Niyamas: The ten ethical principles of Dharma.

Yoga: "Union". The systematic path, discipline, and
philosophy for God-realization.

For authoritative and much more in-depth explanations of these, and
many hundreds more, Sanskrit terms, refer to my book *The Vedic Encyclopedia.*

440

Bibliography - Primary Sources

Anselm, St. *Proslogium*. Trans. S.N. Deane. 2nd ed. La Salle, IL: Open Court Publishing Company, 1962.

Baladeva Vidyabhushana. *The Vedanta-Sutras of Badarayana*. Trans. Rai Bhadur Srisa Chandra Vasu. 2nd ed. New Delhi: Munshiram Manoharlal Publishers, 1979.

The Bhagavad Gita. Trans. Deutsch, Eliot. New York: Holt, Rinehart and Winston, 1968.

Dharmaraja. *Vedantaparibhasha of Dharmaraja*. Sastri ed. and trans. S. S. Suryanarayana. Adyar: Adyar Library, 1942.

Gaudapada. *Mandukyopanishad with Gaudapada's Karika and Shankara's Commentary*, 4th ed., trans. Swami Nikhilananda. Mysore: Ra makrishna Ashram, 1955.

Gautama. *Gautama's Nyayasutras with Vatsyayana Bhashya*, Sanskrit ed. and English trans. Ganganatha Jha, 2 vols. Poona: Oriental Book Depot, 1939.

-----. *The Nyaya-Sutras of Gautama*. Trans. Gangunath Jha. 5 Vols. Delhi: Motilal Banarsidass, 1984.

Harsha. *Sri Harsha's* Khandanakhandakhadya. Trans. Phyllis Granoff. Dodrecht, Holland: D. Reidel Publishing Co., 1978.

Ishvarakrishna. *Samkhyakarika*, 4th ed., trans. S. S. Suryanarayana Sastri. Madras: University of Madras, 1948.

Jaimini. *Jaimini's Mimamsasutra with Shabara's Commentary and Notes*, trans. Ganganatha Jha, 3 vols., Gaekwad Oriental Series, Baroda: 1933-36; reprint Oriental Institute, 1973-1974.

Jiva Gosvamin. *Jiva Gosvamin's Tattvasandarbha*. Trans. Stuart Mark Elk man. Delhi: Motilal Banarsidass, 1986.

-----. *Sri Tattva-Sandarbha*. Trans. and Commmentary Satya Narayana Dasa and Kundali Dasa. New Delhi: Jivas, 1995.

-----. *Bhagavatsandarbha.* Notes Chinmayi Chatterjee. Calcutta: Jadavpur University, 1972.

Kanada. *Vaisheshikasutras of Kanada*, trans. N. Sinha. Allahabad: Panini Office, 1911.

Keshava Mishra. *Tarkabhashyaa of Keshava Mishra*, 2nd ed., ed. and trans. G. Jha. Poona: Oriental Book Agency, 1949.

Krishnadasa Kaviraja Gosvamin. *Caitanyacaritamrita of Krishnadasa Gosva mi.* (ed. and trans., 2nd ed.). London: 1922.

Krishna Yajvan. *Mimamsaparibhasha of Krishna Yajvan*, ed. and trans. Swami Madhavanand. Belur Math: The Ramakrishna Mission Sarada Pitha, 1948.

Kumarila Bhatta. *Shlokavartika of Kumarila Bhatta with the Commentary of Nyayaratnakara of Parthasarathi Mishra*, trans. Ganganatha Jha (Cal cutta: Asiatic Society, 1907), ed. Swami Drankasa Sastri (Banaras: Tara Publications, 1978).

Madhva. *Anubhashya of Madhva.* Bombay: Nirnaya Sagara Press, S. S. Rao, trans., 2nd ed. Tirupati, 1936.

-----. *Madhva Brahmasutrabhashya with Several Commentaries*, 4 vols. R. Rag havacendra (ed.). Mysore: Government Branch Press, 1922.

-----. *Madhva's Commentary on the Brahmasutras.* (Trans. S. S. Rau) Madras: Thompson and Co., 1904.

Madhava Acharya. *The Sarva-Darshana-Samgraha.* Trans. E.B. Cowell and A.E. Gough. The Showkhamba Sanskrit Studies, Vol X. Vara nasi, India: Chowkhamba Sanskrit Series Office, 1978.

Manikana. *A Navya-Nyaya Manual*, ed. and trans. E. R. Sreekrishna Sarma. Adyar: Adyar Library, 1960.

Nimbarka. *Vedanta Parijata Saurabha and Vedanta Kausthubha of Shrinivasa*, trans. R. Bose. 3 vols. Calcutta: Royal Asiatic Soceity of Ben gal, 1940-43.

Panini. *Panini's Ashtadhayi*, ed. and trans. Srisa Candra Vasu, 2 vols.

443

Reprint Delhi: Motilal Banarsidass, 1961.

Patañjali. *Patañjali Mahabhashya*, ed. Vedavrata Snataka, 10 vols. Gurukul Jhajjar (Rohtak): Haryana Sahitya Samsthan, 1961-1964.

-----. *Patañjali's Yogasutra*, ed. and trans. Swami Vijnana Asrama. Ajmer: Sri Madanlal Laksminivas Chandak, 1961.

-----. *The Yoga-Sûtra of Patanjali: A New Translation and Commentary*, Inner Traditions International; Rochester, Vermont, 1989.

Ramanuja. *Sri-Bhashya*. Trans. Swami Vireswarananda and Swami Adidevananda. 2nd ed. Calcutta: Advaita Ashrama, 1986.

-----. *The Vedanta-Sutras with the Sri-Bhashya of Ramanujacharya*, Vol. I. Madras: The Educational Publishing Co., 1961.

-----. *Vedartha-Sangraha*. Trans. S. S. Raghavachar. Mysore: Sri Ramakrishna Ashrama, 1978.

Ramayana, Critical Edition, 7 vols. Baroda: Oriental Institute, 1960-1975.

Shabara. *Shabarabhashya*, with contemporary Sanskrit commentary by B. G. Apte, 6 vols. Poona: Anandashrama, 1931-1934. English trans. G. Jha, 3 vols. Baroda: Oriental Institute, 1973-1974.

Shankaracharya. *Aparokokshanubhuti of Shankaracharya*, trans. Swami Vimuktananda, 2nd ed. Calcutta: Ramakrishna Math, 1955.

-----. *Atmabodha*. Trans. Nikhilananda, Swami. Mylapore, Madras: Sri Ramakrishna Math, 1947.

-----. *Brahma-Sutra-Bhashya*. Trans. Swami Gambhirananda. Calcutta: Advaita Ashrama, 1983.

-----. *Eight Upanisads with the Commentary of Shankaracharya*. Trans. Swami Gambhirananda. 2 Vols. Calcutta: Advaita Ashrama, 1965.

-----. *Upadesha Sahasri of Sri Shankaracharya ("A Thousand Teachings")*. Trans. Mylapore, Madras: Sri Ramakrishna Math, 1961.

-----. *Minor Works of Sri Shankaracharya*, 2nd ed. Bhavagat, H. R. (ed.). Poona Oriental Series No. 8. Poona: Oriental Books Agency,

444

1952.

-----. *Vivekacudamani of Shankaracharya*, 7th edition, Trans. Swami Madhavananda. Calcutta: Ramakrishna Math, 1966.

Shayana. *Rgveda with the Commentary of Shayana*, 2nd ed., 4 vols. Max Mu ller (ed.). London: 1892; reprint: Banaras: Chowkhambha Sanskrit Office, 1966.

Shripati. *Shripati's Shrikara Bhashya*, ed. Hayavadana Rao. Bangalore: 1936.

Srinivasadasa. *Yatindramadipika of Srinivasadasa*. Trans. Adidevananda, Swami. Madras: Sri Ramakrishna Math, Mylapore 1949.

Sureshvara. *The Naishkarmya Siddhi of Sri Sureshvara*. Trans. Alston, A.J. London: Shanti Sadan, 1959.

-----. *The Sambandha-Vartika of Sureshvaracharya*. Trans. Mahadevan, Swami. Madras: University of Madras, 1958.

Svatmarama Yogindra. *Hathayogapradipika by Svatmarama Yogindra*, 2nd ed., trans. Srinivasa Iyengar. Adyar: Theosophical Publishing House, 1933.

Tagare, Ganesh Vasudeo. *The Bhagavata-Purana*. 5 Vols. Dehli: Motilal Banarsidass, 1976.

Tapasyananda, Swami. *Srimad Bhagavata: The Holy Book of God*. Vols. 1-4. Madras: All India Press, 1982.

Udayana. *Nyayakrishnamanjali of Udayana*, ed. and trans. E. G. Cowell. Calcutta: 1864.

Upanishads. One Hundred and Eight Upanishads, 4th ed. W. C. Pancikar (ed.). Bombay: Nirnaya Sagar Press, 1932.

Vadiraja. *Vadiraja's Refutation of Shankara's Non-Dualism: Clearing the Way for Theism*. Trans. Betty, L. Stafford. Delhi: Motilal Banarsidass, 1978.

Vacaspati Mishra. *Nyayavartikatparyantika*. Ed. G. S. Tailanga. Viziana gram Sanskrit Series, no. 9, 1896.

-----. *The Bhamati of Vacaspati on Shankara's Brahmasutrabhashya*, ed. and trans. S. S. Suryanarayana Sastri and C. Kunhan Raja. Adyar: Theosophical Publishing House, 1933.

Vedanta Deshika. *Pañcaratra Raksha of Sri Vedanta Deshika*, critical eds. M. Duraiswami Aiyanjar and T. Venugopalacharya, with notes and variant readings, introduction by G. Srinivasa Murti. Adyar: Adyar Library, 1942.

Venkatacarya. *Vedantakarikavali of Venkatacharya*, ed. and trans. V. Krisna macarya. Adyar: Adyar Library, 1950.

Vishnu-purana, trans. H. H. Wilson. Reprint Calcutta: Punthi Pustak, 1961.

Bibliography - Secondary Sources

Adler, Mortimer J. "The Nature of Natural Law." http://radicalacademy.com/adlernaturallaw.htm.

Agarwal, Vishal. *The Ancient Commentators of Prasthana Trayi.* Unpublished manuscript, 1998.

Balasubramanian, R. *Advaita Vedanta.* Madras: University of Madras, 1976.

-----. "Advaita: An Overview." *Perspective of Theism and Absolutism in In dian Philosophy.* Ed. T.N. Ganapathy. Madras: Vivekananda Col lege, 1978.

Banerjee, N. V. *The Spirit of Indian Philosophy.* New Delhi: Arnold-Heinemann, 1958.

Barua, B. M. *History of Pre-Buddhistic Indian Philosophy.* Calcutta: Calcutta University, 1921.

Bharadwaj, K. D. *The Philosophy of Ramanuja.* New Delhi: Sir Sankar Lall Charitable Trust Society, 1958.

Burlamaqui, Jean-Jacques. *The Principles of Natural Law.* General Books, LLC, 2007.

Carman, J. B. *The Theology of Ramanuja: An Essay in Interreligious Understand ing.* New Haven, Conn., and London: Yale University Press, 1974.

Chaudhuri, Roma. *Ten Schools of the Vedanta.* 3 vols. Calcutta: Rabindra Bharati University, 1981.

Coomaraswamy, Ananda. *Hinduism And Buddhism.* Kessinger Publishing, 2007.

----. *Spiritual Authority and Temporal Power in the Indian Theory of Government,* Oxford University Press, 1994.

----. *What is Civilisation? and Other Essays.* Oxford University Press, 1991.

448

Clooney, Francis X. *Thinking Ritually: Rediscovering the Purva Mimamsa of Jaimini*. Vienna, De Nobili Research Library, 1990.

Devi, Savitri. *A Warning to the Hindus*. Promilla Paperbacks, 1993.

Eliade, Mircea. *Yoga: Immortality and Freedom*. Princeton, NJ: Princeton University Press, 2009.

Evola, Julius. *Heathen Imperialism*. Thompkins & Cariou, 2007.

----. *Metaphysics of War: Battle, Victory and Death in the World of Tradition*. Ed. John Morgan. London: Arktos, 2007.

----. *Revolt Against the Modern World*. Inner Traditions, 1995.

Feuerstein, Georg. *Philosophy of Classical Yoga*. Inner Traditions, 1996.

----. *The Yoga Tradition: Its History, Literature, Philosophy and Practice*. Hohm Press, 2001.

Frawley, David. *Arise Arjuna: Hinduism and the Modern World*. 1995.

----. *Gods, Sages, and Kings*. Lotus Press, Twin Lakes, Wisconsin, 1991.

----. *From the River of Heaven*. Lotus Press, Twin Lakes, Wisconsin, 1990.

----. *Hinduism and the Clash of Civilizations*. Voice of India, 2001.

----. *Universal Hinduism: Towards a New Vision of Sanatana Dharma*. Voice of India, 2010.

----. *Yoga and Ayurveda*. Lotus Press, Twin Lakes, Wisconsin, 2009.

Guénon, Réné. *Introduction to the Study of the Hindu Doctrines (Introduction générale à l'étude des doctrines hindoues*, 1921). Sophia Perennis, 2004.

----. *Man and His Becoming according to the Vedânta (L'homme et son devenir selon le Vêdânta*. Sophia Perennis, 2004.

----. *The Crisis of the Modern World (La crise du monde moderne*, 1927). Sophia Perennis, 2007.

----. *The King of the World*, Collected Works of Réné Guénon. Ghent, New York: Sophia Perennis, undated (originally published 1927)

----. *The Reign of Quantity & the Signs of the Times (Le règne de la quantité et les signes des temps*, 1945). Sophia Perennis, 2004.

Kak, Subhash. "The Assault on Tradition". Vigil, January, 2005.

Lehmann, Jean-Pierre. "The Dangers of Monotheism in the Age of Glo balization". The Globalist Magazine, March 30, 2006.

Prabhupada, A.C. Bhaktivedanta Swami. *Bhagavad-Gita As It Is* (1968).

----. *Dharma: The Way of Transcendence*. Bhaktivedanta Book Trust, 1998.

----. *Easy Journey to Other Planets*. Bhaktivedanta Book Trust, 1970.

----. *Srimad-Bhagavatam* (30 Vols.). Bhaktivedanta Book Trust, 1972–77.

----. *The Science of Self-Realization*. Bhaktivedanta Book Trust, 1977.

Rothbard, N. Murray. *The Ethics of Liberty*. NYU Press, 2003.

Saint-Yves d'Alveydre, Alexandre. *Mission de l'Inde en Europe*. University of Michigan Library, 1910.

Schall, James Vincent. "Natural Law and Economics," *Religion & Liberty*, 3 (May/June, 1993), 3-6.

Scruton, Roger. *Culture Counts: Faith and Feeling in a World Besieged*. En counter Books, 2007.

----. *The Aesthetic Understanding*. St. Augustines Press; 2nd edition, No vember, 1998.

Spengler, Oswald. *Der Untergang des Abendlandes (The Decline of the West)*. Vol. 1&2. General Books, 2010.

Vishvesha Tirtha, Swami. *Gita Saroddhara: Quintessence of the Gita*. Bharatiya Vidya Bhavan, Bombay, 1983.

Waghorne, Joanne Punzo & Norman Culter (eds.). Gods of Flesh / Gods of Stone. Columbia University Press, New York, 1996.

452

CPSIA information can be obtained
at www.ICGtesting.com
Printed in the USA
LVHW081519080419
613369LV00039B/1262/P